EDGAR CAYCE
ON THE REVELATION

EDGAR CAYCE
ON THE REVELATION

A STUDY GUIDE
FOR SPIRITUALIZING
BODY AND MIND

JOHN VAN AUKEN
FOREWORD BY CHARLES THOMAS CAYCE

STERLING PUBLISHING
NEW YORK

Published by Sterling Publishing Co., Inc.
387 Park Avenue South, New York, NY 10016

Distributed in Canada by Sterling Publishing
C/o Canadian Manda Group, 165 Dufferin Street,
Toronto, Ontario, Canada M6K 3H6

Distributed in the United Kingdom by GMC Distribution Services
Castle Place, 166 High Street, Lewes, East Sussex, England BN7 1XU

Distributed in Australia by Capricorn Link (Australia) Pty. Ltd.
P.O. Box 704, Windsor, NSW 2756, Australia

ISBN-13: 978-1-4027-3389-5
ISBN-10: 1-4027-3389-5

Van Auken, John.
    Edgar Cayce on the Revelation : a study guide for spiritualizing body and
mind / John Van Auken.
        p.   cm.
Includes bibliographical references.
ISBN 1-4027-3389-5
    1. Bible, N.T. Revelation—Criticism, interpretation, etc. 2. Cayce, Edgar,
1877–1945. Edgar Cayce readings. I. Title.
BS2825.2.V35   2000
228'.06—dc21

                                                       99–086754

For information about custom editions, special sales, premium
and corporate purchases, please contact Sterling Special Sales
Department at 800-805-5489 or specialsales@sterlingpub.com.

CONTENTS

Foreword .... *vii*

About Edgar Cayce and the Revelation Readings .... *xi*

PART I: THE INTERPRETATION

1   Interpreting the Revelation 1

2   The Twins, the Curse, and the Godling:
    Three Keys to Interpretation 18

3   Spiritualizing the Body: Chapters 1-10 of the
    Revelation 33

4   Spiritualizing the Mind and Applying the Wisdom:
    Interpreting Chapters 11-20 57

5   A New Body, A New Mind: Revelation 21-22 85

PART 2: YOUR PERSONAL REVELATION

6   Experiencing the Spirit Through Prayer and
    Meditation 93

7   Dreams and Visions 115

8   Balance, Patience, and Application: Keys to Success 128

PART 3: THE ORIGINAL MATERIAL

9   Edgar Cayce's Readings on the Revelation 139

10 The Text of the Revelation: World English Bible
    (WEB) Translation 248

FOREWORD

*A*s the new millennium was about to begin, the Sunday, December 26, 1999, edition of the *New York Times* published an article about the future entitled, "Forget the Millennium. Try to Predict One Week." The article included this statement about Edgar Cayce: "Today the world is still intact, despite gloomy predictions from the heavy hitters of prophecy. The mystic Edgar Cayce, who accurately predicted the stock market crash of 1929, predicted the American coasts would flood in 1998." There are also references to predictions of Nostradamus and others in the article.

I was annoyed by the characterization of Edgar Cayce as a doomsday prophet. Prophecy was clearly not the focus of the Cayce readings. But I appreciated the use of the term *mystic* in describing Edgar Cayce. I think of a mystic as one who unlocks secrets or solves mysteries. The term, I am sure, has the same derivation as the word *mystery.* It has been said that a mystic is one who makes the transition from searching for God to spiritually experiencing God.

The psychiatrist, Scott Peck, in characterizing spiritual development, referred to a stage four, which he called mystical/communal. He said, "Seeing a kind of interconnectedness beneath the surface, mystics of all cultures and religions have always spoken in terms of unity and community." To me, the Edgar Cayce material on the Revelation relates directly to this idea. The commentary is not focused on interpretation related to prophesy and predictions of the future; instead, it is focused on unlocking the mysteries of this material. There are many other examples in the Cayce readings of this process, and perhaps Cayce, himself, in the trance state, was an example of such a definition of mystic.

Several of my favorite nuggets from the readings also include the term *mystery:*

> For the time has arisen in the earth when men—everywhere—seek to know more of the *mysteries* of the mind, the *soul's* mind—which man recognizes as existent. 254-52

> As is understood . . . that which is the holding or interesting factor with same is an air of mystery, and the mystery fades when the truth is apparent to the individual . . . 254-46

I think these comments in the readings are related to both the time we are living in and the necessity of and focus on the practical application of these esoteric concepts. The Revelation material in the readings and this book, I think, are important in the same ways.

As I read John Van Auken's manuscript on the Cayce readings' interpretation of the Book of Revelation, I was again reminded of this term *mystic* and these definitions. To me, these profound readings and John Van Auken's commentary are perfect illustrations of this mystical approach. The premise is that this material, written by the disciple John in a state of deep prayer and meditation, is a kind of cryptogram that unlocks the secrets involved in our spiritual development. Another premise is that we are all connected, as souls, in this process of spiritual development. Perhaps most important as a premise is the focus in this material on the necessity for our application of these principles for development to occur. The readings do not simply present a series of esoteric theories, but also the focus on application.

Essentially, the Cayce readings suggest that the Disciple John, the author of this mysterious Bible book, provides a firsthand experience of "the way," through prayer and meditation, to awaken this mental pattern (mind being a much more complex and comprehensive concept in the Cayce readings than in typical physiological or psychological literature) that is an aspect of each of us—the universal Christ Consciousness. The source of the information was John's own higher self, awakened through attunement, and again, an aspect of the potential in each of us. The first third of the book, according to the readings, explains to us, through symbols, our makeup as three-dimensional beings. The last two thirds of the book is interpreted as lessons of application in our spiritual development. John Van Auken does a fine job of leading us through this commentary from the readings. For any student of the Cayce readings, this will be an important resource. John also helpfully mentions other resources available on this same material.

Two additional comments: First, for many people, of the ways the readings have been most beneficial in their personal lives is the insights provided regarding the Bible, even making it come alive. This book will enhance that experience. It's hard to read the Edgar Cayce readings on the Bible and not feel that we know some of the characters in it more deeply. I would encourage the reader of this book to pursue this, especially with regard to the Disciple John. Biblical passages and the Cayce readings painted a portrait of an amazing man in the disciple John, "that Disciple whom Jesus loved," from John's meeting of Jesus as John worked on his fishing nets at the shore to his deep love for and friendship with the Master to his witness of the crucifixion, his caring for the Holy Mother, and his exile on Patmos. A deeper connection with and understanding of this man can only enhance our work with the Revelation material. Second, if, in this time of increased travel opportunities for some of you, it becomes possible to travel to Greece and the Island of Patmos, do it. The readings are clear about the potential of energy and vibrations associated with places and objects (psychometry). Perhaps it's my imagination, but having visited this island of John the Apostle's several times, my feeling is that there is such energy, such peace in this special place.

Charles Thomas Cayce, President
Edgar Cayce Foundation

INTRODUCTION

ABOUT EDGAR CAYCE
AND THE REVELATION READINGS

*E*dgar Cayce (pronounced KAY-see) was born on a farm near Hopkinsville, Kentucky, on March 18, 1877. As a child, he displayed unusual powers of perception. At the age of six, he told his parents that he could see and talk with "visions," sometimes of relatives who had recently died and sometimes even of angels. He could also sleep with his head on his schoolbooks and awake with a photographic recall of their contents, even "seeing" the page upon which the answer appeared. However, after completing seventh grade, he left school—which was not unusual for boys at that time.

When he was twenty-one, Cayce developed a paralysis of the throat muscles, which caused him to lose his voice. When doctors were unable to find a physical cause for this condition, Edgar Cayce asked a friend to help him reenter the same kind of hypnotic sleep that had enabled him to memorize his schoolbooks as a child. The friend gave him the necessary suggestions and, once he was in this trance state, Cayce spoke clearly and directly without any difficulty. He instructed the "hypnotist" to give him a suggestion to increase the blood flow to his throat; when the suggestion was given, Cayce's throat turned bright red. Then, while still under hypnosis, Cayce recommended some specific medication and manipulative therapy to aid in restoring his voice completely. When he awoke, he could speak normally again.

On subsequent occasions, Cayce went into this hypnotic state to diagnose and prescribe healing for others, with much success. Doctors around Hopkinsville and Bowling Green, Kentucky, took advantage of Cayce's unique talent to diagnose their patients. They soon discovered that all Cayce needed was the name and address of a patient to "tune in" telepathically to that individual's mind and body. The patients didn't have to be near Cayce; Cayce could tune in to them wherever they were.

When one of the young physicians working with Cayce submitted a report on his strange abilities to a clinical research society in Boston, the reactions were amazing. On October 9, 1910, the *New York Times* carried two pages of headlines and pictures. From then on, people from all over the country sought "the sleeping prophet," as he was to become known.

The routine he used for conducting a trance-diagnosis was to recline on a couch, hands folded across his solar plexus, and to breathe deeply. Eventually, his eyelids would begin fluttering, and his breathing would become deep and rhythmical. This was the signal to the conductor (usually his wife, Gertrude) to make verbal contact with Cayce's subconscious by giving a suggestion. Unless this procedure was timed to synchronize with his fluttering eyelids and the change in his breathing, Cayce would go beyond his trance state and simply fall fast asleep. However, when the suggestion was made, Cayce would proceed to describe the patient as though the patient were sitting right next to him. His mind functioned much as an X-ray scanner, seeing into every organ of the patient's body. When Cayce was finished, he would say, "Ready for questions." However, in many cases his mind would have anticipated the patient's questions, answering them during the main session. Eventually, he would say, "We are through for the present," whereupon the conductor would give the suggestion to return to normal consciousness.

If this procedure were in any way violated, Cayce would be in serious personal danger. On one occasion, he remained in a trance state for three days and had actually been given up for dead by the attending doctors.

At each session, a stenographer (usually Gladys Davis Turner, his longtime personal secretary) would record everything Cayce said.

Sometimes during a trance session, Cayce would even correct the stenographer's spelling. It was as though his mind were in touch with everything around him and beyond.

As the "readings" Cayce gave were transcribed and collected, each client was identified with a number to keep his or her name private. For example, hypnotic material for Edgar Cayce is filed under the number 294. His first reading for himself was numbered 294-1, and each subsequent reading was numbered consecutively (294-2, 294-3, and so on). Some numbers refer to groups of people, such as the study group readings in the 262 series. Some numbers refer to specific research or guidance readings, such as the 254 series, containing the readings dealing with the overall work of the organization that grew up around Cayce, and the 364 and 996 series containing the readings on Atlantis.

It was August 10, 1923, before anyone thought to ask the "sleeping" Cayce for insights beyond physical health—questions about life, death, and human destiny. In a small hotel room in Dayton, Ohio, a businessman named Arthur Lammers asked the first set of philosophical questions that led to an entirely new way of using Cayce's strange abilities. It was during this reading that Cayce first began to talk about reincarnation as though it were as real and natural as the functioning of the physical body. This concept shocked and challenged Cayce and his family. They were deeply religious people, doing this Work to help others because that's what their Christian faith taught. Reincarnation was not part of their reality. Yet, the healings and help continued to come. So, the Cayce family proceeded with the health material, but cautiously reflected on the strange philosophical information. Ultimately, the Cayces began to accept the idea, though not as "reincarnation" per se. Edgar Cayce preferred to call it "the continuity of life." As a child, he had first read the Bible from front to back, and did so for every year of his life. He felt that it did contain much evidence that life, the true life in the Spirit, is continuous.

Eventually, Edgar Cayce, following advice from his own readings, moved to Virginia Beach, Virginia, and set up a hospital, where he conducted his physical readings for the health of others. He also continued the new type of readings, called "life readings." From 1925 through 1944, he conducted nearly 2,000 life readings, describing the past lives of individuals as casually as if everyone understood reincarnation to be a reality. Such subjects as deep-seated fears, mental blocks, vocational talents, innate urges and abilities, marriage difficulties, child training, etc., were examined in the light of what the readings called the "karmic patterns" resulting from previous lives spent by the individual's soul in the earth plane.

When he died on January 3, 1945, in Virginia Beach, Cayce left more than 14,000 documented stenographic records of the telepathic-clairvoyant readings he had given for more than 6,000 people over a period of forty-three years. They constitute one of the largest and most impressive records of psychic perception ever collected. Together with their relevant records, correspondence, and reports, the readings have been cross-indexed under thousands of subject headings and placed at the disposal of doctors, psychologists, students, writers, and investigators who still come to the Association for Research and Enlightenment (A.R.E.) to examine them. Of course, they are also available to the general public in topical books and complete volumes, as well as on the CD-ROM for PC and MacIntosh computers.

The A.R.E. was founded by Cayce in 1931 as an open-membership research society. It continues to initiate and support investigation and experimentation and conducts conferences, seminars, and lectures. The A.R.E. also has one of the largest and finest libraries of parapsychological and metaphysical books in the world. The Edgar Cayce Foundation was founded to index, catalog, and preserve his Work. Both organizations are headquartered in Virginia Beach, Virginia.

READING AND INTERPRETING CAYCE

Edgar Cayce's readings do present some difficulties in interpretation and understanding. First, they are somewhat difficult to read, mostly due to their syntax and the presence of archaic or biblical terms and style. They are *written* records of a *verbal* presentation, a process that occasionally does not carry the full intent that was expressed, and punctuation can significantly change the meaning or intent of the voiced statement. Also, most of the readings were given to specific people with uniquely personal perspectives and prejudices on the topics being discussed; therefore, the responses were slanted to fit the seeker's perspective. For example, in a reading for one person, Cayce recommended one marriage for life; to another he recommended never getting married; a third he encouraged to marry a second time. Even in the few cases where a reading was intended for broader presentation to many people, the "sleeping" Cayce was still somewhat at the mercy and wisdom of those directing the session and asking the questions. Nevertheless, Cayce, Gertrude, and their assistant, Gladys, were very conscientious people, always seeking to be exact and true to the original intent of the reading. As I indicated earlier, the "sleeping" Cayce occasionally would even stop his direct discourse to give an aside comment to the stenographer about the way she was recording the material, correcting spelling or giving a clarifying explanation of something he had just said. Finally, because some of Cayce's readings cover so many points within one sentence or paragraph, it can be difficult to determine which topic he is referring to when the sentences or paragraphs are so complex.

Despite all this, with practice, one can become familiar enough with the form of the readings—the syntax; terms; the "thys," "thees," and "thous"; the repetitive use of the word "that"; and the complex thought pattern—that one *can* learn to read and understand the Cayce material.

A Study of the Book of Revelation

In the latter half of the 1950s and early '60s, a group at the A.R.E. New York Center, then located at 34 West 35th St., began a seven-year study of Cayce's interpretation of the Revelation. It was their intention to produce a readable version that everyone could use. Their work was later combined with twenty-three of Cayce's readings on the Revelation and published in book form by the A.R.E. Press in Virginia Beach. The book, which is still in print, is titled, *A Commentary on the Book of the Revelation: Based on a Study of Twenty-Three Psychic Discourses of Edgar Cayce.*

In the late 1960s and early '70s, Shane Miller, an artist on the animated feature film *Gulliver's Travels*, completed a series of color-slide transparencies outlining the key parts of Cayce's interpretation of the Revelation. The slides were transferred to film, a soundtrack was added, and it became a frequently shown film around the A.R.E. community. Black-and-white reproductions of some of these slides appear in this book. Throughout the 1970s and early '80s, Everett Irion, a longtime student of the Cayce readings, came from Texas to Virginia Beach to work at the A.R.E. and, ultimately, led another Revelation study group based on Cayce's approach. This resulted in the publication by the A.R.E. Press of *Interpreting the Revelation with Edgar Cayce.* In the 1980s, David McMillin came from the Midwest to Virginia Beach and started a Revelation study group that continues today. It focuses on the original Cayce instruction that the Revelation could help health care workers better understand how the body works. He was joined in Virginia Beach by four others: Douglas Richards, Ph.D., who had been research director at the A.R.E. for several years and was deeply involved in improving his own health through guidance that came through Cayce; Carl Nelson, D.C., who has a large and popular chiropractic practice; Karen Kluge Waller, the mother of a handicapped daughter, who simply wanted the best for her child; and Eric Mein, M.D., who had pursued a medical degree because of his love of the Cayce health concepts and his hope that they could be added to the health care models used today. McMillin, Richards, Nelson, Waller, Mein, and I united to form Meridian Institute, which devotes itself to in-depth health research based on the Edgar Cayce concepts, some of which include concepts in the Revelation.

I have studied and applied the readings and Revelation material in the Cayce legacy for thirty years. I find the Cayce material to be one of the greatest collections of wisdom that I have encountered and an excellent supplement to the biblical stories and lessons. What also impresses me is that Cayce's concepts are so in tune with Western and Eastern spiritual, mental, and physical teachings, from the most ancient to the latest discoveries. The real proof of this work's value, however, has come in the results I have realized in my life by applying these teachings in the little things every day. Early in my study of Cayce's work I read his comments on the Revelation. They were so profound and meaningful to me and to my development as a spiritual person that I never stopped rereading them and discussing them with others who are also seeking to awaken themselves spiritually. Over thirty years, I have written six books based on Cayce's concepts and methods, and my intention in writing this book is to add to the body of existing works on the Revelation, focusing on the spiritualization process in this strange but captivating book of the Bible.

I've divided this book into three sections: interpretation, personal revelation, and the original material. It is my hope that this book will help us to experience God directly and live as cocreators and companions forever! A monumental task, yes; but as you and I know and have heard before, even the longest journey begins with one little step and proceeds step by step. Fortunately, we all have moments of spontaneous enlightenment, even though we must still continue the ongoing development. Those moments give us the strength to continue the spiritualization process.

PART I

THE INTERPRETATION

I

INTERPRETING THE REVELATION

*T*he story of how the Christian Church held on to the book of the Revelation and allowed it into their final authorized canon is about as amazing as the vision it records. All the original manuscripts of the New Testament have been lost. Much of our knowledge today comes from second- to eighth-century Greek manuscripts, from some surviving translations of the first-century material into other languages, and from early church writers who were recording from memory what they had read or what had been told to them by first-century sources.

The most important and oldest manuscripts of all or parts of the New Testament that survive today are written on papyrus and parchment and date back only to the second century. We have no written manuscripts of the Gospels, Epistles, or Revelation dating from the first century. There are several reasons for this. Back then, all literary work had to be copied by hand; there was no printing with movable type (that did not come until A.D. 1450). Also, the scrolls that were used limited the size of a manuscript. Though there are records of Caesar cutting scrolls into small sheets and stacking them like a modern book, it wasn't until the second century that page-books were developed. This development allowed the many scroll manuscripts to be converted to sheets and bound into large books (still handwritten).

Even then, many early churches did not include the Revelation in their sacred literature. The earliest Christian Bible included the Old Testament, the four Gospels, the Acts, and thirteen letters of Paul, I Peter, and I John. Seven books that ultimately became part of the present-day New Testament were generally unrecognized in the first and second centuries: Hebrews, James, II Peter, II and III John, Jude, and the Revelation. Interestingly, the Letter of Barnabas, or the Shepherd of Hermas, was originally accepted as Scripture, only to be rejected later. It wasn't until the fourth century that we saw the first authoritative pronouncements listing the acceptable canon we have today. The criterion for being included in this list was twofold: (1) the work was written by an apostle, and (2) it was in general harmony with the Old Testament and the rest of the New Testament. The introduction to the Revelation, identifying the work as being that of the apostle John's, and its general harmony with the Books of Ezekiel and Daniel won it inclusion into the final authorized canon of the New Testament. The first time all twenty-seven books of the New Testament we have today were listed, including the Revelation, was in St. Athanasius's Festal Letter of A.D. 367.

There are apocalyptic passages in the Gospels: Matthew 24-25, Mark 13, and Luke 21, but the Book of the Revelation is *the* prophecy book of the New Testament, as the Book of Daniel is for the Old Testament. The original name of this most mysterious book of the Bible is *Apokalupsis,* which in Greek literally means "to take the cover off" or "uncover." The Apocalypse or Revelation is the *uncovering* of a spiritual message from God. However, while it may be *called* an uncovering, few readily understand it.

The Revelation is addressed to the seven churches in Asia Minor, mentioned in chapters 2 and 3. It was written at a time of great persecution for those struggling to hold to the tenets and practices of this fledgling faith, particularly during the reigns of Nero in A.D. 37 to 68 and Domitian in A.D. 81 to 96. Domitian actually declared himself *dominus et deus,* lord and god, which the Christian faithful simply could not affirm, and so began the persecutions that resulted in the often-repeated saying, "Rome became drunk on the blood of the saints." This was a departure from Rome's earlier position, which was protective of the fledgling faith, allowing it to develop among the other Jewish sects, as noted in the Acts of the Apostles and Paul's

Epistle to the Romans.

Scholars consider the author of the Revelation to be the apostle John (Revelation 1:1,9; 21:2, 22:8), who also wrote the Gospel and the three Epistles of John. He was arrested along with the apostle Peter. They were tried and convicted of activities subversive to the authority of the government. Peter was sentenced to death by crucifixion. John was sentenced to banishment to the island of Patmos in the Aegean Sea.

According to Edgar Cayce, before they were parted, Peter promised John that he would endeavor to come to him after his death and communicate with him from heaven. In Cayce's interpretation, this promise was an important one, for it was Peter's angelic spirit who later appeared to John twice during his revelation in the form of an angel (Revelation 19:10 and 22:9). In these two appearances, the angel clearly identified himself as one of John's brethren: "I am a fellow-servant with thee and with thy brethren." But his appearance was so wonderful that John could see only an angel.

Traditionally, there are four approaches to interpreting Revelation: (1) preterist, (2) historicist, (3) symbolic, and (4) futuristic.

As the term implies, the *preterist* approach places the events and visions in the past, particularly to the Roman Empire of the first century A.D. The proponents of this view believe that the primary purpose of the book was to encourage the faithful of that time that God would intervene in their immediate struggles. The preterist view explained the symbolic nature of the text as a conscious attempt by the disciple John to hide the real meaning of the text from the authorities and the general public, keeping its message available only to the faithful. The faithful would know that the great whore of Babylon seated upon the seven hills was none other than Rome. The lamb that was slain was Jesus Christ. The bride adorned for her husband was Jerusalem, which God would soon rescue from the beast's (Rome's) control.

The *historicist* interpretation approaches the Revelation as a panoramic view of history from the first century A.D. to the Second Coming of Christ. This was the view of most of the Protestant reformers. They believed that many of the symbols can be associated with various nations and events throughout time, to the present and the near future, when Christ will return in glory and power.

The *symbolic* view maintains that the Revelation portrays the conflict between good and evil throughout the entire span of human history. The book attempts to encourage the faithful to keep up the fight because, despite the magnitude of the challenge and depth of suffering involved in this fight, good will overcome evil in the end and reign forever. This view does not attempt to associate the symbols with nations or events in history, but simply with the various forces that make up the good influence and the evil influence in humanity's journey.

The *futuristic* view holds that, from chapter 4 on, Revelation deals with events at the "end times," as spoken of in the Book of Daniel by the angel Gabriel. According to this view, chapter 1 deals with the past, chapters 2 and 3 tell of things that were present at and shortly following at the time of its writing, and chapters 4 through 22 tell of things that will follow the Age of the Church during the Second Coming of Christ.

Edgar Cayce's approach to the Revelation closely followed the symbolic view, but he took it far beyond the usual symbolic interpretation. In fact, Cayce taught that the whole Bible is a story that is both historic and symbolic and on two levels: one very personal to each soul and the other for all souls as a group. According to Cayce, the Bible tells of our souls' journey (individually and as a group) from our creation in the image of God for the purpose of being eternal companions to God, through the fall from grace and the loss of the Garden, up through the struggles to regain the glory that was ours "before the world was."[1] The Revelation, according to Cayce, is a very special part of the great biblical story and should be studied as a kind of roadmap for the final spiritualization of our bodies and minds. The symbols and scenes in this mysterious book represent experiences and stages through which we pass in our struggle to awaken again spiritually and regain our close connection with God and the Garden we once shared. Cayce said that some symbols and places in the Revelation actually represent *glands* within our bodies and *thought patterns* within our minds.[2] He explained that "the visions, the experiences, the names, the churches, the places, the dragons, the cities, all are but emblems of those forces that may war within the individual in its journey through the material, or from the entering into the material manifestation [i.e., physical body and world] to the entering into the glory, or the awakening in the spirit." (281-16)

This is quite a unique approach to the Revelation. Most interpreters believe that it is a story about the forces in the *outside* world. Cayce acknowledged that it does have that content, but its greater purpose and message are to each individual soul as a map of the spiritual path we travel *within* our bodies and minds to reach the ultimate purpose for our being: oneness and companionship with God and one another. For Cayce, the outer activities and commandments were important, but the inner work was the key to understanding the Revelation. The symbols "represent *self;* self's body-physical, self's body-mental, self's body-spiritual . . . and they are *one* in thee—even as the Father, the Son and the Holy Spirit is one in Him." (281-16)

Why, then, was Revelation written in such a cryptic manner? According to Cayce, it was to keep its spiritual secrets for "those that were, or will be, or may become," through their spiritual seeking, initiated into an understanding of "the glories that may be theirs if they will but put into work, into activity," the guidance and calling found in the text. As the Spirit came to each church in Revelation and spoke to them, so Cayce wanted each of us to ask ourselves: "What is lacking in self? Are ye cold? Are ye hot? Have ye been negligent of the knowledge that is thine? Are ye stiff-necked? Are ye adulterous in thought, in act, in the very glories that are thine?" (281-16)

In every line of the Revelation, every activity, every symbol, we find good and evil rising in a struggle. This struggle, according to Cayce, is within us and is because we were created to be joint heirs with Christ, as sons and daughters of God, to that everlasting glory that may be ours with Him in God. But the material, physical forces, and self-satisfying interests take strong hold of us, and we forget our spiritual destiny. Yet, Cayce did not see the physical as evil or a stumbling block to spiritualization; rather, he saw it as a tool, a stepping-stone to aid in our spiritual struggle if we use it properly, as the Revelation reveals.

Here are some examples of Cayce's interpretation of symbols, scenes, and characters found in the Revelation:

The seven churches—These represent the seven spiritual centers within the body. In classical Hinduism and Buddhism, these centers are called *chakras* (which means "wheels"), spinning wheels of energy located in specific areas of the human body. Cayce correlated these centers to the endocrine glands, which secrete powerful hormone messages directly into the bloodstream, affecting all parts of the body (281-29). Each of the churches represents a specific spiritual center. The virtue and the fault of each church symbolizes the virtue and fault of that spiritual center within us. These powerful centers affect the soul and mind inhabiting the body. Therefore, the Spirit moves through each church, calling on it to overcome its weaknesses and to do what it knows to do, so that the final glory may be achieved, helping us to prepare for the spiritualization of mind and heart described in subsequent chapters of the Revelation.

The seven lamps of fire—These represent the helpful influences that destroy hindrances to the spiritual awakening. They are inner messengers, aids, who stand between the forces of good and evil and become as powers within the nature of man to overcome (281-29). This idea may be an extension of the teaching that angels watch over us. An example of this can be found in Psalms 91:11: "For he will give his angels charge over you, to keep you in all your ways." It may also be the power of our inner conscience that helps us along the way. But with Cayce, it may also be our inner thoughts and chemistry: What thoughts and hormones are we releasing most often? Those that fire up the carnal or violent forces of the body or the gentler, calmer, more uplifting ones, that make the body a temple for the soul?

The four beasts—These are our four fundamental physical natures (desires), which must be overcome. They are also the four destructive influences that "make for the greater desire for the carnal forces." (281-16) The Revelation's description of each adds to our understanding of these forces and how we may subdue their negative qualities. These also represent urges and forces in the four lower, more earthly glands in our bodies. Cayce equated the four lower glands with earthly forces and the three upper glands with heavenly forces. More on this in a later chapter.

The great red dragon—This symbolizes the powerful urge within ourselves that originally so separated us from the Source of Life that we fought with those very influences that would bring the spiritual awakening. The great red dragon is the serpent from the Garden in Genesis (Revelation 12:9) who first aided in our souls' separation from God's presence and the Garden—symbolic of a serpentlike willfulness and reasoning within ourselves, when we were heavenly teenagers with the keys to the car. Now this influence has grown strong and powerful in the form of a great red dragon, ready to devour any new heaven-centered intentions we bring forth in our hearts and minds (281-16).

Mark of the beast—This strange mark, *666*, represents vows and obligations we have made to the work of the beast and how we condemn rather than help any effort to overcome the beast's influence. The beast is like our ego and egocentric interests. It represents the work of self alone, without God's influence. The mark is erased when the work of our hands and the thoughts of our minds are cooperating with God, rather than simply being self-driven. The beast is our lower nature at our most selfish, self-centered, self-gratifying, self-glorifying point of existence.

New heaven and new earth—These represent a new mind and a new heart. Throughout the Old Testament you may have noticed that the Lord made occasional reference to giving us new hearts or "circumcising" our hearts (Deuteronomy 10:16, 30:6; Ezekiel 18:31, 36:26; Jeremiah 4:4). Here, in the final book of the Bible, we have received our new hearts. These also represent a new vibration in the seven spiritual centers. The "wheels" are spinning with a new purpose, a new life force; one that is spiritualizing. Therefore, we have a new body, too; one that helps the heart and mind maintain higher consciousness.

Water of life—This is the transformative, rejuvenative influence of the Spirit of God flowing through our purposes, which have been made pure in "the blood of the Lamb—which is in Jesus, the Christ, to those who seek to know his ways." (281-37) Ingesting this water is cleansing, making us new and reborn. But, once again, it is not actual water that we are talking about. It is the essence of water from within us, as Jesus meant when He said, "He that believeth on me, as the scripture hath said, from within him shall flow rivers of living water." (John 7:38) Jesus' reference to the scriptures is to Isaiah 58:11, where we find a similar comment about the inner water: "And the Lord will guide thee continually, and satisfy thy soul in dry places, and make strong thy bones; and thou shalt be like a watered garden, and like a spring of water, whose waters fail not."

Tree of life—This represents "the sturdiness of the purpose of the individual in its sureness in the Christ". (281-37) The tree's leaves represent our *activities* as healings to others and to ourselves in the material life. The fruits of this special tree are the "fruits of the spirit." Cayce listed them in many of his discourses as: kindness, patience, joy, understanding, gentleness, longsuffering, forgiveness, etc. The tree's ability to bear fruit each month indicates the continuousness of the influence of this sturdiness and these activities that bring forth the spiritual fruits in our lives.

Cayce's interpretations call each of us to participate in a great struggle to be born again in the Spirit and to spiritualize our lives, bodies, and minds. In Revelation 1:10, the disciple John said that he was "in the spirit on the Lord's day." Cayce said that he was in meditation (281-16). In this deep state, he was caught up in the Spirit of God and "turned" (Revelation 1:12) away from the outer world. He began viewing the inner, heavenly world and was told to write what he saw and heard. Cayce said that what John perceived was for his own personal spiritual development, as well as for other souls who, by their own development, could sense the true meaning of this story and its strange imagery and could use it to benefit their own journey. Again, the journey we are speaking of is the journey from a predominantly physical, material being to a predominantly spiritual, celestial being who is sojourning temporarily in the physical world.

The process John went through to have his revelatory experience, combined with the content of the experience, reveals a spiritual, mystical approach to life. The mystical approach is founded upon a belief that each of us can have an immediate, intuitive perception of spiritual truths that transcend ordinary intellectual understanding by experiencing a direct, intimate union of our soul with God. This union occurs through the power and grace of the intercession of Jesus Christ on our behalves, which resulted from His sacrifice and resurrection. Because of Christ's sacrifice and current oneness with the Creator, the veil has been rent in the temple of consciousness. A way is now opened to experience the Spirit of God and the truth directly, not for one or two selected people, but for any and all who seek. As Revelation 1:5-6 states it: " . . . Jesus Christ [is] the faithful witness, the firstborn of the dead, and the ruler of the kings of the earth. To him who loves us, and released us from our sins by his blood; and he has made us to be a kingdom, to be priests unto his God and Father." In Jewish tradition, the high priest entered the holy of holies and experienced direct contact with God. Now, anyone who asks shall receive; anyone who seeks shall find; to anyone who knocks, the door will be opened (Matthew 7:7 and Luke 11:9).

When we look at John's Gospel and Epistles, we find the foundations for his mysticism. The disciple John was the youngest of the twelve apostles and the last to be chosen. Interestingly, his Gospel is more about what Jesus said than what Jesus did and is very different from the synoptic Gospels of Matthew, Mark, and Luke, which are similar in content and sequence. Certain concepts, discussions, and events appear only in John's Gospel, such as the "Word" being incarnate in the flesh in the opening chapter, the Samaritan woman at the well in chapter 4, and Jesus' extensive comments and prayers at the Last Supper in chapters 14-17. The literary style of John's Gospel is also unique. It is uncomplicated, easy to read, with no attempt to tie it all together; each narrative is presented as though it is an isolated event or statement. It is a book of striking contrasts: light and darkness, truth and falsehood, good and evil, life and death, God and Satan. His Gospel is saturated with symbolic representations from ordinary life. For example, Jesus used common things such as water, bread, light, wine, a vine, branches, a shepherd, and so on to convey spiritual truths. Though it contains little or no prophecy (surprising, since the other Gospels do and since John later wrote the Revelation), it is the most mystical of the four Gospels.

For example, in the Gospel of John 1:1-13, we have the wonderful description of the incarnation of the Word. If we translate it as closely to the original Greek as possible, we actually get a better understanding, mostly because we have too narrowly translated a key word in the text. That word is *word!* John used the Greek word *logos,* which means so much more than the English *word.* For example, in chapter 8:43 of the Gospel, John recounted Jesus actually using two different Greek words for *word* to explain to the authorities why they so often did not understand his teachings; in so doing, He gave a key insight into the importance of the word *logos:* "Why do you not understand my words *[lalian]?* It is because you cannot hear my word *[logon]."* *Logos* means the rational principle that governs and develops the whole universe. If we use this definition in the English translation, then it reads much more powerfully. John was trying to convey to us that not only the message or word of God was incarnate in Jesus, but so was the essence of the whole cosmos, the power behind all creation. Also, in the original text of this chapter, there is no masculine pronoun *He* in several passages, as the English versions suggest. It's actually written in the early Greek as "this one," not "he." Here is the text with these adjustments:

¹In the beginning was the Logos, and the Logos was with God, and the Logos was God.

²This one was in the beginning with God.

³All things were made through this one; and without this one was not made anything that has been made.

⁴In this one was life; and the life was the light of men.

⁵And the light shined in the darkness; and the darkness did not comprehend it.

⁶There came a man, sent from God, whose name was John [the Baptist].

⁷The same came for witness, that he might bear witness of the Light, that all might believe through him.

⁸He was not the Light, but came that he might bear witness of the Light.

⁹There was the true Light, even the Light which enlightens every man coming into the world.

¹⁰This one was in the world, and the world was made through this one, and the world did not know him.

¹¹This one came unto his own, and they that were his own did not receive him.

¹²But to as many as received him, gave he the right to become children of God, even to them that believe on his name:

¹³who were born, not of blood, nor of the will of the flesh, nor of the will of man, but of God.

In this same gospel, we also have the mind-opening discussion with the Samaritan woman at the well, in which we learn of the "living water" that later appears in the Revelation and of the nature of God and how best to attune to God, concepts which John certainly needed to know in order to have his great revelation. The first of these two teachings begins in chapter 4:7-15, the second in verses 19-26:

⁷There came a woman of Samaria to draw water: Jesus said to her, "Give me a drink."

⁸(For his disciples were gone away to the city to buy food.)

⁹The Samaritan woman therefore said to him, "How is it that thou, being a Jew, ask drink of me, who am a Samaritan woman?" (For Jews have no dealings with Samaritans.)

¹⁰Jesus answered and said to her, "If you knew the gift of God, and who it is that says to you, 'Give me to drink,' you would have asked of him, and he would have given you living water."

¹¹The woman said to him, "Sir, you have nothing to draw with, and the well is deep; where then do you have that living water?

¹²Are you greater than our father Jacob, who gave us the well, and drank from it himself, and his sons, and his cattle?"

¹³Jesus answered and said to her, "Every one that drinks of this water shall thirst again;

¹⁴but whosoever drinks of the water that I shall give him shall never thirst; but the water that I shall give him shall become in him a well of water springing up unto eternal life."

[15]The woman saith unto him, "Sir, give me this water, that I thirst not, neither come all the way here to draw."

In this scene, we learn of another water, a living water, that, once we have received it, we will never thirst for water again. We will be like a well of our own, with water springing up within us, bringing eternal life.

Then, after Jesus told the woman of events in her life that He could not physically have known, she addressed a key issue about worshiping God that surely helped John to get into the Spirit for his revelation:

[19]The woman said unto him, "Sir, I perceive that thou art a prophet.
[20]Our fathers worshiped in this mountain; and your people say, that in Jerusalem is the place where men ought to worship."
[21]Jesus saith unto her, "Woman, believe me, an hour comes, when neither in this mountain, nor in Jerusalem, shall you worship the Father.
[22]You worship that which you do not know; we worship that which we know, for salvation is from the Jews.
[23]But an hour comes, and now is, when the true worshipers shall worship the Father in spirit and truth: for such people the Father seeks to be his worshipers.
[24]God is a Spirit, and they that worship him must worship in spirit and truth."

The idea that God is a spirit and seeks us to worship Him in spirit is fundamental to understanding the Revelation. We cannot approach these teachings from an intellectual, physical perspective. They require that we evoke or receive the Spirit of God; this Spirit then will lift our spirits up to a level of consciousness from which we can understand the teachings. Jesus touched on this need in His teachings to Nicodemus: "We speak that which we know, and bear witness of that which we have seen; and you do not receive our testimony. If I told you earthly things and you don't believe, how shall you believe if I tell you heavenly things?" (John 3:11-12) Another Scripture concerning the Spirit of God that is relevant to our study of the Revelation is from Joel 2:28-31:

[28]And it shall come to pass afterward, *that* I will pour out my Spirit upon all flesh; and your sons and your daughters shall prophesy, your

old men shall dream dreams, your young men shall see visions:
²⁹And also upon the servants and upon the handmaids in those days
will I pour out my spirit.
³⁰And I will shew wonders in the heavens and in the earth, blood, and
fire, and pillars of smoke.
³¹The sun shall be turned into darkness, and the moon into blood,
before the great and terrible day of the Lord comes.

From the need for spirit to worship the Spirit, the woman at the well
turned to the promise of a Messiah who would help us all. It is always easier
if one descends from heaven to help than if we are asked to lift our minds
and hearts up to heaven to receive help. Therefore, many were waiting for a
special one to descend from heaven, including this Samaritan:

> ²⁵The woman saith unto him, "I know that Messiah comes
> (he that is called Christ): when that One comes, he will
> declare all things to us."
> ²⁶Jesus said to her, "I that speak to you am he."

This ordinary woman, not of the chosen people, drew more out of Jesus
than many others who asked questions of Him. In her discussion with Jesus,
we learn of the water of life, the nature of God, the way to worship God,
and that the fulfillment of the prophecy in Daniel was Jesus of Nazareth.
In a rare self-testimonial, Jesus acknowledged to the woman that He was,
indeed, the prophesied Christ.

"Christ" is a transliteration of the Greek word *christos*, which literally
means "anointed one," a stage in the preparation of the high priest to enter
the holy of holies to meet God directly. The priest's head was to be anointed
with oil, usually olive oil: "Then shalt thou take the anointing oil, and pour
it upon his head, and anoint him." (Exodus 29:7)

This process may also have been experienced by ordinary people, as written in the Psalms. One good example is Psalms 23:5: "Thou hast anointed
my head with oil; my cup runneth over." A better translation of this term
might be "a consecrated one," as in Exodus 29:29: "And the holy garments
of Aaron shall be for his sons after him, to be anointed in them, and to be
consecrated in them." The anointing was to consecrate one for a special
service. The corresponding word for *christos* in Hebrew is *mashiyack*, which
we transliterate to *messiah*. This very specific term is only found in Daniel

9:25-26. *Messiah* means exactly what *christos* means, just in a different language.

There are several scriptural references to the coming of a special one to help the people. The first and most important one is directly from the Lord; as His creation fell from grace in the Garden, He prophesied that the woman's seed would become the redeemer of this situation and would subdue the influence of the serpent and the knowledge of good and evil (Genesis 3:15). The Samaritan woman was obviously familiar with the prophecies and was looking for the messiah to come in her lifetime. John's use of *Logos* lends support to the Messiah-Christ nature of this one.

Many prophets had come and gone, and many roamed the Holy Land in the days of the Samaritan woman, but the truth had gotten lost in the troubles and confusions of the times. For the preceding four hundred years, little had gone well for the faithful among the several sects of the Jews. They had been taught for generations that God would guide, protect, and speak to them. As a group, the chosen people had a history of mystical connection with God and God's immediate participation in their lives. Mystical teachings and tales throughout the Scriptures taught, supported, and gave living examples of this relationship. One is found in Deuteronomy 4:35-36: "Unto thee it was shown, that thou might know that the Lord is God; there is none else besides him. Out of heaven he made you to hear his voice, that he might instruct you; and upon earth he made you to see his great fire; and hear his words out of the midst of the fire."

What impact these words must have had! God is oneness, and there is nothing beyond this oneness. We were first made in heaven to hear God's voice and learn directly from Him and then made again upon earth to see His great fire and hear His words in the fire—the fire of His spirit upon us, as John noted in the beginning of the Revelation. In I Kings 19:9-16, Elijah had a direct experience with God that reveals an inner and outer quality to our spiritualization process. As you read it, notice the symbolic nature of some of the elements in the story: mountain, cave, wind, earthquake, fire, and silence—these same symbols occur in the Revelation.

> ⁹And he [Elijah] came there [Horeb, the mountain of God] to a cave, and lodged there; and, behold, the word of the Lord came to him, and He said unto him, "What are you doing here, Elijah?"
> ¹⁰And he said, "I have been very zealous for the Lord, the God of hosts; for the children of Israel have forsaken thy covenant, torn down thine

altars, and slain thy prophets with the sword. And I, even I only, am
left; and they seek my life, to take it away."

[11]And He said, "Go forth, and stand upon the mount before the Lord."
And, behold, the Lord passed by, and a great and strong wind rent
the mountains, and broke in pieces the rocks before the Lord; but the
Lord was not in the wind; and after the wind an earthquake; but the
Lord was not in the earthquake;

[12]and after the earthquake a fire; but the Lord was not in the fire; and
after the fire a still small voice.

[13]And it was so, when Elijah heard it, that he wrapped his face in his
mantle, and went out, and stood in the entrance of the cave. [Note
that he had not actually left the cave to experience the mountaintop
with the Lord in verse 11. Therefore, he must have experienced this
within his mind.] And, behold, there came a voice unto him, and said,
"What are you doing here, Elijah?"

[14]And he said, "I have been very zealous for the Lord, the God of
hosts; for the children of Israel have forsaken thy covenant, torn down
thine altars, and slain thy prophets with the sword. And I, even I only,
am left; and they seek my life, to take it away." [Later, in verse 18, the
Lord informed Elijah that he was not the only one left; 7,000 others
remained faithful.]

[15]And the Lord said to him, "Go, return on thy way to the wilderness
of Damascus: and when thou comest, thou shalt anoint Hazael to be
king over Syria;

[16]and Jehu the son of Nimshi shalt thou anoint to be king over Israel;
and Elisha the son of Shaphat of Abel-meholah shalt thou anoint to
be prophet in your place." [Elijah had earlier asked to be replaced.]

The important points in these verses are the outer places that represent
inner ones: the cave of consciousness and the mountain of God within the
cave. It is also very helpful to realize that the voice of God is not that of
thunder from the sky, but rather the still, small voice within. Furthermore,
God's voice speaks from within but guides Elijah to outer actions. This is
an important point in the Cayce interpretation: Inner attunement is to be
applied and lived in the outer world among one another. Living the contact
with God in our outer lives is a fundamental teaching that is too often
forgotten. There is a wonderful moment in the Gospel of Mark, 12:28-34,
when a scribe from the Temple was listening to Jesus' discussion with some

Sadducees, Pharisees, and Herodians. The scribe was so impressed with Jesus' answers that he spoke up and asked a question that received an answer that is key to our spiritual journey—the oneness of it all and its inner and outer nature:

> [28]And one of the scribes came, and heard them questioning together, and knowing that he [Jesus] had answered them well, asked him, "What commandment is the first of all?"
>
> [29]Jesus answered, "The first is, 'Hear, O Israel; The Lord our God, the Lord is one [Deuteronomy 6:4];
>
> [30]and thou shalt love the Lord thy God with all thy heart, and with all thy soul, and with all thy mind, and with all thy strength [Deuteronomy 6:5].'
>
> [31]The second is this, 'Thou shalt love thy neighbor as thyself [Leviticus 19:18].' There is no other commandment greater than these."
>
> [32]And the scribe said unto him, "Of a truth, Teacher, thou hast well said that He is one [God]; and there is none other but He.
>
> [33]And to love Him with all the heart, and with all the understanding, and with all the strength, and to love his neighbor as himself, is much more than all whole burnt offerings and sacrifices."
>
> [34]And when Jesus saw that the scribe answered wisely, he said unto him, "Thou art not far from the kingdom of God."

To love God (the Oneness) with all our being and to love our neighbor as ourselves sum up the whole of the laws and prophets. Notice how the scribe's ability to perceive this truth from within himself resulted in Jesus' statement that the scribe was not far from fully realizing the kingdom of God.

The mystical, inner approach to God and to realizing our ultimate nature and destiny is an important key to interpreting the Revelation in a manner that is truly meaningful to us today.

In the vast body of Edgar Cayce's work, he first mentioned the Revelation in a physical health reading for a twenty-year-old woman suffering from seizures (2501-6). In the course of analyzing her problem and suggesting a course of action to help her, Cayce casually mentioned that it would "be very good for the doctor here to read The Revelation and understand it! especially in reference to this body!" Three years later, at an evening gathering of some fifty people in the living room of a close friend, Cayce gave the first reading on the Revelation, reading 281-16. It took all of fifty minutes, but everyone was amazed at the approach Cayce took. His stenographer recorded the reading (see chapter 9 for the complete transcript).

Three years later, members of the Glad Helpers prayer healing group, who had been handpicked by Cayce and worked closely with him, initiated the first of a series of readings on the Revelation, reading 281-28 (see chapter 9 for the complete transcript). That series covered nine readings (281-28 through 281-34, 281-36, and 281-37) and took less than a year to complete, from October 26, 1936, to September 8, 1937. Later, the same group picked up on Cayce's connection between the churches in the Revelation and the endocrine glands in the human body, and several more readings were given specifically on the endocrine glands (281-38, 281-46 through -49, 281-51 through -55, 281-57 and -58, and 281-63).

The Glad Helpers were used to prayer and meditation sessions. It was part of their normal process, ultimately leading to the laying on of hands. A major Cayce teaching identified prayer with lifting oneself up and calling upon God, and meditation with actually entering into direct, conscious contact with God, as the disciple John had done in receiving his revelation. In the third reading on this subject Cayce explained why John was able to take his prayers to a new, deep meditation level:

> . . . the body of the Christ represented to the world a channel, a door, a mediation to the Father. Hence this then may become as the study of self in its relationship to the material world, the mental world, the spiritual world. And this is the manner that has been presented as the way through which each individual would make application of same, of the life of the Christ in his or her own experience. 281-29

John's experience was made possible because Christ is a channel, a door, a mediation to the Father, and each of us can apply this in our lives. The Revelation represented a new connection between God and each of us through Christ. John's vision revealed the transitions, passages, and stages he went through and that we may go through to make a new relationship with God, similar to the one we originally had in the Garden where we walked and talked with Him. Remember, in the Cayce paradigm, characters and events in the Bible not only represent individual souls but also all souls as a group. Adam, therefore, is an individual and a group. The experiences recorded in the Bible are those that all souls experience. My soul and yours were created by God in the beginning, in God's image, and walked and talked with Him in that primeval Garden of the original consciousness. Today, in this present incarnation which so captivates us, it is hard to believe that somewhere within each of us is a godling created in the image of God and who once had regular, conscious contact with its Creator.

* * *

Endnotes

[1]John 17:5 and Cayce reading 1158-9. All cited Cayce readings are in chapter 9: "Edgar Cayce's Readings on the Revelation."

[2]The concept referenced here is in reading 1173-8.

2

THE TWINS, THE CURSE, AND THE GODLING: THREE KEYS TO INTERPRETATION

*I*n the Cayce vision of life and its purpose, we were created first as spirits within the One Spirit, consciousnesses within the Universal Consciousness, minds within the One Collective Mind. We were given complete freedom to do as we chose. This was necessary if we were to become true companions to the Creator, which was our primary reason for being. We had to choose to be companions, however; otherwise, we would only be children, servants, or subordinates to the Creator. We had to be completely free to choose. Also, in order to be companions and not simply reflections of the Creator, we had to become individually unique, knowing ourselves to be ourselves and yet one with the Whole, the Creator. This freedom, this process of individuation, and the ultimate need to be reunited with the Creator of our beings are behind much of what we deal with in life.

We could take a great step forward in this process if we allowed for the possibility that there are two distinct parts to ourselves: one dominant in the physical world and the other lying just behind consciousness. We are familiar with this latter self, even though most of us are not readily conscious of its existence. For example, have you ever awakened with a dream that you wanted to write down, but as you came closer to consciousness, you noticed that your bladder was full, went to empty it, and upon returning to the bedside to write down this significant dream, realized that you had completely lost its contents? You remembered having dreamed, but not the dream itself. How is this possible? It is possible because your outer self, your conscious mind, did not dream the dream. Your inner self did. While you were dreaming, you clearly felt that *you* were dreaming—a you with whom you are very familiar. The "dreaming you" was your deeper self, your subconscious mind, twin to your outer self. As you moved through the veil of consciousness to go to the toilet, so subtle was the shift from inner self to outer self that you did not notice it. As you engaged the somatic nervous system to move the physical body, you completely engaged the outer mind, the outer physical self, and lost conscious connection with the inner mind, the inner self. Nevertheless, when you were in the dreaming mind, you felt that you were in *yourself*, a normal, natural part of yourself. This reflects how natural your deeper, inner self is and how familiar you are with it. So it is with all of us. We know our inner selves, but the veil between the two is so delicate that we do not usually notice our shifting from one to the other. The veil is also so opaque that we cannot normally see through it. We need to work to make this veil more transparent and our sensitivities more subtle. In this way, we can connect our inner self with our outer self and become whole again.

Throughout many of the spiritual teachings of the ages, we find curious tales of two brothers, sometimes twins. One pursues his dreams and desires throughout the world, while the other lingers behind, staying close to the parent or original home. In some of these legends, the worldly one kills the other twin. In other cases, it only seems as though the other is killed. In ancient Egypt, we find tales of Osiris and his brother Set; in Mayan culture, there is the legend of two godly brothers against two earthly brothers; in the Old Testament, we find Cain and Abel, Jacob and Esau; and in the New Testament, Jesus told the parable of two brothers, a prodigal son and his brother who stayed home and helped his parents.

In the legend of Osiris and Set, we have brothers who came out of the heavens into the world together. Set became so jealous of his brother, who was so good and loved by all, that Set killed him. Osiris, upset by his brother's terrible deed, rejected the world as fundamentally evil and left it to those who pursue it. Osiris chose to remain in the netherworld between the outer world and the heavens, and judged anyone who attempted to pass from the world to the heavens. Eventually, Set was subdued by the ancient Egyptian version of a messiah: Horus, the immaculately conceived son of Osiris's widow, Isis.

In the creation legend of the Mayans as recorded in the Popol Vuh, both our heavenly selves and our earthly selves are depicted as brothers. In the beginning, one named 7 Macaw came to life, which fits so well with our symbology of the seven spiritual centers within the physical body. 7 Macaw claimed a place in the cosmos for himself that he did not deserve. He acted and talked like a god, but he was not. He magnified and glorified himself. Therefore, two real gods, *twins* from "the Heart of Heaven," one named Blowgunner (representing the original breath of God) and the other named Jaguar Deer (the magic of God), decided that the self-glorifying 7 Macaw must die because he was neither a heritage nor a legacy with the Heart of Heaven. But 7 Macaw gave birth to two sons who continued in the ways of their father. These two sons were symbolically named Alligator (one who crawls on his belly) and Two-his-leg (one who stands upright and stomps mountains underfoot). They were just like their bragging father, taking upon themselves undeserved glory. The godly hero twins plotted to destroy them all, father and brothers. 7 Macaw was destroyed when the godly twins drew his *pride* from him, for all he was was pride. Alligator was destroyed by magic made by the godly twins. Two-his-leg was destroyed when he ate a bird cooked by the godly twins. The bird is symbolic of a higher, lighter influence that can fly above the earth and its mountains. Ingesting this influence took Two-his-leg's strength from him, leaving him unable to stomp mountains.

In the story of Cain and Abel, we have the two offspring of the fallen Adam and Eve. In Hebrew, the name *Cain* literally means "acquired one," and *Abel* means "a breath." Their names give an insight into their symbolic roles. Cain was immersed in the pursuit of earthly desires. He represents the outer ego self. Abel is identified with the breath that was received from the Lord in the Garden. Cain became a tiller of the soil, while Abel became a shepherd, a "keeper of flocks." In this, we see the further distancing of Cain from the Lord, following in the curse of his father, Adam: " . . . cursed is the ground because of you; through painful toil you will eat of it all the days of your life. Both thorns and thistles it shall grow for you; and you shall eat the plants of the field; by the sweat of your brow you shall eat bread, till you return to the ground, because from it you were taken; for you are dust, and to dust you shall return." (Genesis 3:17-19)

When the two brothers brought their offerings before God, Abel's was pleasing to God, while Cain's was not. Cain became angry, and his countenance fell. Yet, when the Lord saw Cain's anger and low countenance, He instructed Cain: "If you do what is right, will you not be accepted? But if you do not do what is right, then sin is crouching at your door; its desire is to have you, but you must master it." (Genesis 4:7)

In the next tale, we find twins Jacob and Esau, who were very different in their interests and pursuits. Jacob lingered around the tents and talked about life and people's needs. Esau hunted and pursued adventure and life's many pleasures, gratifying his appetites. In a defining moment, Esau's desire to satisfy his hunger caused him to give away his inheritance to Jacob for a pot of lentil soup.

These stories have meaning for us because they reflect a deep truth about us. We are two. If we read Genesis carefully, we see that there were two creations. In the first (Genesis 1:26-27), we were created in the image of God, which is *Spirit*—"God is Spirit" (John 4:23-24). The second was flesh (Genesis 2:5-7), from the dust of the earth. Hence, there are two parts to us, one godly and the other human. Here are those passages from Genesis:

> So God created man in his own image, in the image of God he created him; male and female he created them. Genesis 1:27

> This is the account of the heavens and the earth when they were created. When the Lord God made the earth and the heavens—and no shrub of the field had yet appeared on the earth and no plant of the field had yet sprung up, for the Lord God had not sent rain on the earth and there was no man to work the ground, but streams came up from the earth and watered the whole surface of the ground—the Lord God formed the man from the dust of the ground and breathed into his nostrils the breath of life, and the man became a living being.
>
> Now the Lord God had planted a garden in the east, in Eden; and there he put the man he had formed. Genesis 2:4-8

Notice that, after we were created in Genesis 1 in the image of God (i.e., Spirit), there was still "no man to work the ground." (Genesis 2:5) This was because we were not yet physical. As the last line indicates, God had not "formed" man yet. Then, we see a different level of God, noted by the writer as a change in the name of God. In Genesis 1, God was called *Elohim*. In Genesis 2, He was called *Yahweh Elohim*, which most English translations identify as *Lord God*. This is the aspect of God that created us a second time, in the physical form, "from the dust of the earth." (Genesis 2:7) But the changes continued. Later, in Genesis 3, the Lord God divided us further. Though divine and human, we were originally androgynous, male and female united in each soul, but the growing influence of the duality of the world required that these be divided into separate male and female parts. A deep sleep was cast over us, as individuals and as a group. The deeper, inner part was taken out and separated into a distinct individual portion. This part of us was originally called *chavah*, which literally means *life giver* in Hebrew. Although major changes were occurring at this point in the creation story, we were still immortal beings living in direct contact with the Lord God in the Garden, "naked but unashamed." (Genesis 2:22-25)

Now we can better understand the biblical terms, "son (daughter) of God" and "son (daughter) of man." These represent each of the two major parts of our being: one divine and destined to inherit the kingdom and live with God forever, the other human and destined to yield its temporary dominance to the deeper, eternal part. Yet now, we have become so physically focused that we hardly sense the other, divine self. In fact, this was the main "crime" of which Jesus was accused: He identified Himself too closely with God, calling Himself the Son of God and calling God *Abba*, literally *Papa*. When confronted on this issue, He repeatedly pointed out that even the Scriptures tell us that we are gods, children of the great God, made in His image and destined to eventually reign with Him forever:

I said, "You are gods; you are all sons [and daughters] of the Most High." Psalms 82:6

Jesus answered them, "Is it not written in your Law, 'I have said you are gods'?" John 10:34

Then God said, "Let Us make man [actually, the word is *adam*] in Our image [actually, the Hebrew word is *tselem*, which most closely corresponds to the English word *shadow* or *shade*], according to Our likeness . . . " Genesis 1:26

And God created man [adam] in His own image, in the image of God He created him; male and female He created them. [Note: Male (Hebrew, *ish*) and female *(ishshah)* are at this time still united in one being. They are not separated until Genesis 2:21.] Genesis 1:27

The children of God were created and lived in the heavens, or in the consciousness of God, long *before* they began to live in the flesh on the earth. This is important to remember when trying to understand the strange prophecies and events in the Scriptures, especially in the Revelation.

In addition to our dual nature, there is a curse that we should be aware of because it affects us whether or not we know of it. In the course of using our free will, we made choices that were not compatible with the Creator. These incompatible choices made us feel "naked" in the presence of the All-Knowing, so we sought to hide, as Adam and Eve did in the Garden. There really is no way to hide from the Omnipresent One, no way to keep one's thoughts, desires, and memories from the All-Knowing One so an illusion was developed to help us, until we redeem ourselves and make our minds and hearts once again compatible with the Creator's. This illusion is time and space. These allow us to feel private and have a sense of progress from one less-than-ideal condition to another, more compatible condition. This was a gift from the Creator, symbolized in the Genesis story as clothing (self-privacy) and a place beyond the Garden where we would think God was not with us (i.e., our own space). Time gives us the sense of a sequence or series of actions and thoughts that will ultimately subdue and absolve the incompatible desires, thoughts, actions, and memories—from the Genesis of our separation to the final Revelation in which we unite with God again. According to Cayce, before evolution, there was an involution from spirit into matter. The fall from our original state first occurred in spirit and mind, not in flesh. The flesh is not, in itself, evil or wrong. Self-seeking willfulness is a source of evil. Misuse of free will caused the fall, not the lust of the flesh. Here is a great teaching for our outer selves. Cayce stated that the only sin is self, self without consideration of God and others. This lower, self-centered portion of our being desires to have our complete attention, but we must master it. We must master the urge to seek self's desires with little or no consideration for others and God. This was the original sin in the Garden.

Here's one Cayce reading excerpt on sin:

(Q) What is my worst fault?

(A) What is ever the worst fault of each soul? *Self—self!*

What is the meaning of self?

That the hurts, the hindrances are hurts to the self-consciousness; and these create what? Disturbing forces, and these bring about confusions and faults of every nature.

For the only sin of man is *selfishness!*

(Q) How may it be overcome?

(A) Just as has been given; showing mercy, showing grace, showing peace, longsuffering, brotherly love, kindness—even under the most *trying* circumstances.

For what is the gain if ye love those *only* that love thee? But to bring hope, to bring cheer, to bring joy, yea to bring a smile again to those whose face and heart are bathed in tears and in woe, is but making that divine love *shine—shine*—in thy own soul!

Then *smile*, be joyous, be glad! For the day of the Lord is at hand.

Who is thy Lord? Who is thy God?

Self? Or Him in Whom ye live and move and have thy being—that is *all* in All, God the Father, the Love—the *great* Hope, the Great Patience?

These are thy *all*.

Keep in the way that is arising before thee, more and more. And as ye open thy consciousness to the Great Consciousness within, there will arise more and more the white light.

For He is the light, and the life—eternal. 987-4

If we read Genesis carefully, the first biblical prophecy was " . . . if you eat of it, you will surely die." (Genesis 2:17) The second was the curse placed upon the three main characters in the Garden:

So the Lord God said to the serpent, "Because you have done this, "Cursed are you above all the livestock and all the wild animals! You will crawl on your belly and you will eat dust all the days of your life.

And I will put enmity between you and the woman, and between your offspring and her offspring; he [i.e., her offspring] will crush your head, and you will bruise his heel."

To the woman he said, "I will greatly increase your pains in childbearing; with pain you will give birth to children. Your desire will be for your husband, and he will rule over you."

To Adam he said, "Because you listened to your wife and ate from the tree about which I commanded you, 'You must not eat of it,' cursed is the ground because of you; through painful toil you will eat of it all the days of your life.

It will produce thorns and thistles for you, and you will eat the plants of the field.

By the sweat of your brow you will eat your food until you return to the ground, since from it you were taken; for dust you are and to dust you will return." Genesis 3:14-19

Since the created companions of God chose to disobey, to do as they wanted rather than as they were told, they became like God, knowing good and evil. In one respect, this was a natural stage of their development into true companions, for they were made to become full, cocreative companions with God, not just children or subordinates. They had to freely know themselves to be themselves and yet choose to be one with God. Only in this way could they be companions who chose the companionship, through the good times and bad. However, God did not want the rebellious energy to go on forever, so immortality was lost, and cycles of life and death began. Genesis stated it this way:

And the Lord God said, "The man has now become like one of us, knowing good and evil. He must not be allowed to reach out his hand and take also from the Tree of Life and eat, and live forever."

So the Lord God banished him from the Garden of Eden to work the ground from which he had been taken.

After he drove the man out, he placed on the east side of the Garden of Eden cherubim and a flaming sword flashing back and forth to guard the way to the Tree of Life. Genesis 3:22-24

Now we, the celestial, immortal companions of God, have become predominantly terrestrial, with free will and self-interests dominating, and we are now mortal. We no longer have access to the tree of life; that is, not until we reach the end of this great journey described in the last book of the Bible, the Revelation. Here we find that the tree of life will be given back to us, and we may eat from it and drink the water of life freely. The great story of the two brothers (and daughters) spans their creation and curse in the Garden of Genesis to their regaining a "new heaven" and "new earth" with no more curse, as John revealed in the final chapters of Revelation:

> Then I saw a new heaven and a new earth, for the first heaven and the first earth had passed away, and there was no longer any sea.
>
> I saw the Holy City, the new Jerusalem, coming down out of heaven from God, prepared as a bride beautifully dressed for her husband.
>
> And I heard a loud voice from the throne saying, "Now the dwelling of God is with men, and he will live with them. They will be his people, and God himself will be with them and be their God.
>
> He will wipe every tear from their eyes. There will be no more death or mourning or crying or pain, for the old order of things has passed away."
>
> He who was seated on the throne said, "I am making everything new!" Then he said, "Write this down, for these words are trustworthy and true."
>
> He said to me: "It is done. I am the Alpha and the Omega, the Beginning and the End. To him who is thirsty I will give to drink freely from the spring of the Water of Life." Revelation 21:1-6
>
> Then the angel showed me the River of the Water of Life, as clear as crystal, flowing from the throne of God and of the Lamb down the middle of the great street of the city.
>
> On each side of the river stood the Tree of Life, bearing twelve crops of fruit, yielding its fruit every month. And the leaves of the Tree are for the healing of the nations.
>
> No longer will there be any curse. The throne of God and of the Lamb will be in the city, and his servants will serve him.
>
> They will see his face, and his name will be on their foreheads.
>
> There will be no more night. They will not need the light of a lamp or the light of the sun, for the Lord God will give them light. And they will reign for ever and ever. Revelation 22:1-5

Why is it so important to understand these elements of the Bible before we can understand the prophecies? Because the prophecies are all about the journey after the fall from Spirit and God's company, through the struggles with self-will and self-consciousness in the physical body and the earth, back into the full consciousness and attunement with Spirit, with God, and with one another.

Now, when the Lord condemns or purges the flesh or the Earth, we understand that it is to make room for Spirit, which is the true nature of our eternal being. When the prophecies call for an end to the Earth by fire, flood, plague, famine, and so on, we understand that it is a cry for the rebirth of the cooperating godling by subduing the influences and demands of the selfish self. Then, once Spirit is reborn, we will unite these two aspects of ourselves in a "new heaven" and a "new earth." The curse will be gone. All is new again. Every tear will be wiped away, and joy will be full.

But the coming of the higher self, or the lord, is a stressful process. Like giving birth in the physical, giving birth to the deeper, eternal self requires some "dilation," time, courage, and effort, and with these come pain, suffering, and stress. The coming of the higher self, or the godly self, is so profoundly overwhelming to the earthly self that it is often seen as a disaster for the lower self, the human self. In a manner of speaking, it is the death of the lower self and the birth of the divine self. St. Paul said:

> Listen, I tell you a mystery: We will not all sleep, but we will all be changed—in a flash, in the twinkling of an eye, at the last trumpet. For the trumpet will sound, the dead will be raised imperishable, and we will be changed. I Corinthians 15:51-52

As the life force of the spirit self within us stirs—or, as Daniel put it, "the four winds of heaven churning up the great sea" (Daniel 7:2)—the spiritual centers within the body will begin to whirl, and the great inner powers will be aroused. At first they will be like beasts: "I was like a beast before Thee." (Psalms 72:22) Once subdued, they will serve the new Lord of the house.

According to the Cayce material, most of our human consciousness and energy exist in the lower four chakras. If we never control our urges or aspire to anything greater than self-gratification, then they become the four beasts spoken of in Ezekiel, Daniel, and the Revelation. These represent four earthly influences that take hold of us: sex, possessiveness, violence, and selfishness—the very stuff that every TV adman knows will sell a product. On the other hand, if we do control ourselves and aspire to more, then the life force will create higher energy in these centers, and it will move upward into the top three chakras. There it will be tested again, either to be found beastly or heavenly—and another battle may ensue until the higher self is victorious.

It is a dangerous awakening. One can become a beast or an angel or, as

Cayce put it, a god or a Frankenstein (262-20, 3541-1). It all depends upon the dominant influence: if self-gratification, self-glorification, then the beastly nature takes hold; if attunement and cooperation with God, then the angelic, godly nature takes hold. The spirit of cooperation, mutual respect, and a sense of the oneness of humanity (or the brotherhood and sisterhood) are needed to help all of us rise to higher levels of consciousness, to the original nature of life before the world and separation were.

Here's how the prophets have seen "the great and terrible day of the coming of the Lord." Consider the term *Lord* in this context as a reference to the overself, the godly self, that part that was created in the image of the Creator. From Isaiah to Peter, we have remarkably similar and consistent imagery:

Wail, for the day of the Lord is near; it will come like destruction from the Almighty. Isaiah 13:6

See, the day of the Lord is coming—a cruel day, with wrath and fierce anger—to make the land desolate and destroy the sinners within it. Isaiah 13:9

For the day is near, the day of the Lord is near—a day of clouds, a time of doom for the nations. Ezekiel 30:3

Alas for that day! For the day of the Lord is near; it will come like destruction from the Almighty. Joel 1:15

Let all who live in the land tremble, for the day of the Lord is coming. It is close at hand—a day of darkness and gloom, a day of clouds and blackness. Like dawn spreading across the mountains a large and mighty army comes, such as never was of old nor ever will be in ages to come. Joel 2:1-2

The Lord thunders at the head of his army; his forces are beyond number, and mighty are those who obey his command. The day of the Lord is great; it is dreadful. Who can endure it? Joel 2:11

The sun will be turned to darkness and the moon to blood before the coming of the great and dreadful day of the Lord. Joel 2:31

Multitudes, multitudes in the valley of decision! For the day of the Lord is near in the valley of decision. Joel 3:14

Woe to you who long for the day of the Lord! Why do you long for the day of the Lord? That day will be darkness, not light. It will be as though a man fled from a lion only to meet a bear, as though he entered his house and rested his hand on the wall only to have a snake bite him. Will not the day of the Lord be darkness, not light—pitch-dark, without a ray of brightness? Amos 5:18-20

The day of the Lord is near for all nations. As you have done, it will be done to you; your deeds will return upon your own head. Obadiah 1:15

Be silent before the Sovereign Lord, for the day of the Lord is near. The Lord has prepared a sacrifice; he has consecrated those he has invited. Zephaniah 1:7

The great day of the Lord is near—near and coming quickly. Listen! The cry on the day of the Lord will be bitter, the shouting of the warrior there. Zephaniah 1:14

A day of the Lord is coming when your plunder will be divided among you. Zechariah 14:1

See, I will send you the prophet Elijah before that great and dreadful day of the Lord comes. Malachi 4:5

The sun will be turned to darkness and the moon to blood before the coming of the great and glorious day of the Lord. Acts 2:20

Hand this man over to Satan, so that the sinful nature may be destroyed and his spirit saved on the day of the Lord. I Corinthians 5:5

You know very well that the day of the Lord will come like a thief in the night. I Thessalonians 5:2

But the day of the Lord will come like a thief. The heavens will disappear with a roar; the elements will be destroyed by fire, and the earth and everything in it will be laid bare. II Peter 3:10

All of these statements have been quoted over and over to put the fear of God into people. But what these prophets were seeing was the human self's reaction to the end of its dominance and the return of the divine self, the godling each of us was created to be.

The quote from St. Paul in this list is surprising (I Corinthians 5:5). He actually called for one to be handed over to Satan for purging before the coming of the Lord. But if you recall, this is exactly the mission God gave Satan in the Book of Job:

Then the Lord said to Satan, "Have you considered my servant Job? There is no one on earth like him; he is blameless and upright, a man who fears God and shuns evil."

"Does Job fear God for nothing?" Satan replied. "Have you not put a hedge around him and his household and everything he has? You have blessed the work of his hands, so that his flocks and herds are spread throughout the land. But stretch out your hand and strike everything he has, and he will surely curse you to your face."

The Lord said to Satan, "Very well, then, everything he has is in your hands, but on the man himself do not lay a finger." Then Satan went out from the presence of the Lord. Job 1:8-12

In the ancient Hebrew teachings, Satan (literally, "adversary") is the accuser, as we see when he first spoke to God in the Book of Job, accusing Job of loving God only as long as his earthly self was satisfied. But, he also became God's tester, putting Job to the test of his faith and patience.

Notice also that Satan first asked God to test Job's outer world, his possessions. When Job passed this test, then Satan sought to test the inner world of Job's own being. The inner and outer worlds must be in harmony. We cannot be spiritually seeking within, while hating or cursing everyone and everything outside of us. The ancient Egyptian god Hermes (Thoth) taught long ago: "As within so without, as above so below." We have to live as we believe, act as we think, "walk our talk." The inner and the outer must reflect our beliefs. If not, consciousness fragments and all kinds of dis-ease develop. Cayce said that the two parts of our being literally war with one another (364-7).

Finally, in the New Testament, Satan became the tempter. As the Holy Spirit comes upon us (as it did upon Jesus), we will be led out into the desert to be tested, tempted, and prepared for the coming of the Lord, both within our beings and outside among others and the world—until, like Jesus, we can say, "Be gone Satan, you have no part in me." (Matthew 4:10)

The spiritualization of the "son of man" through the coming of the "messiah" within each of us, is an important stage in our spiritual rebirth. Daniel and the other prophets saw the power of our heavenly (higher) forces come upon our beastly (lower) forces to judge and subdue or even destroy them, in order to control or spiritualize our being.

Here are some descriptions of the coming of the spirit:

> Then there came a voice from above the expanse over their heads [the beasts' heads] as they stood with lowered wings. [The beasts are now in a submissive pose, and the higher self is descending from the higher chakras to take command of the entire body-temple.]
>
> Above the expanse over their heads was what looked like a throne of sapphire, and high above on the throne was a figure like that of a man. [But this is the being with whom God originally shared the Garden.]
>
> I saw that from what appeared to be his waist up he looked like glowing metal, as if full of fire, and that from there down he looked like fire; and brilliant light surrounded him.
>
> Like the appearance of a rainbow in the clouds on a rainy day, so was the radiance around him. This was the appearance of the likeness of the glory of the Lord. When I saw it, I fell facedown, and I heard the voice of one speaking.
>
> He said to me, "Son of man, stand up on your feet and I will speak to you."
>
> As he spoke, the Spirit came into me and raised me to my feet, and I heard him speaking to me. Ezekiel 1:25-2:2

> I turned around to see the voice that was speaking to me. And when I turned I saw seven golden lampstands, and among the lampstands was someone "like a son of man," dressed in a robe reaching down to his feet and with a golden sash around his chest.
>
> His head and hair were white like wool, as white as snow, and his eyes were like blazing fire.

His feet were like bronze glowing in a furnace, and his voice was like the sound of rushing waters.

In his right hand he held seven stars, and out of his mouth came a sharp double-edged sword. His face was like the sun shining in all its brilliance.

When I saw him, I fell at his feet as though dead. Then he placed his right hand on me and said: "Do not be afraid. I am the First and the Last. I am the Living One; I was dead, and behold I am alive for ever and ever! And I hold the keys of death and Hades." [This is the portion of us that died when we left the spiritual attunement for the earthly, physical life. Therefore, it was alive, was dead and behold is alive again.] Revelation 1:12-18

Then I saw another mighty angel coming down from heaven. He was robed in a cloud, with a rainbow above his head; his face was like the sun, and his legs were like fiery pillars. Revelation 10:1

I looked, and there before me was a white cloud, and seated on the cloud was one like a son of man with a crown of gold on his head and a sharp sickle in his hand. Revelation 14:14

Ezekiel and John both saw the beastly urges of humanity make war with the heavenly forces of God and the godlings, but they also saw eventual heavenly victory over evil for all eternity. This is occurring within each of us. We each call forth our best selves, wrestle with our worst selves, and, with the help of God, are ultimately victorious in becoming greater than even the angels for having been put to the test (Hebrews 2).

It is important to keep Hermes's great teaching in mind, because the inner and outer cannot be totally isolated. Ultimately, they are one. For our purposes here, however, we'll look at them separately. The goal is to be predominantly spiritual while temporarily living in the physical.

3

SPIRITUALIZING THE BODY:
CHAPTERS 1-10 OF THE REVELATION

*I*n the first chapter of the Revelation, the disciple John intro-
duced himself and the circumstances surrounding his vision (verses 1-9).
Then, he began describing the vision with the appearance of an awesome
figure who spoke to him, the "Alpha and Omega," who instructed John to
write a message to the seven churches, representing the seven spiritual centers within the body, and explained to John the meaning of the seven stars
and seven golden lampstands (see illustrations 1 through 3).

In his first chapter, John described the encounter this way:

¹²And I turned to see the voice that spake with me. And having turned
I saw seven golden candlesticks;
¹³and in the midst of the candlesticks one like unto a son of man,
clothed with a garment down to the foot, and girt about at the breasts
with a golden girdle.
¹⁴And his head and his hair were white as white wool, *white* as snow;
and his eyes were as a flame of fire;

[15]and his feet like unto burnished brass, as if it had been refined in a furnace; and his voice as the voice of many waters.

[16]And he had in his right hand seven stars: and out of his mouth proceeded a sharp two-edged sword: and his countenance was as the sun shineth in his strength.

[17]And when I saw him, I fell at his feet as one dead. And he laid his right hand upon me, saying, Fear not; I am the first and the last,

[18]and the Living one; and I was dead, and behold, I am alive for evermore, and I have the keys of death and of Hades.

[19]Write therefore the things which thou sawest, and the things which are, and the things which shall come to pass hereafter. Revelation 1:12-19

But John was not the only one to see an awesome figure and seven items that represented the seven centers; both Ezekiel and Daniel reported seeing a similar vision.

Ezekiel began his vision by telling us, "the heavens were opened, and I saw visions of God." (Ezekiel 1:1) In his vision, he saw four beasts, just as Daniel and John did. He saw seven spinning wheels, representative of the seven chakras. He heard a voice instruct him through the battles and challenges involved in the spiritualization process. The imagery was terrifying, but the message was the same as that given to Daniel and John: All the terror, war, and pestilence represent the transformative process from physical, earthy being to spiritual, heavenly being.

Here's an excerpt from Ezekiel's vision:

[25]And there was a voice above the firmament that was over their heads [the beasts' heads]: when they stood, they let down their wings.

[26]And above the firmament that was over their heads was the likeness of a throne, as the appearance of a sapphire stone; and upon the likeness of the throne was a likeness as the appearance of a man upon it above.

[27]And I saw as it were glowing metal, as the appearance of fire within it round about, from the appearance of his loins and upward; and from the appearance of his loins and downward I saw as it were the appearance of fire, and there was brightness round about him.

[28]As the appearance of the bow that is in the cloud in the day of rain, so was the appearance of the brightness round about. This was the

appearance of the likeness of the glory of Jehovah. And when I saw it, I fell upon my face, and I heard a voice of one that spake.

[1]And he said unto me, Son of man, stand upon thy feet, and I will speak with thee.

[2]And the Spirit entered into me when he spake unto me, and set me upon my feet; and I heard him that spake unto me.

[3]And he said unto me, Son of man, I send thee to the children of Israel, to nations that are rebellious, which have rebelled against me: they and their fathers have transgressed against me even unto this very day.

[4]And the children are impudent and stiffhearted: I do send thee unto them; and thou shalt say unto them, Thus saith the Lord Jehovah.

[5]And they, whether they will hear, or whether they will forbear, (for they are a rebellious house,) yet shall know that there hath been a prophet among them.

[6]And thou, son of man, be not afraid of them, neither be afraid of their words, though briers and thorns are with thee, and thou dost dwell among scorpions: be not afraid of their words, nor be dismayed at their looks, though they are a rebellious house.

[7]And thou shalt speak my words unto them, whether they will hear, or whether they will forbear; for they are most rebellious.

[8]But thou, son of man, hear what I say unto thee; be not thou rebellious like that rebellious house: open thy mouth, and eat that which I give thee.

[9]And when I looked, behold, a hand was put forth unto me; and, lo, a roll of a book was therein;

[10]And he spread it before me: and it was written within and without; and there were written therein lamentations, and mourning, and woe. Ezekiel 1:25-2:10

Daniel described his encounter this way:

[5]I lifted up mine eyes, and looked, and, behold, a man clothed in linen, whose loins were girded with pure gold of Uphaz:

[6]his body also was like the beryl, and his face as the appearance of lightning, and his eyes as flaming torches, and his arms and his feet like unto burnished brass, and the voice of his words like the voice of a multitude.

[7]And I, Daniel, alone saw the vision; for the men that were with me saw not the vision; but a great quaking fell upon them, and they fled

to hide themselves.

[8]So I was left alone, and saw this great vision, and there remained no strength in me; for my comeliness was turned in me into corruption, and I retained no strength.

[9]Yet heard I the voice of his words; and when I heard the voice of his words, then was I fallen into a deep sleep on my face, with my face toward the ground.

[10]And, behold, a hand touched me, which set me upon my knees and upon the palms of my hands.

[11]And he said unto me, O Daniel, thou man greatly beloved, understand the words that I speak unto thee, and stand upright; for unto thee am I now sent. And when he had spoken this word unto me, I stood trembling.

[12]Then said he unto me, Fear not, Daniel; for from the first day that thou didst set thy heart to understand, and to humble thyself before thy God, thy words were heard: and I am come for thy words' sake. Daniel 10:5-12

From Cayce's perspective, this figure was the deeper, higher spiritual self. To John, this figure said, "Do not be afraid; I am the first and the last, and the living One; and I was dead, and behold, I am alive forevermore, and I have the keys of death and Hades." (John 1:17-18) As with John, our spiritual selves, made in the image of God and destined to be eternal companions to God, have been dead to us and will remain so until we give birth to them again, as Jesus instructed Nicodemus (John 3:14). The first instruction from the spiritual self was to the seven spiritual centers of the body, represented by the various sevens throughout the initial chapters of Revelation.

The idea that the body possesses seven centers or chakras that may be used for spiritualization dates back to ancient times. One of the first recorded manuscripts to teach this was Patanjali's *Yoga Sutras*, written in the ancient Sanskrit language around 300 B.C. Patanjali was a student and teacher of the most ancient body of religious literature yet found in the world, the Veda (ca. 1200 B.C.).[1] Vedism was the religion of an ancient Indo-European people who settled in India. One of Vedism's key teachings, which eventually made its way into another ancient Sanskrit text, the Bhagavad Gita (ca. 200 B.C.), is that the Supreme Being created our souls with an eternal share of Himself/Herself in each soul, but this share is latent within us and must therefore be awakened (Bhagavad Gita, IX, 7-11). Cayce affirmed this concept when he was asked, "Should the Christ-Consciousness be described as the awareness within each soul, imprinted in pattern on the mind and waiting to be awakened by the will, of the soul's oneness with God?" He answered, "Correct. That's the idea exactly!" (5749-14) Patanjali taught that this latent Presence is in all of creation and, most important to us, *in* each physical body, and it can be awakened. In order to experience this shared Presence of the Supreme Being, Patanjali taught, one needs to elevate the normal levels of body energy and mental consciousness. The levels we find sufficient for everyday life are not sufficient for intimate contact with God.

In the Vedic texts and most other Eastern texts, energy and consciousness were symbolized by the serpent. Judeo-Christian followers often equate evil and Satan with the serpent, but the teachings of Christ and Moses also contained serpent images as part of spiritualization. Recall a teaching Jesus gave to Nicodemus during a secret, nighttime visit from this high-ranking member of the Sanhedrin (John 3). Nicodemus wanted to learn more, and Jesus gave him three major teachings. The first was that we must be born again; we have been born physically, but we need to also be born spiritually. The second teaching was that no one ascends to heaven but those who first descend, even the son of man, referring to the involution of spirit into matter prior to our evolution up through matter. All of us, whether we remember it or not, have a portion within us that first descended from heaven.

Key to our study in this chapter, however, is the third teaching: "As Moses raised the serpent in the desert, so must the son of man be raised up to eternal life." Jesus was referring to the time when Moses left the kingdom of Pharaoh (so symbolic of the outer ego and worldly pursuits) to search for God in the desert. In his search, he came upon a deep well around which seven virgins were attempting to water their flocks. Seven virgins? Daughters of a priest? These must be symbolic of the seven spiritual centers, the seven chakras, the seven churches. Moses helped them and, ultimately, married the eldest one. Afterward, he met God in a burning bush and, for the first time, was instructed in how to transform his staff into a serpent and raise the serpent up again into a staff (Exodus 2, 3, 4). Later, when he had all the people out in the desert with him, Moses was instructed by God to place a "fiery" serpent upon a raised staff, saying that anyone who was bitten by a serpent would be healed when that person looked upon the raised one (Numbers 21:8-9). Here again, I believe the writer was trying to convey more than a literal, physical story to us. We also see that the serpent can be both poisonous and healing. The one that crawls on the ground is poisonous and deadly, but when the serpent is raised up and "fiery," it is healing.

We have to go back to the Garden of Eden to fully understand this, because Adam and Eve were not the only ones to fall in the Garden; the serpent fell also. The serpent represents the life force and consciousness within each of us. This energy can be harmful if misused, but raising it is a key step along the path that leads to the glory of direct consciousness with God and His Presence within us. In the teachings of Patanjali and Cayce (264-19, 262-87, 444-2), the life force within the body can lower or raise our vibrations and consciousness. Jesus and Moses taught that the serpent represents energy within us that must be raised up in order to realize eternal life and engage us in communication with God.

The process of raising the energy begins with an understanding of where the energy is in the body, how it is raised, and the path it follows through the body. According to the Yoga Sutras, the energy is "coiled up" like a serpent *(kundalini)* in the lower part of the torso. It moves up the spinal column *(sushumna)*, through the spiritual centers *(chakras* [wheels] or *padmas* [lotuses]), to the base of the brain, through the brain, and over to the brow. The path of the kundalini through the body is represented by a cobra in the striking position or by a shepherd's crook (a staff with a large hook on the upper end, flared out at the very tip). Many books today teach that the kundalini culminates at the crown of the head, but the more ancient images and teachings, as well as Cayce's, always depicted it culminating at the forehead. This will cause some confusion among many who have studied and practiced for years using the crown chakra as the highest spiritual center in the body. Cayce insisted that the true path of the kundalini comes over through the crown chakra and into the third-eye chakra on the brow (281-54).

The seven spiritual centers are connected with the seven endocrine glands within the body: (1) testes or ovaries, (2) cells of Leydig, (3) adrenals, (4) thymus, (5) thyroid, (6) pineal, and (7) pituitary. They are also connected with major nerve ganglia or plexuses along the spine (pelvic or lumbar, hypogastric or abdominal, epigastric or solar, cardiac, pharyngeal or throat, and the brain itself). Cayce recommended that meditators have osteopathic adjustments to their spines for better flow of the kundalini energy (281-12). (These days, osteopathy has moved away from physical adjustments, leaving that area to chiropractors and, in some cases, massotherapists.)

Let's examine what John's spiritual self had to say about each spiritual center, beginning with the lowest center and moving up through the body to the highest. In each case, John's spiritual self first described a characteristic of himself that was related to that specific church, center, and gland. Then, he acknowledged the center's strengths or virtues, followed by the center's shortcomings or vices. Finally, he gave the center a directive, a command. Interestingly, in Pantanjali's teachings, the forehead center was called *ajna*, which literally means "a commandment" or "an order." These commandments are given to each center by the spiritual self. Remember, Cayce stated that John's experience is an excellent reference for all of us to work with in our own practice.

The Seven Churches: The Seven Spiritual Centers
Revelation 1-3 (Illustrations 4-10)

The Church of Ephesus: First Center (Gonads)

In John's vision, the portion of our spiritual selves that holds the seven stars (identified as the seven angelic forces overseeing each chakra) and walks among the seven golden lampstands (identified as the actual glands in the body) said that this first center's virtue is that it has toiled and persevered and that it cannot stand evil or false spirituality. Nevertheless, its weakness is that it has left its first love. It must, therefore, remember from where it has fallen, repent, and do the first deeds. Despite all appearances to the contrary, we are celestial, spiritual beings first. We descended from heaven into matter and this world. These outer influences have taken hold of us. They possess us. We feel completely terrestrial and physical, subjects of this world. This first chakra reflects that loss. It must reverse its focus from worldly realities to include only spiritual realities, remembering that it originally loved the spiritual things and God, who is a spirit (John 4:24).

In many of the ancient texts, reversing the flow of energy in the body is a major technique for spiritualizing the body. In illustration 38, we see a Taoist diagram of a breathing technique in which the mind visualizes energy rising up the back of the body with every inhalation of the breath, uniting with the Great Spirit's breath, and then descending down the front of the body with every exhalation, bathing the body in raised, spiritualized energy. The sexual glands or chakras have the life force of the body "coiled" within them. This needs to be awakened and drawn upward through the body, to the brain, and over to the forehead. There it needs to be united with our spiritual ideal, or our image, concept, or consciousness of God and our godly nature. Then, with this first love restored, the body will be bathed in the resurrected spirit and vibration. Over time, the body will become spiritualized again.

In its final comment to this center, the spirit promised that if this center spiritualizes itself, it will be allowed to eat from the tree of life again in the Paradise of God (Revelation 2:7). In other words, it will regain its immortality and its companionship with God in the Paradise lost in Genesis.

The Church of Smyrna: Second Center (Cells of Leydig)

As the spiritual self turned its attention to the church of Smyrna, it identified itself as being the first self and the last self, which was dead and is now alive again. It acknowledged that this center, the navel or lower abdomen chakra, had suffered much tribulation, poverty, and slander from those claiming to be true spiritual seekers but who are of "the synagogue of Satan." (Revelation 2:9)

Cayce identified the second and the sixth spiritual centers as the "seat of the soul." (294-142) The soul's companion is the subconscious mind, according to Cayce (3744-3). These two abide in the autonomic nervous system of the body and directly affect the endocrine glands and their hormones. Their primary points of contact are the second and sixth chakras. The spirit was aware of the soul's and subconscious mind's poverty and tribulation in a purely physically driven body with little or no spiritual nourishment. When we are predominantly in our outer egos and conscious minds, our souls and deeper minds suffer and starve. Despite this, the spirit said that the soul is rich and it should not fear its trials and imprisonment in the body; at the death of the body, the spirit will give it "the crown of life." (Revelation 2:10)

The spirit warned that this center lets fear take hold of it and it must let go of fear. The spirit promised that if this center stops being afraid and doubting the truth, it will not suffer the "second death." Cayce said that the second death is when those who have gained understanding again fall away into self-exaltation, accentuating the ego rather than the soul-self, and suffer the death of the truth a second time. If this spiritual center lets go of fear, it will never fall away again, never again suffer death of the truth. Cayce explained it this way: "For there is set before thee good and evil, life and death; choose thou. For the spirit of truth maketh alive. Fear, doubt, condemnation, bringeth doubt, illness, fear, and then dissolution (disillusion?); and the hill to be climbed again." (1261-1) In other readings, Cayce said that doing what we know is right, despite the challenges, will remove fear. We certainly don't want to climb the hill again or experience the death of the truth a second time.

The Church of Pergamos[2]: Third Center (Adrenal Glands)

As the spirit approached this third center, it described itself as the one with a two-edged sword, revealing this center's power to wield a weapon that can cut for good or evil. The spirit acknowledged that this center held fast to "my name" and did not deny "my witness, my faithful one"; even though this center is "where Satan's throne is" and "where Satan dwells." (Revelation 2:13) Over and over in the Cayce volumes, we find the concept that within each of us is both the Holy One and the Evil One, wrestling for power and control over us.[3] Thus, this center is a most dangerous and potentially powerful chakra, given the energy of the solar plexus and the adrenal glands' "fight-or-flight" hormones. In many yoga texts, its power is often identified as second only to the crown chakra. According to Cayce, during physical growth or meditation, if balance is maintained, the energy of the life force, the kundalini, crosses the solar plexus each time it passes to another center (281-53).

This center is also the place of anger (281-54), impulsive reactions, and spirit-killing urges. The spirit identified its weaknesses and vices as eating things "sacrificed to idols" and committing "acts of immorality." The spirit said that, uncontrolled, this center throws "stumblingblock[s]" in the way of our spiritual efforts. It must stop. If it does, then the spirit promised that it would "eat of the hidden manna" and "receive a new name." (Revelation 2:14-17)

Cayce said that "my name" in verse 13 referred to our eternal name that uniquely identifies each of us from among the rest of creation (281-31). Somehow, deep within us, we have not fully denied this aspect of ourselves; we have not killed the witness to our spiritual nature. If we spiritualize this center, then a new name will be given to us, a name that only we who receive it will know. John received his name written upon a white stone, indicating that it would endure, or, as we would say, "It's written in stone."

The manna referred to this center's desires for physical gratifications, often symbolized as bread; yet, as Jesus so wonderfully put it, we do not live by bread alone, but by every word that comes out of the mouth of God

(Matthew 4:4). These words from God's mouth, Cayce said, are the hidden manna (281-31). As the spirit warned, it will come upon this center "quickly with the sword of my mouth" (Revelation 2:16) if it doesn't overcome its negative influences.

The Church of Thyatira: Fourth Center (Thymus Gland)

Next the spirit moved to the fourth center, identifying itself as the Son of God, with eyes like fire and feet like fine brass. In other words, it had the vision of the spirit and the understanding that comes only from being tested in the furnace of life. It acknowledged that the heart chakra has charity, faith, patience, service, and works, with the most recent works being greater than the first works. There is also one major issue with this center: It lives life without love or spirit, seeking only gratification and pleasure. This is represented by the false prophet Jezebel, whose motto was "Get all you want, no matter how you obtain it,"[4] and by acts of fornication, which is sex without vows, here representative of living physically without spiritual ideals. Then the spirit warned that, unless the heart center changed, it would suffer "great tribulation" in the bed it had made for itself. When Cayce was asked about the great tribulation, he answered:

> The great tribulation and periods of tribulation . . . are the experiences of every soul, every entity. They arise from influences created by man . . . Man may become, with the people of the universe, ruler of any of the various spheres through which the soul passes in its experiences. Hence, as the cycles pass, as the cycles are passing, when there *is* come a time, a period of readjusting in the spheres (as well as in the little earth, the little soul—seek, then, as known, to present self spotless before that throne; even as *all* are commanded to be circumspect, in thought, in act, to that which is held by self as that necessary for the closer walk with Him. In that manner only may each atom (as man is an atom, or corpuscle, in the body of the Father) become a helpmeet with Him in bringing that to pass that all may be one with Him. 281-16

The spirit went on to promise that, if this spiritual center changed, then spirit would "give him the morning star." (Revelation 2:28) The morning star is any bright planet seen in the eastern horizon before sunrise. Venus is the most brilliant planet in our solar system and often appears as the morning star. In astrological traditions, Venus represents love, harmony, and beauty. As we will see later in this chapter, Cayce identified the planet Venus with the heart chakra (281-29).

The Church of Sardis: The Fifth Center, (Thyroid Gland)

The speech delivered by the spirit identified this center with the throat. The spirit explained that speech came from "the seven spirits of God and the seven stars," (Revelation 3:1) which are the sum total of all seven centers acting in unison with God's will. The spirit acknowledged that this center has good deeds, a name, is alive, and that only a few aspects of its activities are "defiled." Nevertheless, it is dead to the real truth and is imperfect. The spirit encouraged this center to strengthen itself because it was closer to death than it realized. If it strengthened itself spiritually, then it would be clothed in white raiment, its name would not be blotted out of the Book of Life, and the spirit would confess its name "before my Father and his angels." (Revelation 3:5)

Notice how much of this center is identified with will and speech. Cayce said that one of the major steps to full spiritual consciousness is letting our will become subordinate to God's will. He often recommended an affirmation, such as this one from the Search for God® study group readings:

> Thy will, O God, be done in me, through me, as Thou seest; for the desire of my heart is that I may be the channel of blessings to others in the ways and manners Thou seest; not my way, O Lord, but Thy way. 262-64

This is reminiscent of Jesus' intimate prayer sessions with the Father in the Garden of Gethsemane, in which He prayed three times for the Father to remove the cup of crucifixion from Him, but only if it was the Father's will, not just Jesus's will. At the end of the third prayer, Jesus knew it was the Father's will that He drink from this cup, because despite the physical outcome, spiritual glory would be realized and the flesh would be raised up again to life spiritualized and everlasting.

The Church of Philadelphia: The Sixth Center (Pineal Gland)

As the spiritual self approached the sixth center, located deep within the brain, it referenced that part of itself that is "holy, true, has the key of David, opens and no one can shut, shuts and no one can open" (Revelation 3:7). Which is to say that only the spiritual part of our being can allow the spiritual process to proceed. This is considered to be one of the most holy centers in the human body. It is the place of "the holy mount" of God, according to Cayce (2501-7). If we enliven this center with spirit and spiritual intentions, then we draw all the lower centers up to this high place and unite them with God's Spirit.

The spirit acknowledged the works of this center, that it is has kept His word and not denied His name. This center knew the truth of its spiritual nature, and, despite how weak it had become from material struggles, it retained the truth of its real nature and purpose for life. This was the only center with which the spirit finds no fault. There is nothing this center had to do except continue to hold on to its truth. Therefore, the spirit promised to draw all the cells of the body before it and make them bow to its truth. It also promised to keep this center from the temptation that had and was coming to the rest of the body: to test the body's true desires, whether they were spiritual or strictly material and self-centered.

In Patanjali's arrangement (illustrations 34 and 35), the crown chakra is the highest center in the body. The kundalini, having risen up the spine, moves through the brain, to the brow, culminating at the opening of the crown. In Revelation 3:11, the spirit actually mentioned the "crown" in reference to this center. In Cayce's arrangement (illustration 36), the energy flows up the spine, through the brain, to the pineal gland, opening this crown chakra, but then flows to the forehead, which to Cayce was the highest center, the pituitary gland.

If we fully awaken this center, then the spiritual self promised to make us "a pillar in the temple of my God" and that we will "never go out from it again." (Revelation 3:12) The spirit will also write the name of God, God's city, and its new name upon us.

The Church of Laodicea: The Seventh Center (Pituitary Gland)

Finally, the spiritual self arrived at the highest center in the body. The aspect of the spiritual self that was in this center is "the Amen, the faithful and true witness, the beginning of the creation of God" (Revelation 3:14). This is the master gland of the body. But the spirit was upset with this center because it was "neither cold nor hot." Because the seventh center was lukewarm about the spiritualization process, the spirit was ready to "spit you out of my mouth." (Revelation 3:15-16) This center said that it was rich and needed nothing, but the spiritual self challenged that it was actually "wretched and miserable and poor and blind and naked", harkening back to the original sin in the Garden (Revelation 3:17). Amazingly, this center had no redeeming qualities and no virtue to acknowledge. It was stagnant and lukewarm, contributing nothing to the overall spiritualization of the body. The spirit therefore warned it to get truth forged in the fires of the spirit, white garments of purity so that its nakedness would be clothed, and eye salve to anoint its eyes to see the real truth. However, in a backhanded way, the spirit also acknowledged its love for this center, saying: "Those whom I love, I reprove and discipline." (Revelation 3:19)

THE THRONE, TWENTY-FOUR ELDERS, SEVEN SPIRITS, LAKE OF GLASS, AND FOUR BEASTS: A NEW CONDITION THROUGHOUT THE BODY REVELATION 4-5 (ILLUSTRATIONS II-I4)

Once the spirit addressed and awakened all seven centers within the body to the spiritualization process, it took the body to a new level of vibration. Now a throne was in the midst of heaven, and the higher, spiritual self was seated upon this throne. Around the higher self and the throne were the twenty-four elders, who Cayce identified as the twelve paired (24 total) cranial nerves within the brain. Energy was being emitted from the brain ("flashes of lightning and sounds and peals of thunder"), and the seven chakras and glands were turned toward the throne ("seven lamps of fire burning"), the seven spirits of God in the midst of the throne (Revelation 4:4-5). Before the throne were the four beasts we first saw in Ezekiel's and then in Daniel's visions, and now, here again, in John's vision (see illustration 37). We find these same beasts represented in ancient Egyptian mysticism as the four children of Horus. Horus was the messiah of the ancient Egyptians, rescuing the world from his uncle Set's domination (Set is ancient Egypt's Satan). The four children of Horus are wrapped like mummies on a lotus, subdued and intoxicated with the fragrance of the great flower. They stand before the throne-seated Osiris, Horus's father and guardian of the way through the Netherworld.

According to Cayce, these beasts are "the four destructive influences that make the greater desire for the carnal forces, that rise as the beasts within self to destroy." (281-16) We have learned what these destructive influences are from the spirit's comments to the first four churches: (1) leaving our first love; (2) fear; (3) anger, impulsive reactions, and spirit-killing urges; and (4) living life without spiritual purposes and ideals. All of these destructive influences were personified in Cain. Though he first sought God's love, he later didn't desire it. He killed his brother impulsively in anger and spitefulness, only to then become so afraid that he could not go on without God's promise of protection. Finally, he went out to live life for himself and his own gratification, without any spiritual interests or intentions. Satan claimed that Job was the same way, having no interest in God and the Spirit, and would curse God to His face if He touched Job's material, physical life and being. Cayce said that these destructive influences must be met (281-16), as God said to Cain, "Sin is couching at the door, its desire is for you, but you must master it." (Genesis 4:7)

As the Revelation continued, the four lower glands were raised to higher vibrations, turning away from material, earthly pursuits and contributing to the spiritualization of the body: "the four beasts gave glory and honor and thanks to him who sits on the throne" (Revelation 4:9). When they did this, it affected the cranial nerves ("the twenty-four elders will fall down before him who sits on the throne"), and they, in turn, began to contribute to the spiritualization of the body ("cast their crowns to him who sits on the throne") (Revelation 4:10). Then the spiritual self was able to open the seals on each of the spiritual chakras of the body. Cayce stated that the book with the seven seals is the human body (281-29). The only part of us that is truly worthy to do this is that part that has crucified self-centered desire sufficiently to allow God's will to fully enter. This one was identified in the Revelation as "the Lion of the tribe of Judah, the root and offspring of David" (Revelation 5:5), all terms associated with the Messiah, only this is the little messiah within each of us, our spiritual self reborn, created by God and sent to redeem our physical selves. This self has so made its will subordinate to God's that it is represented as a lamb. It is in the spirit of the Lamb of God that we may safely open the seals of the spiritual centers of our bodies.

THE SEVEN SEALS AND SOUNDINGS
CLEANSING AND UNITING THE SEVEN CENTERS
REVELATION 6-II
(ILLUSTRATIONS 15-20)

Once the seven spiritual centers were awakened, the higher self and the life force were raised and again seated upon the throne, the lower urges were turned away from their interests, and the cranial nerves were firing with spiritual influences, there began a series of cleansings through the seven bodily centers. Prompted by John's vision of the four colored horses, Cayce picked up on the colors for each center and proceeded to add musical notes, key words from the Lord's Prayer, the four elements, the endocrine glands, and even planets within our solar system! There is so much information that the original group working with Cayce created charts. Subsequently, the New York City group created a chart of their own. Therefore, I've also created a chart based on the originals but with supplemental information (see illustration 33).

We might ask, how could the planets in the solar system have any relevance to the spiritual centers and endocrine glands in our bodies? Cayce's answer was that we are parts of the Universal Consciousness, and, as such, we have a relationship to the Universe and all that is in it (2984-1). At first glance, it may seem paradoxical that these outer influences are also within us spiritually, mentally, and physically; that universal "things," such as planets, find a relating point within our physical bodies. But, as the ancient Egyptian god Hermes (Thoth) said: "As within, so without; as above, so below." It is not so much the occult science of astrology that we are referring to as it is the microcosmic and macrocosmic nature of life. The human body is arranged in a manner that reflects the arrangement of the universe. Here's one of Cayce's best explanations of this:

As we find, Mercury, Jupiter, Mars, Saturn, Venus—with Mars in an abstract position—all becoming a part of this entity's experience; not because of bodily birth but because of the *entity* as a soul.

For the entity finds itself body, mind and soul, and recognizes—or may become aware of the manifestation of the Godhead in the Father, the Son, the Holy Spirit. *He finds himself then a counterpart, a shadow of all that is; and that within his own self each cell of its body is but a miniature of the universe without its own body* [author's emphasis], its own cell of positive and negative force that applies to the material, the

mental and the spiritual. Indeed then the body is the temple of the
living God, where He hath promised to meet thee in thy searching,
in thy seeking to know what ye may do; not for the gratifying of thine
own selfish self alone but to fulfill the purpose for which ye came into
being—to be then an emissary, and advocate—yea, a sign; that others
who have lost their way—as *ye* may have lost thine may take hope and
gain more awareness of the God-force that *is* latent and manifested
within thine own self. 1776-1

Following this philosophical line of thought, each spiritual center in
the body has a corresponding relationship with the seven primary colors
of the spectrum, the seven basic notes of the Western musical scale, seven
key words in the Lord's Prayer, and seven planets within our solar system.
Nevertheless, Cayce did hedge his teaching on this in several readings, explaining that these correlations that we are making are only *relatively* correct
because of the many variables in human spiritual development that would
cause another color, note, word, or planet to better represent that center: (1)
at that particular time in a person's development, or (2) for that individual
soul's unique experiences and, therefore, influences. For all of us generally,
however, these are relatively correct as we have them in the charts here.[5]

Cayce said that going through the opening of the seals and the sounding
of the trumpets actually is going through the purifications that influence
spiritual development through the vibrational changes in the body (281-31).
The way these purifications are described in the Revelation sounds as if they
are terrifyingly devastating to the physical self. However, Cayce explained
that, as progress is made toward giving birth to the spiritual self (which
occurs later in chapter 12 of the Revelation), the physical self must become
more humble, meek, longsuffering, and patient. It must decrease, while the
spiritual self increases, as John the Baptist said of himself and the coming
Jesus. Cayce said that the devastating sufferings represent those influences
that meet and conquer self for the greater spiritual development and oneness of the individual's purposes and desires (281-31). The two parts of our
being can end up at war with one another unless these cleansings occur and
a singularity of purpose is achieved by subduing earthly desires and accentuating heavenly, spiritual desires. The fire is to purify; the hail, to crystallize
opposing purposes into oneness of purpose. Fewer and fewer of self's desires
and more and more of God's desires are depicted as the destruction of one-
third of the earth, the sea, and the heavens occurs, followed by the falling of

a great star from heaven and representing the coming of heavenly influences upon the earthly self. The Sun is darkened so that the Son may give a new light to the body. All the terrifying events that occur during the opening and sounding of the seven spiritual centers under the influence of the higher self upon the throne of consciousness are symbolic of this great transition, this great preparation for the birth of the new, God-centered self.

Let's go through the opening of the seals and the soundings of the trumpets for each center. Though these are done separately in the Revelation, we will do them together here for the sake of clarity and focus.

Opening the First Seal and Sounding the First Trumpet
The White Horse—Conquering—One-third of the Earth Burned

The higher self, in the spirit of the Lamb, and in coordination with God's will, opened the seals of the body. When the first seal was opened, out came the first of the four horsemen, riding a white horse, wearing a crown, and carrying a bow. His mission was to conquer the negative influences and win this center for the spiritual self.

The outer things that are related to this center are the color *red*, the note *do,* the word *bread* in the Lord's Prayer, the planet *Saturn,* the element *earth,* and, of course, the church of Ephesus, the gonads, and the beast like a calf. In the Cayce cosmology, the influence of Saturn is to recast all "insufficient matter" or "spiritualize" the flesh (900-10, 311-2, 3346-1). Here we see the white-horse rider conquering flesh for the spirit.

When the sounding occurred, hail and fire, mixed with blood, were thrown down upon the earthly influences. Cayce said that hail is symbolic of "crystallizing" or uniting ideals under the spiritual influence, fire is purifying earthly influences, and the blood of the Lamb of God symbolizes our being cleansed from all sin (a clear reference to I John 1:7). Here is an example of Cayce's view on the metaphysical and, for that matter, the physical power of the blood:

> (Q) Please give advice which will aid me, physically, mentally and spiritually, in fulfilling my destiny in life of aiding my fellow man.
> (A) Manifesting in self that which is meted to the body, mentally, physically, spiritually, that is necessary to bring those influences within self, those conditions mentally and physically within self, as to cleanse or to make more in accord with that which is the birthright of

every physical being—to be perfect within itself, through the blood as cleanseth from unrighteousness in material, in the mental, and in the spiritual plane. Hence, as there is created that consciousness within self of being whole, or one with that Creative Energy as manifested by Him, through those channels that have been set as the ways, the manners for perfecting of such a consciousness within self, then may the body be that channel to be the greater blessings to those about body. But use that thou hast in hand day by day! For, that which is used gives the ability, the understanding, to apply that which may be needed from day to day. 264-38

The first sounding also burned up one-third of the trees and grasses of the Earth, symbolic of removing a significant portion of the earthly influences.

Opening the Second Seal and Sounding the Second Trumpet
The Red Horse—War—One-third of the Sea Became Blood

When the second seal was opened, out came a horseman wielding a great sword and riding a red horse. His mission was to take peace away from the Earth and make men slay one another. The spirit cannot allow us to be terrestrial, earthly beings forever; we must be forced to seek the spirit, even it means war.

The outer things that are related to this center are the color *orange,* the note *re,* the word *temptation* in the Lord's Prayer, the planet *Neptune,* the element *water,* and, of course, the church of Smyrna, the cells of Leydig, and the beast like a man. In the Cayce cosmology, the influence of Neptune is to accentuate the mystical-spiritual forces in our lives (900-10, 2029-1, 2281-1).

When the second sounding occurred, a great mountain, burning with fire, was thrown into the sea, causing one-third of the sea to become blood (the cleansing concept again). One-third of the sea creatures died and one-third of the ships were destroyed—again, symbolic of reducing the earthly, bodily influences to allow for more spiritual influences.

Opening the Third Seal and Sounding the Third Trumpet
The Black Horse—Famine—A Great Star Fell from Heaven

When the third seal was opened, out came a horseman with a pair of scales in his hand, riding a black horse. His mission was to measure out limited portions to the Earth, allowing more room for spiritual influences, but he was instructed not to harm the oil and the wine, symbolic of those things that are gained only through experiences that squeeze the deeper essences out of life and grow wiser with age.

The outer things that are related to this center are the color *yellow*, the note *mi*, the word *debts* in the Lord's Prayer, the planet *Mars*, the element *fire*, and, of course, the church of Pergamos, the adrenals and solar plexus, and the beast like a lion. In the Cayce cosmology, the influence of Mars is to accentuate temper, madness, and contention (900-10, 830-1, 265-1), also associated with adrenaline that flows into the bloodstream from this center.

When the sounding occurred for this center, a great star from heaven fell to the Earth, which Cayce said is the coming into the body of heavenly influences. One-third of the water of the Earth became bitter, and many men died from drinking it. Again, this is a symbolic way of saying that the earthly influences are becoming less desirable, less tasty, causing earthly influences to be subdued and heavenly ones to be magnified.

Opening the Fourth Seal and Sounding the Fourth Trumpet
The Pale Horse—Death and Hades—The Heavens Were Darkened

When the fourth seal was opened, out came a horseman named Death, and Hades was following him. Death rode a pale or ashen horse. His mission was to kill one-fourth of the Earth with sword, famine, pestilence, and wild beasts, making more room for spiritual influences.

The outer things that are related to this center are the color *green*, the note *fa*, the word *evil* in the Lord's Prayer, the planet *Venus*, the element *air*, and of course, the church of Thyatira, the thymus, and the beast like an eagle. In the Cayce cosmology, the influence of Venus leads one to be loving, considerate, even-tempered, and interested in art, music, and beauty (900-10, 342-2, 451-2), all benevolent features of the heart chakra.

When the fourth trumpet was sounded, one-third of the sun, moon, and stars were smitten, so that their light was darkened. As we mentioned earlier, Cayce said that this was to make room for the light of the Son, awakening the body to the true, eternal, inner light that God will bring with Him. After this sounding, an eagle was seen flying in midheaven, saying "Woe,

woe, woe, to those who dwell on the earth, because of the remaining blasts of the trumpet of the three angels who are about to sound!" (Revelation 8:13) Cayce identified these four lower centers with the earthly portion of our bodies, and the next three higher centers with the heavenly part of our body. Therefore, it is not surprising that "those who dwell on the earth" are going to have great woe when the heavenly influence comes into full glory throughout the body. The body will lose much of its earthly urges and desires, leaving those who have feasted on these and developed appetites for them to suffer the next three woes.

Opening the Fifth Seal and Sounding the Fifth Trumpet
The Martyrs—White Robes—The Bottomless Pit

When the fifth seal was opened, the souls of the martyrs came out from beneath the altar in heaven. They had been slain for their testimony to the word of God. They now wanted to know how much longer God was going to tolerate the negative influences in the Earth. They were given white robes and told to rest a little while longer. Soon the process of enlightenment would be completed.

The outer things that are related to this center are the colors *gray* or *blue,* the note *so,* the word *will* in the Lord's Prayer, the planet *Uranus,* the element *ether,*[6] and, of course, the church of Sardis and the thyroid. There is no beast because we have moved beyond the earthy-earthly portion of the body. In the Cayce cosmology, the influence of Uranus brings forth the extremes in temperament, enthusiasm, zeal, likes and dislikes, and an interest in the unusual, and the psychic (524-2, 421-5, 900-10, 2136-1). This center is also related to the harbinger or herald and, therefore, to John the Baptist, who baptized with cleansing water, called for repentance, and prepared the way for the coming of the One who baptizes with fire and resurrection.

When the fifth sounding occurred, the star that had fallen from heaven and the key to the bottomless pit were given to the fifth angel, or heavenly influence, which we have identified earlier with the church of Sardis and God's will rather than our will. The angel opened the bottomless pit, which Cayce said is symbolic of all those things within us that are "the most uncomely," that are far from the presence of God. These must have the light shone upon them and be destroyed by the angel of the abyss: *Abaddon* in Hebrew, and *Apollyon* in Greek, meaning respectively, *destruction* and *destroyer.* These incompatible things within us, Cayce said, are "lost in the beauty of the Son", and our human selves arise to "the glory of the star as in the Son (not sun, but Son)" (281-31). Though this woe causes many to seek death, the transformation of these hidden evils will leave us lighter, purer, and more compatible with the coming Spirit, which is all-knowing and omnipresent, from Whom nothing can be hidden. The pit must be opened and cleared of its darkness.

Opening the Sixth Seal and Sounding the Sixth Trumpet
The Earthquake—The Wrath of the Lamb—The Four Angels and Their Army

Once the pit was opened and cleared, great earthquakes occurred within the body, the sun was completely blackened, the moon was turned to blood, the stars fell from heaven like figs from a tree shaken by a great wind, the sky was split apart like a scroll, and the rulers of the Earth searched for places to hide from the rising presence of the Lamb and its wrath. The Bible is filled with prophecies of this moment, spoken of as the "great and terrible day of the coming of the Lord" (Joel 2:11) and usually followed by the question, "Who can stand against Him?" (Malachi 3:23; Joel 2:11). Here, these words come to life in the final line of Revelation 6. The body was falling away from its earthly appetites, the rising spiritual vibrations were opening the hardened flesh body like a great earthquake, and the stars of heaven's energy were coming down upon the enlivened, sanctified vessel that the body had become.

When the sixth trumpet was sounded, heaven released four angels who had been prepared for this very "hour and day and month and year," (Revelation 9:15) to cleanse one-third of the Earth further. Then, out of heaven descended the higher self, clothed in a cloud, with a rainbow around his head, a face like the sun, feet like fire, and in his hand was the little opened book, representing the now-opened body. He placed his right foot on the sea and his left foot on the land, representing his power over the body's emotions and flesh. He cried out, and seven peals of thunder rumbled throughout the sanctified body, now the temple of the living god, made in the image of the Most High God. John was not allowed to tell us what the seven peals of thunder uttered throughout his body; each of us will have to experience that for ourselves. The godly self declared that there would be no further delay; when the seventh angel sounded, then the mystery of God was finished. Then this godly portion of John's being handed him the little book and told him to eat it. John reported to us that it was sweet in the mouth but bitter in the belly, and Cayce explained that this is a reference to spiritual truths being beautiful to look at and sweet in the tasting, but at times bitter in the applying and living of them in daily life (281-32). Here are the Cayce readings' further comments on this important phase of the Revelation process:

> . . . How did the Son in the earth become as an intermediator between sinful man and an All-Wise, All-Merciful God? By going through or experiencing, or in giving to, through the very sufferings in the body, the right, the purpose, the aim to be in that position!
>
> Now, man having attained same by this study must prophesy—apply—prophesy *is* apply—before many in many experiences, in many ways, in many environs, in many lands. All of these are a part and parcel of same. How did He put it as He gave, "I will bring to your remembrance *all* things, from the foundations of the world."
>
> Then as it has been experienced by those who have taken hold of, who have combined the book (that is the book of Life), into the experience, it becomes within its body then a part and parcel of—and is to be expended in its relationships to the environs in that of prophecy, yes; in experiences before kings, yes; yea as beggars; yea as rulers; yea as those in authority; yea as those authoritative over.
>
> *Think* of how this is shown in the life of the Master Himself; He that made man, yet under the authority and the will of man by the mere giving of self in the experience of passing through same. Not that these were needed other than that it might be fulfilled, what? Prophecy, as had been given in man's search for God.
>
> Then as this has been found, as is illustrated here by John, in the taking of the book and in becoming these, each then must pass in its experience through the same sources. 281-32

The outer things that are related to this center are the colors *purple* or *indigo*, the note *la*, the word *name* in the Lord's Prayer, the planet *Mercury*, the "element" *cloud* (a higher vibration of water[7]), and, of course, the church of Philadelphia and the pineal gland. In the Cayce cosmology, the influence of Mercury brings the mental powers as reasoning rather than simply sentiment (945-1, 412-5, 900-10).

Opening the Seventh Seal and Sounding the Seventh Trumpet
Silence for Half an Hour—The Golden Censer with Incense—
The Kingdoms of the World and the Lord United

Finally, the seventh seal was opened, and there was silence in heaven for about half hour (Revelation 8:1), the ultimate achievement of attunement to God, as stated by the psalmist: "Be still, and know that I am God." (Psalms 46:10) The seven angels, or angelic influences of the seven spiritual centers of the body, stood before God. They received the seven trumpets to begin the seven soundings. Another angel burned incense in a golden censer. The fragrance of the incense was added to the prayers of the saints and went out before God. Then, the angel threw the censer to the Earth, causing peals of thunder, flashes of lightning, and earthquakes.

When the seventh trumpet was sounded, loud voices from heaven cried out, "The kingdom of the world has become the kingdom of the Lord, and of His Messiah; and He will reign forever and ever." (Revelation 11:15) The twenty-four elders (twelve paired cranial nerves) worshipped God, saying, "We give Thee thanks, O Lord God, the Almighty, who is and was, because Thou has taken Thy great power and has begun to reign." Then all cells of the body were judged according to their level of attunement and atonement with this new reign. The temple of God was opened, and the ark of the covenant appeared in the temple, causing flashes of lightning, peals of thunder, earthquakes, and a great hailstorm. The physical body had now reached a level of cleansing, vibration, and attunement to become the temple of God. Cayce described it this way:

As the Book of Life then is opened, there is seen the effect of that which now has been attained by the opening of the system, the body, the mind; all of those effects that have been created by the ability of the entity to, in the physical . . . attune self to the consciousness of being at-one with the divine within.

Now we see those in the material world using these influences for self-exaltation, self-indulgence, self-glorification; and yet we see those using same for the glory, the understanding, the knowledge, the wisdom of the Father. 281-33

*   *   *

Endnotes

[1]The oldest Hebrew text is "The Book of the Law" dating to 621 B.C.

[2]Also known as *Pergamum*.

[3]A good sample can be found in reading 262-117; see chapter 9.

[4]In I Kings 21:7, Jezebel said, " . . . arise, and eat bread, and let thy heart be merry: I will give thee the vineyard," which she later obtained by deceit and murder.

[5]Cayce's comments on this are throughout so many readings that it is impossible for me to reference them all. But for a sense of his position, see readings 281-29 and 281-30 in chapter 9.

[6]I realize this may be controversial, so consider these readings: 3744-5, 281-3, 281-27, and 195-70 (see chapter 9).

[7]This also may be controversial, so consider these readings: 262-49, 294-17, 440-10, 585-10, and 1877-2 (see chapter 9). Also consider the scriptural passages in Daniel 7:13, Matthew 24:30 and 26:64, and Revelation 1:7.

4

SPIRITUALIZING THE MIND
AND APPLYING

THE ROD, THE TEMPLE, TWO WITNESSES,
AND THE SEVENTH ANGEL
REVELATION 11
(ILLUSTRATIONS 20-22)

Spiritualizing the body has reached such a level in this vision that our attention now turns to spiritualizing the mind and applying the wisdom in one's life. In this section, we will discover our mind and its perspective on the size and nature of heaven. We will meet two witnesses who have helped us know the truth innately and emotionally. We will face up to two beasts that have and do still challenge us in this spiritualization process: fear and double-mindedness. We will witness the birth of our new selves and face our greatest accuser. We will overcome a flood of emotions and the fall of our egocentric selves. Finally, we will unite with the spiritual portion of our minds and be judged according to all we have done with the gifts of free will and life.

This section begins with the disciple John receiving a measuring rod with which to measure "the temple of God, and the altar, and them that worship within." (Revelation 11:1) Cayce explained that the measuring, which also occurs in the prophet Ezekiel's vision, is a sign that to each of us is given the freedom and power to set the metes and bounds of our temple, our heaven. Here are Cayce's words on this:

(Q) What is meant by the symbol of the "reed like unto a rod" with which John was told to measure the temple? Revelation 11. Please explain.

(A) How again has it been given by Him? "With what measure ye mete it shall be measured to thee again." Know that he had acceded to the point wherein he is to set the metes and bounds (John as an individual). Ye, your own souls as individuals, who will you put in your heaven? Ye of a denomination, ye of a certain creed, ye of a certain measurement, with what measure ye mete it is measured to thee again.

This then is an illustration that to each there is given, what? All power to set that as the metes and bounds of what heaven in itself shall be to those who would gather these, or those, or the self. What would be heaven to a soul that built it for its individual self? Heaven, yes—but alone!

Those that will measure then, those that will set metes and bounds—how has it been given oft? When ye name a name, or when ye give metes and bounds, ye forget that God's force, God's power is *infinite!* and this is beyond the comprehension of the finite mind. Yet as is illustrated here to John, as is illustrated to thee, thou art given—with the understanding—as to what the metes and bounds shall be. As to the numbers as seen, as understood, these become as parts of its own understanding. 281-32.

Cayce identified this temple as the mind. He explained that the tabernacle and the holy mount that appeared many times in the Scriptures and ancient legends were metaphors or patterns for the mind and the mind's connection to God. Throughout history, spiritual seekers met God by entering the tabernacle or going up on the mount. Measuring the temple indicates that our understanding has now reached a point that we realize the need for a *unified* activity with the Creative Forces, or the power of God (281-32). He further explained that, as in the ancient physical temple, a veil shields the holy, inner realms of our mind from the worldly thoughts and images of our outer mind. John next spiritualized his mind, uniting the inner and outer mind through a series of cleansings. Ultimately, this process, which John exemplified, leads us to a new wholeness that is consciously aware of God and God's mind with us in our daily lives, just as God was in the temple and with the people of ancient Israel.

The temple was described first in Exodus 25. Moses went up on the Mount of God and returned with the word of God commanding a new temple to be built. The temple is seen again in the Book of Ezekiel (Ezekiel 40-42), when Ezekiel had the same experience as the disciple John, even to being given a reed with which to measure the temple. The temple was also explained in detail by the disciple Paul in his letter to the Hebrews.

Let's begin our study of the temple with God's first words about the subject in Exodus 25: 8-9:

> ⁸And let them make me a sanctuary, that I may dwell among them.
> ⁹According to all that I show thee, the pattern of the tabernacle, and the pattern of all the furniture thereof, even so shall you make it.

It was to be a sanctuary that would allow the infinite God to dwell in the finite world with us. Moses manifested this temple with poles and curtains, as God revealed to him from the holy mount. Ezekiel and John experienced the temple while "in the spirit," both being told to measure it and understand its true nature. Paul remarked how the old, physical temple had become an inner, heavenly temple, through Jesus Christ, resulting in God dwelling within each of us.

The ancient temple described by God to Moses had a court and a tabernacle. The tabernacle was composed of two separate parts: the "holy place," and the "most holy place," often called the "holy of holies." These three areas (court, holy place, and holy of holies) were separated by three distinct veils or curtains, symbolic of the three levels of being (physical, mental, and spiritual) and the three levels of the mental (conscious, subconscious, and superconscious). One large curtain surrounded the whole temple. Through the first curtain, one entered the court of the temple. Another curtain surrounded the tabernacle. Through the second curtain, one entered the first chamber room of the tabernacle, the holy place, which then led to the third curtain, shielding the holy of holies. Special poles were designed to hold these curtains. The whole temple was portable. It could be disassembled and reassembled as the tribes traveled or camped, following God's guidance. Each of the three areas of the temple contained specific items. In the court was the water basin for cleansing and purification and the altar for sacrificial offerings. On the ground inside the chamber of the holy place, to the south side of the chamber, was the large menorah of seven candles. To the north side of the chamber was the bread of the presence of God (sometimes referred to as the "showbread") on a table. In the next and last inner chamber, the holy of holies, was the ark of the covenant and an altar with incense, where God had promised to meet the high priest directly (see illustrations 41 through 44).

You can see how this arrangement would lend itself to a series of steps that would help the ancient seekers make a transition from outer life to inner attunement with God. First was the process of cleansing and absolution and the offering up of one's earthly pleasures (prized lambs, goats, grains, and so on). Then, upon entering the first inner chamber, one would light the seven candles, representing the raising of vibrations in the spiritual centers of the body. In this same chamber was the bread of the presence of God, which symbolized the nourishment that would result from contact with God in the next chamber. Finally, one would enter the holy of holies to make connection with the covenant between God and human. The ark contained three items: (1) the tablets of the ten commandments (which are the covenant: *If you keep these commandments, then I will be your God*); (2) the staff that came alive again by budding, belonging to the first high priest, Aaron; and (3) the manna that fell from heaven to feed Israel in the desert, forever symbolic of God's ability to care for us no matter what the physical limitations. The ark was made of acacia wood covered in gold. Two kneeling cherubim were atop the ark, wings bent in a submissive, humble manner, and amid them was the "mercy seat" to help the less-than-worthy to experience God (see illustration 43).

In Hebrews 9, Paul called us to realize the greater truth of the temple (or sanctuary) arrangement and its purpose for us, emphasizing Christ's role in lifting us to this new level:

[1]Now even a first covenant had ordinances of divine service, and its sanctuary, a sanctuary of this world.

[2]For there was a tabernacle prepared, the first, wherein were the candlestick, and the table, and the showbread; which is called the Holy place.

[3]And after the second veil, the tabernacle which is called the Holy of holies;

[4]having a golden altar of incense, and the ark of the covenant overlaid

round about with gold, wherein was a golden pot holding the manna, and Aaron's rod that budded, and the tables of the covenant;

[5]and above it cherubim of glory overshadowing the mercy-seat; of which things we cannot now speak severally.

[6]Now these things having been thus prepared, the priests go in continually into the first tabernacle, accomplishing the services;

[7]but into the second the high priest alone, once in the year, not without blood, which he offereth for himself, and for the errors of the people:

[8]the Holy Spirit this signifying, that the way into the holy place hath not yet been made manifest, while the first tabernacle is yet standing;[1]

[9]which is a figure for the time present; according to which are offered both gifts and sacrifices that cannot, as touching the conscience, make the worshipper perfect,

[10]being only (with meats and drinks and divers washings) carnal ordinances, imposed until a time of reformation.

[11]But Christ having become a high priest of the good things to come, through the greater and more perfect tabernacle, not made with hands, that is to say, not of this creation,

[12]nor yet through the blood of goats and calves, but through his own blood, entered in once for all into the holy place, having obtained eternal redemption.

[13]For if the blood of goats and bulls, and the ashes of a heifer sprinkling them that have been defiled, sanctify unto the cleanness of the flesh:

[14]how much more shall the blood of Christ, who through the eternal Spirit offered himself without blemish unto God, cleanse your conscience from dead works to serve the living God?

Later in the same chapter Paul continued:

[18]Wherefore even the first covenant hath not been dedicated without blood.

[19]For when every commandment had been spoken by Moses unto all the people according to the law, he took the blood of the calves and the goats, with water and scarlet wool and hyssop, and sprinkled both the book itself and all the people,

[20]saying, This is the blood of the covenant which God commanded toward you.

²¹Moreover the tabernacle and all the vessels of the ministry he sprinkled in like manner with the blood.

²²And according to the law, I may almost say, all things are cleansed with blood, and apart from shedding of blood there is no remission.

²³It was necessary therefore that the copies of the things in the heavens should be cleansed with these; but the heavenly things themselves with better sacrifices than these.

²⁴For Christ entered not into a holy place made with hands, like in pattern to the true; but into heaven itself, now to appear before the face of God for us.

Here, we see Paul guiding us to understand that the physical is a metaphor, a pattern of the heavenly. The external temple of old is a metaphor and pattern of the real temple within us. The blood sacrifice of old is a metaphor and a pattern of a truer sacrifice. Now each of us is learning that the real sacrificial offering in the temple of our consciousness is our selfish self, crucifying our desires, that we may approach God more closely, as exemplified by Jesus Christ, the pattern for each soul to follow.

According to Cayce, the court outside of the temple that John referred to in Revelation 11:2 is the outer environment of physical activity and influence; the inner temple court is the area where the body and mind meet their "sacrificial forces," just as in the ancient temple. The greater spiritual forces, Cayce said, are met in the holy of holies. John was told not to spend time measuring the court outside of the temple, that it had been left to be "trampled" upon by the "nations" for three and one-half years, a recurring measurement of time mentioned throughout the Scriptures, called a half-cycle, a whole cycle being seven years. This is simply a representation of a limited period of time in which the outer self will have to endure the challenges to spiritual growth that come from earthly influences and self-seeking.

Now the vision moves away from measuring the temple and introduces us to the two witnesses. Most students of the Revelation interpret the two witnesses as Moses and Elijah, the two who appeared with Jesus on the mount during His transfiguration (Matthew 17:3). Some identify them as Enoch and Ezekiel. Paul identified Enoch as a witness:

By faith Enoch was translated that he should not see death; and he was not found, because God translated him:² for he hath had witness borne to him that before his translation he had been well-pleasing unto God. Hebrews 11:5.

Elijah is often identified as a witness because of this passage in II Kings 2:11-12, that is reminiscent of Enoch's earlier experience:

> [11]And it came to pass, as they [Elijah and Elisha] still went on, and talked, that, behold, there appeared a chariot of fire, and horses of fire, which parted them both asunder; and Elijah went up by a whirlwind into heaven.
> [12]And Elisha saw it, and he cried, "My father, my father, the chariots of Israel and the horsemen thereof!" And he saw him [Elijah] no more.

But once again, Edgar Cayce, from his deep, meditative state, identified the two witnesses of the Revelation as parts of our individual minds (281-33). One witness is the mental-physical mind and the other is the mental-spiritual mind—one the "conscious" mind and one the "superconscious" mind. Cayce explained that the subconscious is the bridge between these two, which unites one's human self with one's divine self. We are microcosmic trinities: beings who are physical, mental, and spiritual, with minds that are conscious, subconscious, and superconscious, each corresponding to three basic realms of earth, netherworld, and heaven. According to Cayce, the superconscious is a witness because of the "innate forces" that come from its contact with the spiritual realms. As Jesus noted to Nicodemus, no one ascends to heaven who did not first come down from heaven (John 3:13). This heavenly memory deep within us causes us to innately feel or sense that there is more to life than the physical. We may not know why we sense it, but it is with us and has been with most of humanity throughout the ages. Therefore, it is a witness to the truth. On the other hand, the conscious mind is a witness because of the "emotional effect" of its experiences in material life. Our emotions are a witness that there is more to us than the physical. Where does a tear come from? A smile? A frown? The people and circumstances around us touch places within us that are deeper than the circumstances and interactions we have with them. Two characters on the long-running television series *Star Trek*—Mr. Spock (the Vulcan) and Data (the android)—experienced life *without* emotion. For them, logic ruled. Humans are simply not this way; even the most stoic occasionally weep, smile, and become angry. There is more to us than biological processes and electrical brainwaves. Within us is a depth of being which is beyond physical life. Therefore, the conscious, emotional part of ourselves is also a witness to the greater truth.

"These then are the witnesses," said Cayce, "the innate and the emotional; or the spiritual-mental, the physical-mental . . ." (281-33)

I would be remiss as the author if I didn't relate to you that Cayce took this conscious witness idea beyond our normal Western beliefs, stating that the emotions are not only from this life, but from previous lives as well. The concept of reincarnation is a difficult one for Western spiritual seekers. Our perspective usually is based on three key biblical passages that seem to counter any idea of reincarnation. The first is Genesis 3:19: "By the sweat of your face shall you eat bread, till you return unto the ground; because from it you were taken: for you are dust, and to dust you shall return." The second is Ecclesiastes 3:20: "All go to the same place. All came from the dust and all return to the dust." Finally, the most often quoted biblical counter to reincarnation is Hebrews 9:27: "And as it is appointed for men once to die, and after this the judgment:" Each of these passages is true, yet the idea of reincarnation is not necessarily excluded in them. How can this be? We were created twice in Genesis. Once in chapter 1, in the spirit, and again in chapter 2, from the dust of the earth. The Ecclesiastes quote is often taken out of the context of its preceding and following verses. Verse 19 compares humans and our life with that of the animals, noting that there is no difference; we die just like them and return to the dust of the earth as they do. Then verse 21 asks a key question: "Who knows the spirit of man goes upward, and the spirit of the beast goes downward to the earth?" Yes, our physical, earthly part does return to the dust of the earth, but our spirit rises upward and lives on.

Consider how the disciples questioned Jesus as to why the prophecy of the return of Elijah as forerunner to the Messiah[3] was not fulfilled, to which Jesus replied that indeed the prophecy had been fulfilled, but no one recognized the forerunner, causing the disciples to realize that John the Baptist was the reincarnation of Elijah (Matthew 17:13). Jesus said in Matthew 11:13-15, "All the prophets and the law prophesied until John [the Baptist]. And if ye are willing to receive it, this is Elijah, that is to come. He that hath ears to hear, let him hear." Jesus' teaching to Nicodemus that no one ascended to heaven except those who had already descended from heaven (John 3:13), certainly leaves room for our heavenly part to have been involved in other times and places, perhaps even other incarnations. Also consider that Jesus said that this generation would not pass away before all the prophecies of the end times had been fulfilled and that they would see the son of man coming in glory, yet all the listeners died, apparently without this happening (Matthew 24:34).

Could it be that their souls would return again to see this fulfilled? In two passages, the disciples seemed to reveal their belief in previous lives. In John 9:1-2 we see, "As he [Jesus] passed by, he saw a man blind from his birth. And his disciples asked him, saying, 'Rabbi, who sinned, this man, or his parents, that he should be born blind?'" Obviously he would have had to sin before his birth in order to be born blind. The disciples certainly seemed open to this possibility. In Luke 9:19, they shared with Jesus these comments of the people: "Some say you are John the Baptist [who had been executed earlier]; but others say, Elijah; and others say that one of the old prophets is risen again." This surely expressed a basic acceptance among the people that major prophets may reincarnate. It's interesting to note the angel's comments to Zacharias upon announcing the conception of his son, John the Baptist: "And he shall go before his face [the Lord's] in the spirit and power of Elijah, to turn the hearts of the fathers to the children, and the disobedient to walk in the wisdom of the just; to make ready for the Lord a people prepared for him." (Luke 1:17) The "spirit and power of Elijah" had returned with a mission.

Nevertheless, while it is hard to make an argument for reincarnation from the Western scriptures, there are passages that leave room for its consideration. Even St. Paul's statement, that we have only one life to live and then the judgment, can be true and still leave room for reincarnation as part of the greater plan. The outer, earthly self does have one life, and then it dies, but the soul lives on. Many near-death experiencers record seeing their lives pass before them in panorama. A self-judgment of every thought and deed in the life takes place, but in a loving spirit and usually with an unconditionally loving being standing nearby. For each life there is a death, a judgment, but this does not necessarily negate the opportunity for a soul to return to a new physical life in order to improve upon itself and be judged again. The belief that life is eternal also does not negate the concept of reincarnation. Additionally, some of the great minds of the church have written openly about preexistence of the soul and, in some cases, about reincarnation and karma. Here are a few quotes to consider:

> We were in being long before the foundation of the world; we existed in the eye of God, for it is our destiny to live in Him. We are

reasonable creatures of the Divine Word; therefore we have existed
from the beginning, for in the beginning was the Word.
                              —St. Clement of Alexandria (A.D. 150-220)

Every soul . . . comes into this world strengthened by the victories
or weakened by the defeats of its previous life. Its place in this world,
as a vessel appointed to honor or dishonor, is determined by its previous merits or demerits. Its work in this world determines its place in
the world which is to follow this.
                              —Origen (A.D. 185-254), *De Principiis*

. . . it is absolutely necessary that the soul should be healed and
purified, and if this does not take place during its life on earth, it must
be accomplished in future lives.
                              —St. Gregory (A.D. 257-332)

The message of Plato, the purest and the most luminous of all
philosophy, has at last scattered the darkness of error, and now shines
forth mainly in Plotinus, a Platonist so like his master that one would
think they lived together, or rather—since so long a period of time
separates them—that Plato was born again in Plotinus.
                              —St. Augustine (A.D. 354-430)

This next reference brings to mind Plato's comments on the soul's journey through many lifetimes, leading for better or worse, meeting karma
along the way:

Know that if you become worse you will go to the worse souls, and
if better, to the better souls; and in every succession of life and death
you will do and suffer what like must fitly suffer at the hands of like.
                              —Plato (582-507 B.C.), *The Republic*

As we return to the Revelation, the two witnesses—or as the vision later
called them, "the two olive trees and the two candlesticks, standing before
the Lord of the earth" (Revelation 11:4)—had power and went about
prophesying for a set period of time. Then, the beast came out of the abyss
to make war against them, overcame them, and killed them. Their dead
bodies lay in the street of the great city, which is "mystically called Sodom

and Egypt, and where also their Lord was crucified." The "people and tribes and tongues and nations looked at their bodies" for three-and-one-half days, not allowing them to be buried. Those who dwelt on the earth rejoiced over them. But after the three-and-one-half days "the breath of life" came back into them from God, and they rose again, "causing a great fear to fall upon all who saw." Then the two witnesses were "called up to heaven, and a great earthquake felled a tenth of the city and seven thousand people died, and the rest were so terrified that they gave glory to the God of heaven."

Cayce explained these passages:

> . . . The Master gave, "Before the world was, I AM! Now if ye abide in me and I in the Father, then I will bring to thy remembrance *all things*—from the foundations of the world!"
>
> Yet these are as dead, or the only consciousness that arises from same is that which is fanned into life or activity by the application of the laws concerning same. Hence they are as dead, yet become alive again by remembrance, by the application of thought. In what? The light of that which has been attained by the entity or soul that has applied the former lessons in its experience. 281-33

He continued:

> As has been so oft given, all places—as Egypt or Sodom or the Crucifixion, or the Lord—are conditions, circumstances, experiences, as well as individual places. Then in the minds of those who would attempt or that would seek knowledge, they represent their own experiences. Thus these to the people represent—Egypt, the release from bondage; Gomorrah, as a reckoning with sin—as the Lord was crucified there. As has been given, there has never been an experience when His Christ-mas, His death, His birth, wasn't an experience of the age, the people. Though it may go under many names, as an individual may be under many names, in many environs, there is one—*one* that ever comes as is shown in that later given as to those who have the name in the hand, in the head or in the forehead and the like; that is, what is the intent and purpose. Just as the Savior of the world, as Lord, as Christ—what do these as names indicate? That which is as a help in a time of trouble alone? or that to glory in, in thy joy, thy gladness, thy happiness? How many, O how many have

there been that have laughed with God, that have wept with Jesus, that have gloried with the Christ! or rather has it been, "My happiness and my joy is of myself"?

No condemnation; but rather is there the pattern pointed to as was set by Him. He was *all* things to *all* men; rejoiced with those that did rejoice; He wept with those that wept. He was glad, He was happy, He was sorry, He kept the faith.

(Q) What is signified by the revival of these witnesses?

(A) How hath He given? "If ye meditate on these things, I will bring to thy remembrance all things." The reviving, the renewing, by the abilities of the soul to take hold upon the witnesses of the life itself! And what is life? God! 281-33

As Revelation 11 closes, the seventh angel sounded a trumpet and loud voices in heaven said, "The kingdom of the world has become the kingdom of our Lord, and of his Christ: and he shall reign for ever and ever." (Revelation 11:15) The twenty-four elders worshipped God again, and "the temple of God which is in heaven was opened; and the ark of His covenant appeared in His temple, and there were flashes of lightning and sounds and peals of thunder and an earthquake and a great hailstorm." (Revelation 11:19)

Cayce's study group asked, as we all ask, *When?* "Help us understand how time should be interpreted," they said. In explaining this, Cayce responded:

Remember, as has been given to him that was given a measure, as a mete, as a rod to measure heaven—as to how large his heaven would be. All right! Then we have as to how much time—What is time? Is it a record merely of the events of self or of the glory of God? What is the extent of the glory of thy heaven or of thy God? This is as a reckoning. Yet as is shown by the indication of so many days, so many weeks, it is the *inclination* of the individual mind in materiality to set (as was said of John) metes and bounds; and we judge from—How many days or years have ye set? Nineteen thirty-seven (1937) is what? And thy Lord has been continuous! yet ye say only 1937! 281-33

THE HALF-WAY POINT

Now we approach the halfway mark in the Revelation. Cayce told his study group that, thus far, the book had been "the study of the body, the mind, the soul; the physical body, its attributes; the mental body, its associations and attributes; the soul body and its attributes." (281-33) Now we have reached the point that these understandings are to have their influences *actively* in human experience, in application in an individual's life. The last half of the Revelation, Cayce said, refers to the application and the effect or influence of these teachings on an individual's life (281-33).

THE MOTHER,
THE RED DRAGON, AND THE CHILD
REVELATION 12
(ILLUSTRATIONS 23 AND 24)

Cayce said that this chapter is to show to each person what the soul has passed through in creation, in the earth, and in meeting the many challenges (281-33).

The chapter begins, "A great sign appeared in heaven: a woman clothed with the sun, and the moon under her feet, and on her head a crown of twelve stars; and she was with child; and she cried out, being in labor and in pain to deliver the child. And another sign appeared in heaven: and behold, a great red dragon having seven heads, ten horns, and on his seven heads were seven crowns." Clearly a serious encounter was being set up. Symbolically, Cayce identified the woman with the primeval mother, the source of all materiality and all that is good and spiritually helpful in materiality (281-33). Her attire identifies her with the creation in Genesis: sun, moon, and stars, and Cayce added that she is also the Earth, Mother Earth. She was to deliver "the outgrowth of the application of the Word . . . upon self. For the child . . . is born of application of the elements in the body (physical, mental, and spiritual) of the individual," Cayce said (281-34). Those who apply the fruits of the spirit and seek the light through the experiences in materiality gain so much more understanding than even the angels, that someday they will judge the angels. The mother has provided this realm and its opportunities for our spiritual growth. Cayce explained:

> . . . The material plane is a channel, a way and manner through
> and in which each soul, all souls may grow in grace and knowledge
> and in understanding—thus it behooves all souls that they be oft in
> prayer, oft in those periods when there *is* an entering into the holy

of holies as within, and of the rededicating of self for that of being a channel through which the knowledge of God's love for His children may flow to others. 1751-1

Now the mother wanted to deliver us to our glory that we might reign for evermore. As Cayce stated it, " . . . ye have reached to that understanding of thy perfection with God, how in materiality ye may attune the attributes of self." (281-13)

But the red dragon swooped around, attempting with all its might to stop this from happening, hoping to devour the child as soon as it was born. When the child was born, a war broke out in heaven between the dragon and the archangel Michael. The dragon was thrown out of heaven. The dragon is then identified as "the serpent of old," the devil, or Satan, "who deceives the whole world," (Revelation 12:9) emblematic of our rebellious forces and tendencies, even though John had now attained the Book of Life in his body! These must be met, Cayce said (281-33). In Genesis 4:7, we are instructed by God to subdue these influences, to master them.

Once the dragon was thrown out of heaven, a loud cry went up, "Now the salvation, and the power, and the kingdom of our God and the authority of His Christ have come"—and here comes the important part—"for the accuser of our brethren has been thrown down, who accuses them before God day and night." (Revelation 12:10) This line is important for each of us to comprehend, because the accuser is within us. It is the doubter, the less-than-worthy one, and the naked part of our conscience that cannot allow itself to enter into God's all-seeing, all-knowing presence—the beginning of all the trouble in the Garden:

> "Adam, where are you?" asked the Lord God.
> "I'm hiding," replied Adam.
> "Why are you hiding?" asked the Lord God.
> "Because I am naked," answered the man. Genesis 1:9-11

"Who told you that you were naked?" asked the Lord God. He might well have gone on to comment, "You were naked yesterday and you had no problem being in my presence. What makes today so different?" Of course, no one told Adam he was naked but the accuser within his own conscience. This accuser must be dealt with, for it keeps each of us from realizing our destiny, our purpose for life: companionship with God and all of His creation. Another example of this is found in the Old Testament book of Zechariah, when Joshua was presented to the Lord: " ...Joshua the high priest standing before the angel of the Lord, and Satan standing at his right hand to *accuse* him. And the Lord said to Satan, 'The Lord rebuke you, O Satan! The Lord who has chosen Jerusalem rebuke you! Is not this [Joshua] a brand plucked from the fire?' Now Joshua was standing before the angel, clothed with filthy garments, and the angel said to those who were standing before him, 'Remove the filthy garments from him.' And to him he said, 'Behold, I have taken your iniquity away from you, and I will clothe you with festal robes.'" (Zechariah 3:1-4) Later, the Lord said, "I will remove the guilt of this land in a single day." (Zechariah 3:9) A little later, the Lord said this was accomplished "not by might, nor by power, but by my Spirit." (Zechariah 4:6) The garments of our consciousness are soiled from our self-centered activities and thoughts, but the spirit can and will cleanse them in a moment, rebuke the accuser in our minds, and remove the guilt.

The Revelation goes on to explain that the biggest contributors to throwing the accuser out of heaven are the "blood of the Lamb," "the word of their testimony," and the fact that they "did not love their life even to death." The latter comment is reminiscent of Jesus's saying that whoever finds one's life loses it, and whoever loses one's life finds it (Matthew 10:39), and another teaching by Jesus: "Except a grain of wheat fall to the earth and die, it abides by itself alone; but if it die, it bears much fruit." (John 12:24)

If we're not careful, the Revelation passages can leave us with the impression that spiritual growth is made through self-sacrifice alone. Self-sacrifice is important to spiritual development, but it is not the quintessential ingredient. "Go and learn the meaning of this: 'I seek mercy, not sacrifice,'" Jesus instructed (Matthew 9:13, 12:7). Mercy rather than sacrifice is the greater expression of love and, after all, "God is love." (I John 4:8, 4:16) Nevertheless, we are cleansing and subduing our earthly selves and desires to make room for heavenly desires and spiritual influences.

The dragon was persistent and returned to persecute the mother. "Two wings of the great eagle were given to the woman" in order for her to escape from the dragon by flying away from his presence for "the time and times and half time," (Revelation 12:14), a quote directly from Daniel 7:25 concerning a time limit on the power of the beast. Cayce explained that these wings represent "flight from materiality into those influences through which

the body may rest within itself; as physical, or the mental flight, or that to
the astral forces . . . " (281-33) As for "the time and times and half time,"
Cayce had these two comments:

> . . . as He gave in those days, "the time and times and a half times
> shall pass, and *then* shall man come to know that in the temple, in
> the tabernacle of his *own* temple will he meet his God face to face!"
> 257-201
> These changes in the earth will come to pass, for the time and
> times and half times are at an end, and there begin those periods
> for the readjustments. For how hath He given? "The righteous shall
> inherit the earth." Hast thou, my brethren, a heritage in the earth?
> 294-185

The serpent made another attack upon the woman, this time with a
river of water out of its mouth to cause her to be swept away by the flood,
but the earth helped by opening up and swallowing the flood, an action
which enraged the dragon. As you might expect, Cayce identified the river
of water as a flood of emotions "upon the influences of the body in all of its
relationships to the activities in its relationships to others." He warned us
that, in the experience of individuals in the earth, "the flood of emotions . .
. make for doubt, fears, tribulation, disturbances, anxieties," but "the earth
aids in the quieting of the influence." (281-34) This is a wonderful insight
from Cayce. So often, spiritual teachers can see only the weaknesses and
sins of the flesh and the earthly aspects of our being. But Cayce knew that
the body is as wonderful an instrument for enlightenment as it is for sin
and self-seeking. The Earth, too, is as grand a place for manifesting the
love, kindness, understanding, and patience of God as it is for sinning and
self-seeking. Here we see that the Earth and the earthly influences help us
deal with the flood of emotions and challenges of the negative influences.
As helpful as this is, there's more yet with which to deal. Two beasts are
coming that we must face up to and overcome.

Two Beasts
Revelation 13

We should begin this next phase of the enlightenment process, said
Cayce, by *visualizing fear*, in the form of a beast, like the leopard with seven

heads and ten horns (281-34). By our seeking understanding, we have also aroused influences that bring fear. The leopard's seven heads symbolize the *vices* of the seven spiritual centers within us, and these cause us to see aspects of ourselves that we fear. The fear takes ten different forms, as the ten horns on each of the seven heads of the leopard indicate. The leopard rose out of the sea, symbolic of the depths of emotion and unseen influences that normally lie below the surface of consciousness. Because we are opening up the body and mind, and seeking to shine our light upon all aspects of our being, we now see the normally unseen. The dragon, symbolic of our rebellious spirit, gave his power to this beast that brings fear upon us. The leopard approached, speaking blasphemous things aloud and with a blasphemous name upon its head. It makes war with the spiritual influences that are arising within us, causing fear to take hold of us. Fear is one of the most commonly addressed issues throughout the Scriptures. Jesus addressed it many times. Here's an example from Matthew 10 that fits with our current passage in the Revelation:

> [26]Fear not them [those who confront your spiritual efforts]: for there is nothing covered, that shall not be revealed; and hid, that shall not be known.
> [27]What I tell you in the darkness, speak ye in the light; and what ye hear in the ear, proclaim upon the house-tops.
> [28]And be not afraid of them that kill the body, but are not able to kill the soul: but rather fear him who is able to destroy both soul and body in hell.
> [29]Are not two sparrows sold for a penny? and not one of them shall fall on the ground without your Father's leave:
> [30]but the very hairs of your head are all numbered.
> [31]Fear not therefore: ye are of more value than many sparrows.

Revelation 13 moves from its focus on fear to "those whose names are not written in the Book of Life." Cayce explained (281-34) that these are those who are seeking the spiritualization "for impunity's sake or only for the momentary conscience's sake." They "acknowledge the Way," but they follow "closely after the flesh, or the indulgences of the emotions of the body alone, without consideration of others, without other than self's own interest—as is shown by the beast that is loosened—these are they whose names are not written, and these are they who are easily led about by every wind that bloweth." (281-34) We must seek with purpose, with direction, putting our belief, faith, trust, and works in Him. "Having tasted of the tree of life, the knowledge of God," Cayce said, "make thyself and thy calling and thy election *sure* in that ye faint not when ye see these troubles, these disturbances that are only of the earth-earthy, that only the emotions of the desires of self's own show coming to pass in thine experience." (281-34) Fear not at the approach of the first beast.

Now the second beast appeared. It had two horns, spoke like a dragon, made signs and miracles, and had the power to deceive. Cayce identified this two-horned beast as "double-mindedness." (281-34) It reflects our human tendency to seek and serve mammon and God, to apply the truths we've learned not just for virtue's sake, but to impress others or gain an advantage. Misapplication of the truths through double-mindedness is this deceptive beast. Cayce said, " . . . though ye may have done this or that, though ye may have healed the sick, though ye may have cast out demons in my name, I know ye not; for ye have followed rather as the beast of self-aggrandizement, self-indulgence, self-glorification . . . " (281-34)

Of course, the most famous aspect of this second beast is the number 666, the mark of the beast (see illustration 22). The mark must appear on the right hand and the forehead of everyone who wants to buy or sell. Verse 18 says: "This calls for wisdom: let him who has understanding reckon the number of the beast, for it is a human number . . . " According to Cayce, it represents the vows and obligations, the buying and selling we make to the work of the beast, rather than the work of God (281-34). The reading exclaimed, "One Lord, one faith, one God, one baptism, one way!" Jesus addressed it this way in John 6:

> [26]Verily, verily, I say unto you, Ye seek me, not because ye saw signs, but because ye ate of the loaves, and were filled.
> [26]Work not for the food which perishes, but for the food which abides unto eternal life, which the Son of man shall give unto you: for him the Father, even God, has sealed.

Cayce expanded on this by explaining that the reason 666 is a "human number" or sometimes translated as a "number of a man" is because it represents only the work of human hands, without consciousness of God and God directing. He said that this influence penetrates individuals, groups, and organizations, and binds us with vows and obligations to the beast's work

(281-34), again touching on Jesus' guidance that we cannot serve mammon and God. It's important that we understand that this is not necessarily about our *jobs*. We are talking about including God and God's guidance in our labor, our efforts, and our lives, not working simply for our own interests and gratifications, as Jesus was sensing from those who had eaten of the loaves He had provided. The key to overcoming the second beast is seeking God's guidance and including God in our thoughts and lives. Thereby, God may be glorified through our thoughts and lives.

When Cayce was asked to comment upon the words "Here is wisdom", he said:

> That as ye have gained by the analysis or the study of the activity and influence of the spirit of truth throughout the whole members of thy body, physical, mental and spiritual, and have come to the knowledge of that which has first been given, that there is only *one* God, *one* Christ, one faith, one baptism; or as Christ hath given—this is the whole law; to love the Lord thy God with all thy mind, thy body, thy soul; thy neighbor as thyself. This is the whole law. This is wisdom. This is knowledge. Knowing that those things which have been put on through the activities of the elements within thine own forces of thy body and mind are but as the stepping-stones to the knowledge that God is in and through *all* and in Him ye live and move and have thy being. When this is fully comprehended, fully understood, ye have the working knowledge of God in the earth. 281-34

In illustration 40, we see a Gnostic depiction of the kundalini of the body going through the various spiritual centers, each corresponding to numbers and meanings from the mystical Cabala. The Cabala is a system of esoteric concepts developed by Jewish rabbis from about the seventh to eighteenth centuries, reaching its peak in the twelfth and thirteenth centuries. It is based on a mystical method of interpreting the Scriptures to penetrate sacred mysteries, much as we are attempting to do with the Revelation. In this illustration, we see how the number 666 corresponds to the highest possible achievement of the lower mind. Without the influence of the Spirit and the submission of the human portion, one cannot break through to full spiritual achievement. This is why the number is a human one and is limited to our lower, beastly nature. One must take the next step, letting go of the lower self in order for the higher self to be born. As we find in this illustration, the

next step is the Way of the Cross and the glory of the higher mind, which
is the Lamb, and the next stage in the Revelation.

The Lamb, the New Song,
and the Angels' Call
Revelation 14

Cayce commented that we have now reached a place in the Revelation
that begins with "assurance to the individual" who has "put on the whole
armor, with the full understanding," assurances of "great help in those periods of temptation or trial." (281-36)

The Lamb appeared with 144,000 whose names were written in the Book of
Life, and harpers sang a new song that no one could learn but the 144,000.

Cayce said that the Lamb is the mind-spiritual that has "so raised the
body as to become as a new being . . ." (281-36) The 144,000 are those sealed
in the spirit. In the body, they are the "spiritualized cellular structure of the 12
major divisions of the body" (281-29). (For more information plus a diagram,
see the section on the twelve gates in the next chapter.) The harpers' new
song represents the "new experience that comes to each soul. Let's keep it
individual, see? The new experience that comes to each soul, as to the assurance of that help when necessary of the saints of the Father." (281-36)

In verse 13, John heard a voice telling him to write this: "Blessed are the
dead who die in the Lord from henceforth: yea, says the Spirit, that they
may rest from their labors; for their works follow with them." Cayce said
that this refers to:

> . . . the changes that have come and the assurance that has come
> to each individual who has recognized that the Lamb (or the Christ),
> or the activities of Jesus becoming the Christ are the assurance of the
> activity of the Christ in the passage from the material plane to the
> celestial. For as He preached to those bound even in the shadows of
> death, loosened that which made it possible for them to become again
> conscious of the opportunities for reconstructing of themselves in the
> experiences through which error had come, so blessed then are they
> who die in the Lord—for the body alone is bound. 281-36

Next, six angels appeared, and five had messages. The first called out in
a loud voice, "Fear God, and give him glory; for the hour of his judgment

is come: and worship him that made the heaven and the earth and sea and fountains of waters." (Revelation 14:7) The second called out, "Fallen, fallen is Babylon the great, that hath made all the nations to drink of the wine of the wrath of her fornication." (Revelation 14:8) The third called out, "If any man worships the beast and his image, and receives a mark on his forehead, or upon his hand, he also shall drink of the wine of the wrath of God, which is prepared unmixed in the cup of his anger; and he shall be tormented with fire and brimstone in the presence of the holy angels, and in the presence of the Lamb: and the smoke of their torment goes up for ever and ever; and they have no rest day and night, they that worship the beast and his image, and who receives the mark of his name." (Revelation 14:9-11) The fourth angel called out in a loud voice, "Send forth thy sickle, and reap: for the hour to reap is come; for the harvest of the earth is ripe." (Revelation 14:15) The fifth angel called with a loud voice, "Send forth thy sharp sickle, and gather the clusters of the vine of the earth; for her grapes are fully ripe." (Revelation 14:18) Cayce explained that these five angels and their comments are calls to "those individuals who have and are a part of the active force in a material world" who are "to work, to give forth, to give out of their strength, theirselves in active service and not as those that would rest" but as "the reapers, as the harvesters—which to the individual mind means labors for a definite purpose and service." (281-36)

During the angels' callings, a white cloud appeared and one seated upon the cloud was like a son of man with a golden crown and a sharp sickle in his hand. He represents our spiritual self realized. It is this part of us that needs to be up and doing, for at this stage of our development the opportunities are great and the harvest is ripe.

THE SEVEN PLAGUES AND
THE TEMPLE OF THE TABERNACLE OF WITNESS
REVELATION 15
(ILLUSTRATION 25)

Next came the "seven angels with seven plagues which are the last for with them the wrath of God is ended." (Revelation 15:1) This event is as wonderful as it is terrible because it is the culmination of the spiritualization process. Cayce began his explanation of this chapter by saying, "He hath not willed that any soul shall perish but hath with every ill provided a means, a way." (281-36) The pouring out of the plagues is the meeting of self, Cayce said. It is the final cleansing that prepares us for the great work or service that we may render as pure channels of God's light and love in our lives and to this world (281-36).

The "temple of the tabernacle of witness," (Revelation 15:5), which is opened in heaven and came with the seven angels, is "the Book of Life, or the Book of Revelation; that is, of the individual, see?" (281-36) The final verse of this chapter reads, "The temple was filled with smoke from the glory of God and from his power, and no one could enter the temple until the seven plagues of the seven angels were ended," (Revelation 15:8), which Cayce explained as "the final steps in the abilities of the individuals for their effective service, or filled with the smoke as the glory of the Father, see? This is the temple of the body, and—as such—where the Lord hath promised to meet those that are faithful and true." (281-36)

The Seven Bowls
Revelation 16
(Illustrations 26 and 27)

These bowls or vials of God's wrath being poured out upon the earth were, according to Cayce, "the fulfilling of the law." (281-36) This is the carrying forth in the earth of the law (God's wrath) in active force: each individual meeting self according to the laws and commandments of God and one's conscience and purification needs, enabling us to enter completely into the tabernacle to meet God, face to face, without condemnation or unworthiness. According to Cayce, all the vials symbolize the same thing: "effective activity upon the various conditions that have become a part of the errors in those that have the mark of the beast." (281-36) In other words, they each represent a specific cleansing required to meet various errors that keep our lower minds from letting go of sin and the guilt of sin, and allowing our higher minds to come fully into the presence of God. These purifications are necessary and are the final stage of the spiritualization process.

The Whore of Babylon
And the Fall of Babylon
Revelation 17-18
(Illustrations 28 and 29)

"Babylon symbolizes self," Cayce said (281-36). This chapter is the final chapter for the selfish, self-centered, self-seeking aspect of our being. The effects of the fall of self are described in chapter 18.

For us to fully understand the concept of the fall of self, we need to explore two key teachings in the Cayce volumes. The first relates to a major goal for each soul:

> Though all are as one, remember it has been given that the purpose of the heart is to know *yourself* to *be* yourself and yet one with God even as Jesus, even as is represented in God the Father, Christ the Son, and the Holy Spirit; each knowing themselves to be themselves yet *one!* 281-37

In the following Cayce reading, he stated this all-important goal and then explained how best to realize it:

> In analyzing self and these emotions—know that it is not by chance that the entity enters any given experience, and that the associations or activities with individuals are not by chance. For, in the spiritual you live and move and have your being in your Maker. He has not willed that any soul should perish, but has with every temptation, with every trial, given opportunities, friends, connections, associations in which the choice by self will bring those privileges as well as opportunities for making hardships or temptations into stepping-stones in your experience.
>
> Know that it is not all just to live—not all just to be good, but good *for* something; that ye may fulfill that purpose for which ye have entered this experience.
>
> And that purpose is that you might know yourself to be yourself, and yet one with the Creative Forces, or God.
>
> Then, study to show thyself approved unto thy ideal.
>
> What, then, *is* thy ideal?
>
> You find yourself a body, a mind, a soul; each with its attributes, manifesting in a material world. And you realize that the body, the mind and the soul are one—and that confusion may cause detrimental influences to body, to mind or to soul.
>
> Then, you must have your ideal as to spiritual values, as to spiritual imports in your experience. And know—whatever may be your desire,

it must have its inception in *spiritual* attitudes.

What, then, is your spiritual ideal?

In your mental body you find at times confusion, as indicated. But what is your mental ideal? One willing to pay the price in study, in application, that you may gain the proper concept not only of your relationships to spiritual forces from within and without, but your relationships with your fellow man in every phase of your experience?

Then, your ideal is not what you may acquire by "Gimmie—Gimmie—Gimmie," but "What may I do, what may I give, in my relationships to others to make that association the *beautiful experience*," for which ye long so always!

Then the ideal is, "What may I do or be to others, that they may be better, may have a greater concept of the purposes of life, by even being acquainted or associated with myself?"

This should be your ideal, in your material life.

It is not that the body is all of meat, nor all of position, nor all of that activity in a social manner, nor all of play or work—but *all* of these enter into the experience. Just as the mental and spiritual body apply, or need, or rely upon the attributes of the phases of the whole, so is it necessary that there be the ideal in the material relationships. And these also must, as in mind, have a spiritual conception—if you would grow in grace, in knowledge, in understanding.

Then, as you find: If you would have friends, show yourself to be a friend to others. If you would have love in your life, it is necessary that you be *lovely* to others. If you would have that in your material experience to supply the physical needs of the body, the gratifying or satisfying or contenting of self in its relationships to material things, *work* in such a manner that others may be *inspired* by that manner in which you conduct yourself.

Not as one afraid—neither as one that is unmindful of the body needs or the body privileges. But abuse *not* your opportunities, if you would be the gainer in this experience. 2030-1

If knowing self is important to the spiritualization process, then why do we have this all-important step of the fall of self? The answer is found in the second teaching that Cayce expounded upon often: the crucifixion of the selfish, self-centered self, so that the true self may arise. We must subdue "those influences which constantly seek expressions of self rather than of a living, constructive influence of a *crucified* Savior. Then, crucify desire in self; that ye may be awakened to the real abilities of helpfulness that lie within thy grasp." (2475-1)

Here's another of his comments about the fall of self:

> ... what is the purpose of the Revelation: Was it for the purpose of confusing, of being mysterious? ... Rather was it not to present it that each entity, each soul, might find within itself that which answers to that within, that makes the real answer to that as was before stated, "My Spirit beareth witness with thy spirit"? And until the answer is in accord, in attune, [and there is] the consciousness of the prompting of the ability in a manifested material world to make same practical?
>
> Then as the progress is made, as the understanding comes more and more, *never, never* does it make the manifested individual entity other than the more humble, the more meek, the more longsuffering, the more patient. Of this ye may be sure.
>
> Then in all of the experiences of the opening of the centers as are represented, and those vibrations that find expression in the various temperaments of individual souls, these come not as justifications in *self* but justification in the Lamb of God! 281-31

We must come to know ourselves to be our true selves, yet one with God and all of Creation. We must do this not to glorify self, but rather to magnify God and God's love in and through us. This includes crucifying self-exalting activities, attitudes, and selfish desires in order for us to fully realize the glory that is ours in a unified life with God.

The fall of self is the fall of those aspects of our being that limit us from realizing our true potential and joy. That is why all of heaven shouts with joy when Babylon, the self, is fallen.

HALLELUJAH!
THE MARRIAGE OF THE LAMB
REVELATION 19-20
(ILLUSTRATIONS 30 AND 31)

As we have seen through the whole of Revelation, the activities, angels, dragons, earthquakes, various beasts, and a whore have all symbolized influences upon and aspects of the body, mind, and spirit. Now we are ready for the marriage of the Lamb. The Lamb represents the spiritual mind, according to Cayce (281-36). The individual has been raised to such a level of vibration and consciousness that it can realize its association with the spiritual, and it has become a new being, a spiritualized being, a God-conscious being, motivated by the spiritual influences. This achievement caused a great multitude in heaven to cry out, "Hallelujah!" An angel told John to write: "Blessed are those who are invited to the marriage supper of the Lamb." (Revelation 19:9)

Then the heavens opened, a white horse was seen, and "he who sat upon it was called Faithful and True," with a name inscribed which "no one knows but himself," and on his robe and thigh were inscribed "King of kings and Lord of lords." (Revelation 19:11, 12, 16) This rider represents our spiritual selves in the microcosmic interpretation. In the macrocosmic, he "is the symbol of the messenger; and this is Christ, Jesus, the messenger," said Cayce (281-37). He wore a robe dipped in blood, symbolizing the sacrifices made along the challenging way to spiritual consciousness. The two beasts and the kings of the earth were defeated by this rider and his armies. The dragon ("the serpent, who is the Devil and Satan" Revelation 20:2) was bound for a thousand years and thrown into the bottomless pit. In explaining the meaning of Satan being bound for a thousand years, Cayce widened his normal focus of interpreting Revelation for the individual, to one of a global view:

> . . . in the same manner that the prayer of ten just should save a city, the deeds, the prayers of the faithful will allow that period when the incarnation of those only that are in the Lord shall rule the earth, and the period is as a thousand years.
>
> Thus is Satan bound, thus is Satan banished from the earth. The desire to do evil is only of him. And when there are—as the symbols—those only whose desire and purpose of their heart is to glorify the Father, these will be those periods when this shall come to pass.
>
> Be *ye all determined* within thy minds, thy hearts, thy purposes, to be of that number! 281-37

Next is a curious passage in chapter 20, speaking of two resurrections and deaths, the first and the second. Cayce explained this as: "The first [resurrection] is of those who have not tasted death in the sense of the dread of same. The second [resurrection] is of those who have *gained* the understanding that in Him there *is* no death." (281-37) In another of his readings, Cayce expanded this, saying: "How is the way shown by the Master? What is the promise in Him? The last to be overcome is death. Death of what? The *soul* cannot die; for it is of God. The body may be revivified, rejuvenated. And it is to that end it may, the body, *transcend* the earth and its influence." (262-85)

After the thousand-year period during which the Earth and those in it had no evil to contend with, Satan and his followers were loosed again for a little while. They marched up against the saints and the holy city, but were ultimately destroyed in a fire from heaven. Now "a great white throne comes down from heaven," and "he who sits upon it opens the Book of Life" and judges all "by what was written in the Book, by what they had done." (Revelation 20:11, 12) This represents one's higher, spiritual mind reviewing all aspects of one's being, determining what is and has been good and constructive and what has been evil and destructive. This brings great knowledge to one's consciousness. Here are some valuable words from Cayce on gaining knowledge:

> As has been said, man must overcome through the knowledge and association of that knowledge with God's word made manifest in the flesh. The last to be overcome is death, and the knowledge of life is the knowledge of death. See? Any who may seek knowledge is seeking the greatest gifts of the gods of the universe, and in using such knowledge to worship God renders a service to [his] fellow man. For, as given, the greatest service to God is service to His creatures; for, as shown in the Holy One, without spot or blemish, yet gave Himself that others through Him might have the advocate to the approach to the Father without fear; in that He had passed through the flesh and the rules of the earthly, fleshly existence, taking on all the weaknesses of the flesh, yet never abusing, never misusing, never misconstruing, never giving to others a wrong impression of the knowledge of the universe; never giving any save loving brotherhood; the desire to stand in the place of him that would receive condemnation for wrong committed by or in the body; never relying on any who would bring reproach for knowledge, or place such conditions in the hands of him who disregards such understanding of God's laws.
>
> Then, in asking for such knowledge through any of the means of communication of the universal forces (that only take of a small por-

tion of the great storehouse), beware that such knowledge is directed in the channel that give succor and aid, and stands in that way and manner as was given by Him who was given to the world as an ensample and made Himself of no estate that He might give, give, give to all peoples, no matter what clime, what race, what color. They that would seek Him earlier will find Him and, in time, have life and have life more abundantly. 254-17

*   *   *

Endnotes

[1]But was destroyed shortly after this in A.D. 70 and remains so to this day.

[2]See Genesis 5:24.

[3]This prophecy occurs in a few places, but is most frequently identified with Malachi 4:5.

5

A NEW BODY, A NEW MIND
REVELATION 21-22

(ILLUSTRATION 32)

*A*nd I saw a new heaven and a new earth; for the first heaven and the first earth passed away, and there is no longer any sea. And I saw the holy city, new Jerusalem, coming down out of heaven from God, made ready as a bride adorned for her bridegroom. And I heard a loud voice from the throne saying, "Behold the tabernacle of God is among men, and He shall dwell among them, and they shall be His people, and God Himself shall be among them. And he wiped away every tear from their eyes; and there shall no longer be any death; there shall no longer be any mourning, or crying, or pain; the first things have passed away." Revelation 21:1-4

This passage has carried the hopes and expectations of so many Christians for so many generations, and in the spirit of its words it has done so for non-Christian spiritual seekers as well. When will God be fully among us? When will there be no more death, no more mourning, crying, or pain? Cayce said that this time is near. He says the "time and times and half times are at an end" and "the readjustments" will occur soon (294-185). But he instructed us not to get lost in the waiting, to be up and doing:

> Though the very heavens fall, though the earth shall be changed, though the heavens shall pass, the promises in Him are sure and will stand . . .
>
> For in deed and in truth ye know, "As ye do it unto thy fellow man, ye do it unto thy God, to thyself." For, *self* effaced, God may indeed glorify thee and make thee *stand* as one that is called for a purpose in the dealings, the relationships with thy fellow man.
>
> Be not unmindful that He is nigh unto thee in every trial, in every temptation, and hath not willed that thou shouldest perish.
>
> Make thy will then one with His. Be not afraid . . .
>
> These changes in the earth will come to pass, for the time and times and half times are at an end, and there begin those periods for the readjustments. 294-185

In responding to a direct question about this passage in the Book of the Revelation, Cayce asked:

> Can the mind of man comprehend no desire to sin, no purpose but that the glory of the Son may be manifested in his life? Is this not a new heaven, a new earth? For the former things would have passed away. For as the desires, the purposes, the aims are to bring about the whole change physically, so does it create in the experience of each soul a new vision, a new comprehension. 281-37

In response to a question about the "New Jerusalem" and "no death" concepts, Cayce said:

> Those then that are come into the new life, the new understanding, the new regeneration, there *is* then the new Jerusalem. For as has been given, the place is not as a place alone but as a condition, as an experience of the soul.
>
> Jerusalem has figuratively, symbolically, meant the holy place, the holy city—for there the ark of the covenant, the ark of the covenant in the minds, the hearts, the understandings, the comprehensions of those who have put away earthly desires and become as the *new*

purposes in their experience, become the new Jerusalem, the new undertakings, the new desires. 281-37

He also said that Holy Jerusalem is that estate that is attained through the purification processes that occurred earlier in the Revelation (281-37). Now we have come to the holy purpose and the holy of holies becomes our dwelling.

THE TWELVE GATES

The twelve gates to Holy Jerusalem represent "The twelve manners, the twelve ways, the twelve openings, the twelve experiences of the physical to all, and those that have all been purified in purpose for the activities with same." (281-37) But Cayce gives no further description of these twelve gates. However, his earlier work on the twelve tribes of Israel and the twelve major divisions of the body may be a good starting point to understand the twelve gates. You may recall that the temple with the sacred tabernacle was located in the middle of the camp of the twelve tribes of Israel. The twelve tribes may well symbolize the twelve manners, ways, openings, and experiences that lead to the temple and the holy of holies.

The twelve tribes were first arranged into four camps, with three tribes in each cam, (see illustration 45). The camp of Judah was to the east, Reuben to the south, Ephraim to the west, and Dan to the north. The temple was aligned east to west, with its entrance facing east and the holy of holies toward the west. Of course, the tribe of Levi (the thirteenth tribe, but not to be numbered among them, according to the Lord) camped directly around the temple and managed it. The meaning of the names of the tribes may give us some further insight into the twelve manners, ways, openings, and experiences.

Judah means "praise," or "praising the Lord," as his mother explained when she named him (Genesis 29:35). Reuben means "seeing" or "see, a son." (Genesis 29:32) Ephraim means "bearing fruit," or "fruitfulness." Dan means "to judge." (Genesis 30:6) These four tribes are the four major directions of the camp: east, south, west, and north. Certainly these directions would be gateways into the camp and, eventually, into the tabernacle. Praising, seeing, bearing fruit, and judging would appear to be the first four fundamental ways to the temple in the center. With Judah (praising), camped the tribes of Issachar and Zebulun, which mean, respectively, "hiring," (Genesis 30:18) as in employing help, and "dwelling" or "dwelling with me." (Genesis 30:20) With Reuben (seeing) camped the tribes of Simeon and Gad, meaning, respectively, "hears me" (Genesis 29:33) and "with fortune" or "fortune has come." (Genesis 30:11) With Ephraim (bearing fruit) camped the tribes of Mannasseh and Benjamin, meaning, respectively, "forgetting my toil" and "son of my old age." However, Benjamin's mother named him "Ben-oni," which means "son of my sorrow," for she died giving birth to him. Finally, with Dan (judging) camped the tribes of Asher and Naphtali, meaning, respectively, "happiness" (Genesis 30:13) and "wrestling" or "my wrestling." (Genesis 30:8) Here is the arrangement:

The Twelve Tribes of Israel

Four Camps

Tribes	Meanings
1. Judah	praising
Issachar	hiring help
Zebulun	dwelling with me
2. Reuben	see
Simeon	hears me
Gad	with fortune
3. Ephraim	bearing fruit
Mannasseh	forgetting my toil
Benjamin	son of my old age
4. Dan	judging
Asher	happiness
Naphtali	my wrestling

Having arranged these and connected them with their meanings, one could say that the twelve gates to the holy temple are: (1) praising the Lord, (2) hiring His help, (3) inviting Him to dwell with me, (4) allowing others to see what the Lord has brought me ("see, a son"), (5) knowing that the Lord hears me, (6) knowing that the Lord sends with fortune (as in opportunity), (7) being fruitful, (8) forgetting my toil, (9) expecting good things even in old age or sorrow, (10) judging wisely, (11) living in happiness, and (12) wrestling with the issues and challenges of life. This all leads us to the tribe of Levi, which means "attached" or "joined," as this tribe was connected to the temple and the ceremonies that led to meeting God.

On his deathbed, Jacob, the father of these twelve tribes, commented on the destiny of some of his sons, from whom the tribes were named. This gives us some further insight into the tribes and, therefore, the gates. He said that "judging" (Dan) is a "serpent in the way, biting at the horse's heels and causing the rider to fall backwards."[1] As we know, Jesus instructed us to avoid judging others because that judgment comes back upon us. Jacob further said that letting others *see* what the Lord has done for you (Reuben) has the potential to bring strength, dignity, and power, but if "boiled over like water," it defiles us. There is such a fine line between letting our light be seen and showing off or exalting ourselves and our ways, that it is dangerous, like boiling water. Jacob also warned against anger and self-will, noting that Simeon (God hears me) and Levi (I'm attached to God) let anger cause them to kill a man. How many men have died in the name of God? Righteousness can be taken too far. Add a little anger and self-will to it and we have a holy war, a righteous reason to kill. Jacob warned against this, cursing anger as a force that "divides" and "scatters." The twelve gates or ways have to be balanced with the overarching ideal expressed in humility, meekness, and patience.

Jacob is an interesting metaphor. The name *Jacob* means "one who takes by the heel." This is a fascinating name, since the Lord explained to Adam and Eve as they were leaving the Garden that the redeemer of the situation would subdue the serpent's influence by putting his heel upon its head. Later, Jacob's name was changed to *Israel*, meaning "one who contends with God," as he did with the angel of the Lord to gain understanding about heavenly things. Subduing the serpent-influence of self and contending with God to learn the truths are two good ways to give birth to the twelve ways and enter through the twelve gates.

Returning to the Revelation, we find John once again measuring the holy city. Cayce explained that John had now gained a new understanding and, therefore, needed to measure again to know his new self and its relation to all of life. "Though all are as one," Cayce said, "remember it has been given that the purpose of the heart is to know *yourself* to *be* yourself and yet one with God even as Jesus, even as is represented in God the Father, Christ the Son, and the Holy Spirit; each knowing themselves to be themselves yet *one!* So the measurements for those . . . that become attuned to the new purpose, the new desire, the new hopes, the new Revelation, the new understandings to do the will of the Father with the will of that made perfect on the Christ." (281-37)

Now we come to the final chapter and see a river of the water of life, clear and crystal, coming from the throne of God and of the Lamb, and the tree of life yielding its fruits every month, and whose leaves are for the healing of the nations. There is no longer any curse. We see God's face, and His name is written on our foreheads. All are invited to "take the water of life freely." (Revelation 22:17)

Cayce explained that the tree of life planted next to the water of life represents the "sturdiness of the purpose of the individual in its sureness in the Christ." (281-37) He said that the leaves of the tree of "our sureness in Christ" are for the healing of all whom we contact in material life and beyond, and that this is continuous, as symbolized by the tree yielding its fruit monthly:

> As the river, the water, the life represents the active flow of the pur-
> pose of the souls of men made pure in same. Then they flow with that
> purpose from the throne of God Itself, made pure in the blood of the
> Lamb—which is in Jesus, the Christ, to those who seek to know His ways.
> 281-37

*   *   *

Endnotes

[1] All of these comments may be found in Genesis 49:1-27.

PART 2

YOUR PERSONAL REVELATION

6

EXPERIENCING THE SPIRIT
THROUGH PRAYER AND MEDITATION

Studying the Revelation is important, but the real test is in experiencing it firsthand. St. John said that he experienced his revelation while he was "in the spirit on the Lord's day." (Revelation 1:10) Prayer followed by meditation is part of Cayce's recommendations for experiencing our own personal revelation and spiritualization process. Here are some key Cayce teachings about prayer and meditation, followed by a step-by-step meditation process.

Cayce taught that prayer is:

1. "the *making* of one's conscious self more in attune with the spiritual forces that may manifest in a material world" (281-13)

2. "the concerted effort of the physical consciousness to become attuned to the consciousness of the Creator" (281-13)

3. "supplication for direction, for understanding" (1861-19)

He taught that meditation is:

1. "prayer, but is prayer from *within* the *inner* self, and partakes not only

of the physical inner man but the soul that is aroused by the spirit of man from within" (281-13)

2. "listening to the Divine within" (1861-19)

There are examples of Jesus' practice of seeking time and space for Him to enter into His inner sanctuary:

> After he had dismissed them, he went up on a mountainside by himself to pray. When evening came, he was there alone. Matthew 14:23

> One of those days Jesus went out to a mountainside to pray, and spent the night praying to God. Luke 6:12

> Then Jesus went with his disciples to a place called Gethsemane, and he said to them, "Sit here while I go over there and pray." Matthew 26:36

> Very early in the morning, while it was still dark, Jesus got up, left the house and went off to a solitary place, where he prayed. Mark 1:35

Cayce said, meditation:

> ... properly done must make one *stronger* mentally, physically, for has it not been given? He went in the strength of that meat received for many days? Was it not given by Him who has shown us the Way, "I have had meat that ye know not of"? As we give out, so does the *whole* of man—physically and mentally become depleted, yet in entering into the silence, entering into the silence in meditation, with a clean hand, a clean body, a clean mind, we may receive that strength and power that fits each individual, each soul, for a greater activity in this material world. 281-13

The psalmist wrote: "Be still and know that I am God." (Psalms 46:10) The Cayce readings say, " . . . body, mind and soul make up thy tabernacle." (1479-1) In reading 2067-1, Cayce identified the outer court of the temple as the body, the inner court as the mind, and the holy of holies as the spirit. Each person is the temple of the living God, laid out just as the outer temple.

Cayce instructed us to enter into the closet of our inner selves and pour out our selfness that the inner self may be filled with the Spirit of the Father in His merciful kindness to men (281-13). He said:

> ... *Definite* conditions ... arise from within the inner man when an individual enters into true or deep meditation. A physical condition happens, a physical activity takes place! Acting through what? Through that man has chosen to call the imaginative or the impulsive, and the sources of impulse are aroused by the shutting out of thought pertaining to activities or attributes of the carnal forces of man. That is true whether we are considering it from the group standpoint or the individual. Then, changes naturally take place when there is the arousing of that stimuli *within* the individual that has within it the seat of the soul's dwelling,[1] within the individual body of the entity or man, and then this partakes of the individuality rather than the personality. 281-13

Cayce explained that, during prayer and meditation, the energy "rises from the glands known in the body as the lyden, or to the lyden [cells of Leydig] and through the reproductive forces themselves, which are the very essence of Life itself within an individual—see? for these functionings never reach that position or place that they do not continue to secrete that which makes for virility to an individual physical body." (281-13) He further explained the power of holding a high ideal during the meditation process:

> If there has been set the mark (mark meaning here the image that is raised by the individual in its imaginative and impulse force) such that it takes the form of the ideal the individual is holding as its standard to be raised to, within the individual as well as to all forces and powers that are magnified or to be magnified in the world from without, *then* the individual (or the image) bears the mark of the Lamb, or the Christ, or the Holy One, or the Son, or any of the names we may have given to that which *enables* the individual to enter *through it* into the very presence of that which is the creative force from within itself—see? 281-13

We may not see clearly now, but in time and through practice, we will. Cayce continues his teaching on meditation, saying:

The spirit and the soul is within its encasement, or its temple within the body of the individual—see? With the arousing then of this image, it rises along that which is known as the Appian Way, or the pineal center, to the base of the *brain*, that it may be disseminated to those centers that give activity to the whole of the mental and physical being. It rises then to the hidden eye in the center of the brain system, or is felt in the forefront of the head, or in the place just above the real face—or bridge of nose, see? 281-13

From here, Cayce began teaching about cleansing and purifying one's body and mind for the meditation session. He said, "First, *cleanse* the room; cleanse the body; cleanse the surroundings, in thought, in act! Approach not the inner man, or the inner self, with a grudge or an unkind thought held against *any* man! or do so to thine own undoing sooner or later!" (281-13) He wanted us to "*Find* that which is to *yourself* the more certain way to your consciousness of *purifying* body and mind, before ye attempt to enter into the meditation as to raise the image of that through which ye are seeking to know the will or the activity of the Creative Forces; for ye are *raising* in meditation actual *creation* taking place within the inner self!" (281-13) Once the cleansing is completed, he instructed us to:

Sit or lie in an easy position, without binding garments about the body. Breathe in through the right nostril three times, and exhale through the mouth. Breathe in three times through the left nostril and exhale through the right. Then, either with the aid of a low music, or the incantation of that which carries self deeper—deeper—to the seeing, feeling, experiencing of that image in the creative forces of love, enter into the Holy of Holies. As self feels or experiences the raising of this, see it disseminated through the *inner* eye (not the carnal eye) to that which will bring the greater understanding in meeting every condition in the experience of the body. Then listen to the music that is made as each center of thine own body responds to that new creative force that little by little this entering in will enable self to renew all that is necessary—in Him. 281-13

For most of us, going within is illogical. There is nothing within us but flesh and blood and a mind filled with the thoughts and concerns of daily life. But the sacred teachings of many of the great religions of the Earth and

Edgar Cayce teach otherwise. The sanctuary is within us. Ezekiel received this message in his vision when the Lord said, "Because you have defiled my sanctuary with all your vile images and detestable practices, I myself will withdraw..." (Ezekiel 5:11) This certainly sounds like the Lord is speaking of our inner sanctuary, where earthly, self-centered images often crowd out those that would reveal our true nature and destiny. Cayce insisted that:

> ... the body is indeed the temple of the living God, and He has promised to meet thee there, in the holy of holies, in the Mount within. 1152-2

> "There I shall meet thee, in the mount of thyself." For thy body indeed is the temple of the living God; there He may meet thee as ye turn within. There ye may find the greater understanding; for He hath not left His children empty-handed; for He has prepared the way. 882-1

During the great exodus, God had the seekers build a sanctuary so that He could dwell among them. God promised to meet their high priests in the sanctuary, face to face. Paul later wrote to the Hebrews about a new sanctuary and a new covenant, not built by humans for God, but by God through Christ. This sanctuary is *within* us, and Christ's sacrifice has made us all priests. Now we may enter into this new holy of holies within our hearts and minds.[2] As Jesus instructed the woman at the well, "Believe me, the hour comes, when neither in this mountain nor in Jerusalem shall you worship the Father ... But the hour comes, and now is, when the true worshipers shall worship the Father in spirit and truth: for such does the Father seek to be his worshipers. God is a Spirit: and they that worship him must worship in spirit and truth." (John 4:21, 23-24)

In the Psalms, we find many references to meditation. Here are a few:

> I remember thee upon my bed, And meditate on thee in the night-watches. Psalms 63:6

> Mine eyes anticipated the night-watches, That I might meditate on thy word. Psalms 119:148

> I remember the days of old; I meditate on all thy doings; I muse on the work of thy hands. Psalms 143:5

Of the glorious majesty of thine honor, And of thy wondrous works,
will I meditate. Psalms 145:5

One of the most fascinating insights Cayce gave us is about the holy
mount of God, which appears in so many key moments in the Scriptures.
Three of the most notable are Mount Sinai with Moses and Joshua, Mount
Horeb with Elijah, and the mount of transfiguration with Jesus and three
of His apostles, Peter, James, and John. Cayce described the Mount Sinai
event in vivid detail in reading 440-16:

> Though they had seen the Lord Jehovah descend into the mount,
> they had seen the mount so electrified by the presence of the od of
> the people and ohm of the Omnipotent to such an extent that no
> living thing could remain in the mount or on same, save those two
> [Moses and Joshua] who had been cleansed by their pouring out of
> themselves to God, in the cleansing of their bodies, in the cleansing
> of their minds.

Cayce's reference to the "od of the people" refers to a term coined by
Reichenbach (1788-1869) to explain an unseen force in nature that manifests itself in magnetism, hypnotism, and light, called the "odic force." "Od"
is most likely derived from the Greek word *hodos,* which means path or way,
and is used in such modern electrical words as anode and cathode. Cayce's
use of the word "ohm" is most probably referring to the term coined by one
of Reichenbach's contemporaries, Georg Simon Ohm (1789-1854). This
term is a measurement of electrical resistance. However, the way Cayce used
the term in the readings is not like this at all. He was equating the ohm force
with electricity in general.

Therefore, we could translate this mount experience as, "The magnetism
of the people's hearts and minds seeking God so long and so hard had attracted the Omnipotent to descend upon the mount, and It brought with
It the powers of the Omnipotent, powers which destroy as well as enlighten
(the ohm of electricity)."

During meditation, the mount is equated with the sixth spiritual center
of the body, and the holy of holies with the seventh.

Another major mount experience came when Jesus ascended the mount
with His three disciples and was transfigured. In this vision on the mount,
the law and prophets were represented in the physical, the mental, and the

spiritual: in Moses (physical), Elijah (mental), and the Christ (spiritual). If you recall, during the transfiguration, the disciples saw Moses and Elijah with the transfigured Jesus. Each represented an aspect of the path or way to spiritual breakthrough. Moses led the way out from the lower self's control (symbolized by Pharaoh and the captivity in Egypt). Moses then struggled through the desert to the mount of God, where he learned from God directly, face to face. However, Moses ultimately could not enter the Promised Land, as the physical self does not inherit the Kingdom. Therefore, the mental self (symbolized by Elijah) seeks God throughout the earth but does not find Him in the earth; not in the lightning, earthquake, fire, or wind. It is not until he backs up to the mouth of the cave (enters within his deeper consciousness) and hears "a still, small voice" within his own head that God comes fully into his consciousness. Finally, the spiritual seeker, through the *Emmanuel* (literally, "God with man") phase of development, fills the flesh and the mind with the Holy Spirit, causing human and Divine to be one, consciously one—companions eternally.

You may recall a teaching that cost Jesus many of His followers: that we must eat His flesh and drink His blood. This Scripture, taken from John 6:53-69, says:

> [53]Jesus therefore said unto them, Verily, verily, I say unto you, Except ye eat the flesh of the Son of man and drink his blood, ye have not life in yourselves.
>
> [54]He that eateth my flesh and drinketh my blood hath eternal life: and I will raise him up at the last day.
>
> [55]For my flesh is meat indeed, and my blood is drink indeed.
>
> [56]He that eateth my flesh and drinketh my blood abideth in me, and I in him.
>
> [57]As the living Father sent me, and I live because of the Father; so he that eateth me, he also shall live because of me.
>
> [58]This is the bread which came down out of heaven: not as the fathers ate, and died; he that eateth this bread shall live forever.

Many listeners were so turned off or confused by this teaching that they said, "This is a hard saying; who can hear it?" (verse 60) and stopped following Him. Jesus explained that these words were Spirit, coming from heaven, yet He turned to His chosen apostles and asked, "Will you also go away?" Of course, Peter replied for them all, " . . . to whom shall we go? You have the words of eternal life. And we have believed and know that you are the Holy One of God." (verses 67-69) Cayce addressed this teaching in his meditation training, saying: "Be sure it is Him we worship that we raise in our inner selves for the dissemination; for, as He gave, 'Ye must eat of my *body;* ye must drink of *my* blood.' Raising then in the inner self that image of the Christ, love of the God-Consciousness, is *making* the body so cleansed as to be barred against all powers that would in any manner hinder." (281-13)

In meditation, we raise ourselves to the mount of God within us and meet God in the holy of holies within us. The experience gradually spiritualizes us. The following is a typical Edgar Cayce method of meditation. If one attempted to outline the steps in a typical Edgar Cayce meditation session and added to it the spiritualization process described in the Revelation, it would look something like this:

1. Cleanse self and surroundings.
2. Set the ideal.
3. Stretch the body and do the head-and-neck exercises.
4. Take a comfortable position (sitting or reclining).
5. Say prayers. This would include a prayer of protection and, since it is the Revelation process, the Lord's Prayer should be said, keyed to the seven spiritual centers within the body.
6. Do the breathing exercise(s).
7. Do three incantations (chants), usually "aarrrr-eeee-oooo-mmmm." Since it is the Revelation process, this incantation should be used to raise and move the life force through the seven centers along the kundalini path.
8. Recite an affirmation, first aloud, then quietly within. Since it is the Revelation process, you might use something like this:

Father God, Mother God, cleanse me and my seven spiritual centers that I may enter into your loving Presence. Spiritualize my body, my mind, and my soul that I may be your companion. Lift me above myself to complete oneness with Your Infinite Spirit. Draw me into Your Presence. Then, make me a pure channel of Your love, patience, peace, and understanding to all I meet each day; not to magnify me, but to magnify You.

9. Using your imaginative forces, see, feel, know that the spirit affirmed in the words of the affirmation is raising you to higher levels of vibration

and consciousness and to closer attunement with your ideals and God.

10. When you sense the Spirit of God, rise up to It and abide there in silent receptivity, stating in your heart and mind, "Not my will, but Thy will be done."

11. Let the Spirit of God cleanse and spiritualize you, physically, mentally, and spiritually.

12. When you sense that the attunement is shifting or completed, begin to bring forth in the mind's eye others who have asked for your prayers or who need help or about whom you have concern. Let the vibrations, consciousness, and spirit of the attunement flow to them. Be a pure channel, with no personal opinion of how this should best be done or what is best for the recipient to receive. Let God's will flow cleanly through you to them.

13. If you have a personal concern, bring it up at this time. Hold it forth in your mind before God's mind and, like Jesus in the Garden, *feel* God's guidance concerning it. Repeat this enough times so that you feel certain about God's feelings. If this cannot be achieved, then leave *expectantly*, for it will come to you another way at another time.

14. Begin to rebalance the body and mind for normal functioning in this world, but with the essence, the vibration, the spirit of the attunement. Do not leave supercharged energy in the upper portions of your body, however. Distribute this throughout your body, equally.

15. Now, get up and go live life in a manner that is compatible with your attunement and growing development. Live in the "fruits of the spirit," which are love, joy, kindness, gentleness, patience, longsuffering, understanding, peace, and so on. Let your outer life reflect your inner life.

16. Repeat this process on a daily basis.

Let's examine some of the details of these steps.

First, cleanse your surroundings, your body, and your mind in a manner that is sufficient to you. Then, set your ideal. What is your ideal physically, mentally, and spiritually? This is so individual and so dependent upon where we are in our lives and our development that it is very difficult for someone else to set our ideals for us. Nevertheless, as a model to give us some idea of how this is done, let me outline a typical ideals list following Cayce's instructions.

A Sample Ideals List

Physically: Decide what you consider to be your ideal body, ideal day, ideal work, ideal recreation, ideal diet and exercise, and so on. How would you prioritize these and budget time for them? Note any reasons why you select these as your physical ideals. What is your motivation for selecting them? Cayce encouraged us to write these down, but to be prepared to change them as we develop.

Mentally: Decide what you consider to be your ideal mental disposition, attitude, thinking process. How do you want to use your mental powers in thinking about others, about yourself, about life, and so on? What do you want your mind to be thinking upon, studying, building toward? How would you prioritize these and budget time for them? What motivates you to select them? Again, write all of this down and review it from time to time, being prepared to change it as you develop.

Spiritually: Decide what you consider to be your spiritual ideal. Here's one of Cayce's comments on the spiritual ideal:

> Know that the purpose for which each soul enters a material experience is that it may be as a light unto others; not as one boastful of self or of self's abilities in any phase of the experience, whether mental or material, but living, being in spirit that which *is* ideal and not idealistic alone, nor the unattainable.
>
> For, as He hath given—if ye would know the Spirit, or God, search for Him; for happy ye will find Him.
>
> Thus—in that consciousness of daily living and being that which is in keeping with the ideal—life and its problems becomes not a burden, but opportunities—for the greater expressions and expansions of self in knowing that as ye sow daily the fruit of the spirit, ye need not worry nor fret thyself as to its growth. *God* giveth the increase. Hence be not weary in well-doing. 641-6

The spiritual influence in our lives is noncorporeal, nonworldly. It seemingly comes from out of nowhere. You can know this influence if you seek it, but you ultimately will feel the results of its presence rather than see it. St. John wrote in his first epistle that God is love, and no one has "seen" God, but those who have love in them know God and have Him in them and with them. (I John 4:8-16) Writing down the spiritual ideal can be difficult. I've seen people simply write the word "love" for their spiritual ideal. Cayce recommended that we develop this beyond just a one-word ideal. He wanted it to be a practical thing in daily living, speech, thinking, and activity. How does the spiritual influence find a practical, daily presence in your life? This is what you need to consider and write down as your spiritual ideal. I found reading the Sermon on the Mount to be an excellent way to prepare for determining one's spiritual ideal.

EXERCISES

Now, you have some preparatory exercises you have to do. The kundalini pathway begins at the base of the spine, follows the spinal column to the base of the brain, then proceeds to the center of the brain and on to the brow. That fluid, along with the hormones, is part of the chemical changes of meditation. The nerves that run up the spine and throughout the body are part of the electrical pathway. You need to loosen all these up and get them flowing better, because they tend to get congested and sluggish.

One of Cayce's most frequently recommended stretching exercises is to stand up, roll on the balls of the feet and stretch upward, with the arms and hands trying to touch the ceiling. Once you have stretched upward, alternately stretch each arm and side like a cat does on the carpet—reaching with one side and then the other side. Then, bend over to touch your toes while continuing the alternate stretching of the sides, all the way down to the hips and legs. This loosens up the spinal column, which has the fluid and nerves in it. Do about three of these stretches.

When you finish with that, Cayce recommended a very specific head-and-neck exercise. Bend the head forward, touching the chin to the chest, while feeling the stretch down your back. Do three of these. Now, lift the head up, elongating the neck, and bring the head backward, feeling the stretch down the front of the body and spine. Do three of these. Now tilt the head three times toward the left shoulder, feeling the stretch on the right side of the body; then three times to the right shoulder, feeling the stretch on the left side of the body. When you have completed this, rotate the head and neck three times in a clockwise direction, followed by three rotations in a counterclockwise direction. Go slowly, feeling the stretching throughout the body and spine. This gets the circulation of the blood, the lymph, and the electrical energies moving well throughout your body, and the spinal fluid moving much freer. If you feel any more stiffness, you can now stretch it out anyway you'd like.

The Position

In the Eastern world, positions for meditation, or *asanas* (Sanskrit for "seats"), are very important. Cayce allowed for much more flexibility, requiring only that the spine be straight. He basically suggested a position that you can comfortably maintain for at least a half hour. In all my years with the Cayce organization, I've seen many different positions, but the most common is sitting upright in a chair, spine straight, feet on the floor, hands in the lap. During the final meditation stage of channeling God's spirit to others, many Cayce students rotate their wrists so that their palms are up and open, feeling that the energy flows out of the palms. Others let the energy flow out of their mind's eye, leaving their palms in whatever position is comfortable. Cayce was also a teacher and, for that matter, a practitioner of the lying-down position, with his head and feet on a north-south axis with the poles of the Earth, usually with the head toward the north. In this position, he always insisted that the hands cover the solar plexus. This is because there are two primary portals through which the soul may leave the body: the solar plexus and the crown of the head (the soul originally enters the body through the soft spot on top of the baby's head). Cayce did not want us to leave the body through the solar plexus during meditation. In fact, he did not encourage out-of-body travel at all, but rather wanted us to travel through dimensions of consciousness.

Prayers

Cayce stressed this stage of preparation. One must pray to a level that produces a real sense of the protection and power of Christ and God with us. Here is one of Cayce's comments on this:

> Then as ye open in thy meditation, first surround thyself with the thought, the prayer, the desire that Jesus, in His promises, guide thee in thy seeking.
> *Then* ye have set yourself aright.
> Then again as ye raise thy power of vibratory forces through thy body, ye give thyself in body, in mind, in purpose, in desire, into the hands, into the keeping of His purposes with thee. 853-9

Cayce developed several prayers for protection during meditation. Here are a few examples:

My Father and my God, as I (Name thine own name) approach the throne of grace and mercy, seeking to be a better channel through which the blessings and the knowledge of my Lord and my Savior, as manifested through Thy son, Jesus, the Christ, may now be manifested in the earth, my I, as Thy servant, choose the way I should go. 262-72

Our Father and our God! Let Thy love so overshadow us that we may have naught but Thee in our minds and in our purposes! And may Thy ways be our ways! Put away from our thoughts those things that would make us afraid, and help us to boldly approach the throne of mercy and grace and ask in Jesus' name that which we ought to ask for. 281-39

Our Father our God! In Thy love, in Thy mercy, be Thou nigh unto us as we approach Thy throne seeking help and aid from the cares of every soul in this world! 281-40

Father, who art in heaven! Hallowed be Thy name. In Thy care and thy promises, through the Christ, we seek to approach the throne of mercy and grace. Pardon Thou my shortcomings, and use my mind, my body, my life, in such a way and manner that it may induce others to glorify the Christ, our Lord, our Brother, now. 538-47

Father, God, Maker of heaven and earth! I am Thine—Thou art mine! As I claim that kinship with that holy love, keep Thou me in that consciousness of Thy presence abiding with me: that I may be that channel of blessings to others, that I may know Thy grace, Thy mercy, Thy love—even as I sow such to my fellow man! 987-4

Over the years, members of the Glad Helpers prayer healing group developed this prayer of protection to be used prior to entering meditation:

As we approach the throne of power, might, grace, and mercy, we wrap about ourselves the protection found in the thought of Christ, in the love of God-consciousness.

Cayce encouraged us not to just say the words by rote, but to see, feel, and know that what we are saying is happening! This will create real protection.

THE LORD'S PRAYER WITH KEY WORDS

One of the most fascinating concepts Cayce explained was that Jesus taught His disciples how to use His prayer for meditation, identifying key words in the prayer for each spiritual center. Here is that prayer with the key words:

Prayer and Key Word	Order/Gland/Center
Our Father who art in *Heaven*	Seventh/Pituitary/third eye
hallowed be Thy *name*	Sixth/Pineal/Crown
Thy kingdom come, Thy **will** be done; on Earth as it is in Heaven.	Fifth/Thyroid/Throat (Heaven represents the three upper upper chakras, Earth the lower four.)
Give us this day our daily *bread;*	First/Ovaries-Testes/Root
Forgive us our **debts** as we forgive our debtors.	Third/Adrenals/Solar Plexus
Lead us not into *temptation;*	Second/Leydig/Lyden
but deliver us from *evil;*	Fourth/Thymus/Heart
For Thine is the *kingdom,*	Fifth/Thyroid/Throat
and the *power,*	Sixth/Pineal/Crown
and the *glory* forever.	Seventh/Pituitary/Third Eye

The last three key words are not given in the Cayce reading but were developed by those who applied this prayer in their meditation sessions. They have become a part of the Cayce legacy. The order is curious, but this is how Cayce gave it (281-29). When asked how best to use the Lord's Prayer in meditation, Cayce answered:

As in feeling, as it were, the flow of the meanings of each portion of same throughout the body-physical. For as there is the response to the mental representations of all of these in the *mental* body, it may build into the physical body in the manner as He, thy Lord, thy Brother, so well expressed in, "I have bread ye know not of." 281-29

BREATHING EXERCISES

Cayce taught some breathing exercises, but he also commented favorably upon the known yoga breathing techniques with which so many of us have become familiar:

These exercises [yoga breathing] are excellent . . . Thus an entity puts itself, through such an activity [yoga breathing], into association or in conjunction with all it has *ever* been or may be. For it loosens the physical consciousness to the universal consciousness . . . Thus ye may constructively use that ability of spiritual attunement, which is the birthright of each soul; ye may use it as a helpful influence in thy experiences in the earth. 2475-1

Cayce's best-known breathing exercise is the alternate nostril method. It begins with a deep, slow inhalation through the right nostril, filling the lungs and feeling *strength!* Then comes a slow exhalation through the mouth. During the inhalation, strength should be felt throughout the body. As you do this right-nostril-and-mouth breathing, let your focus be upon the whole of the body. Do three of these inhalations and exhalations. Now, shift to inhaling through the left nostril, but this time exhale through the right nostril, not through the mouth. This time feel the *gentle* opening of your body to the spiritual influence. As you do this left-right nostril breathing, keep your focus on the third eye and crown chakra, letting the other centers open toward these two. This will not be difficult because the sixth and seventh centers have a natural *magnetism*—just as the snake charmer's music does for the rising serpent.

When you have finished this breathing pattern, go through the Lord's Prayer again slowly, directing your attention to each chakra as you recite the phrase and key word.

Another excellent breathing technique that has found favor among deep meditators in the Cayce community was originally taught in the Taoist text, *The Secret of the Golden Flower*.[3] It is described as *the circulation Consciousness and Life*, and goes like this:

> Breathe through your nostrils in a normal manner. With each inhalation, however, *feel* or *imagine* the life force being drawn up from the lower parts of the torso to the crown of the head and over to the third-eye center on your brow. Hold the breath slightly, and sense the union of the finite with the infinite, of the dark (yin) with the light (yang). As you exhale, *feel* or *imagine* the consciousness and life force *bathing* the chakras as they descend through each to the lowest center. Pause, then inhale, while again feeling or imagining the drawing upward. Repeat this cycle at a comfortable pace, using your consciousness and breath to direct the movement in synchronization with the inhalations and exhalations. As the breath and life forces rise, feel or imagine how they open the chakras. As they descend, feel how they bathe the chakras. Take your time; again, consider this an integral part of the meditation process. Do about seven to twelve cycles of inhalations and exhalations (see illustrations 37 and 38 for a visual sense of this process).

INCANTATIONS/CHANTS

Raising one's vibrations and consciousness through incantation was recommended by Cayce and has been a major part of meditation techniques around the world for centuries. Incantation or chanting for meditation is an *inner sounding* that vibrates, stimulates, and lifts the life force. It is done in a droning manner, with a monotonous, humming tone, vibrating the vocal cords and then directing this vibration to the three major chambers in the body: abdominal, pulmonary, and cranial. Feel the sound vibrating your chakras. Feel the chakras being tuned to the specific sounds and their unique vibrations. Then, carry your consciousness upward as the sounds move upward and change. Do this chanting three or more times or until you feel yourself carried or lifted by the sounds.

Here are some of Cayce's best commentaries on sounding and chanting for higher attunement during meditation:

(Q) What is the note of the musical scale to which I vibrate?

(A) As we have indicated, Ah—This is not R, but Ah—aum [A U M], see? These are the sounds. Those that respond to the centers of the body, in opening the centers so that the kundaline forces arise to that activity through those portions of the body. Sound these, and ye will find them in thyself. They are the manners or ways of seeking.

For as ye have understood, if ye have read Him and His conversation with His friends, His disciples as respecting John—John was a great entity, none greater. And yet the least in the kingdom of heaven was greater than he. What meaneth this manner of speech?

They that have wisdom are great, they that have understanding as to the manner to *apply* same for the good of self *and* others—not for self at the expense of others, but for others—are in the awareness of the kingdom.

Thus, as to the note of thy body—is there always the response to just one? Yes. As we have indicated oft, for this entity as well as others, there are certain notes to which there is a response, but is it always the same? No more than thy moods or thy tendencies, *unless* ye have arisen to the understanding of perfect attunement.

When a violin or an instrument is attuned to harmony, is it out of tune when struck by the same motion, the same activity? Does it bring forth the same sound?

So with thy body, thy mind, thy soul. It is dependent upon the tuning—whether with the infinite or with self, or with worldly wisdom. For these, to be sure, become the mysteries of life to some—the mysteries of attuning. What seek ye? Him, self, or what?

He is within and beareth witness.

The tone, then—find it in thyself, if ye would be enlightened. To give the tune or tone as Do, Ah—aum—would mean little; unless there is the comprehending, the understanding of that to which ye are attempting to attune—in the spiritual, the mental, the material.

There *is* music in jazz, but is there perfect harmony in same?

There *is* harmony in a symphony, as in the voices as attuned to the infinite—a spirit and a body poured out in aid or the search for the soul.

There is no greater than that as may be expressed in that of, "O my son Absalom, my son, my son Absalom! would God I had died for thee, O Absalom, my son, my son!"

To what is this attuned? What *is* the note there?

That as of the realization of the lack of training the mind of the son in the way of the Lord, rather than in the knowledge of controlling individuals.

This, then, is indeed the way of harmony, the way of the pitch, the way of the tone. It is best sounded by what it arouses in thee—where, when, and under what circumstance. 2072-10

But as we find it can be accomplished much more satisfactorily within self by the right character of meditation and breathing exercise—which would be those with the body seated *in* what is ordinarily termed as Chinese or Japanese fashion, and with the chant that has been a portion of the body—of the Ar-ar-r-r—e-e-e—o-o-o—m-m-m, in the deep breathing and the circular motions of the body, and the carrying of the directing of the spiritual influences and the mental activity to the glandular forces of the body; raising these *within* self, and directing them to that to be accomplished would be the manner.

Not that this becomes as an Egyptian or an East Indian chant, but keeping the mental attitude of the Christ-Consciousness within that is purifying, is magnifying the abilities for peace, quiet, yet *attuning* self to the aliveness of not only the emotions but to the mental application for *constructive* experiences in the body and mind.

These are much better than depending upon either suggestion from without or the application of any form of electrical or mechanical appliance for the raising of the vibrations for *this* body, [275].

This would not do for *all* but can be accomplished within self. 275-45

Just as has been indicated through this channel for many, the entity will find that there are the combinations of that ye call the scale—or those harmonies set to the Ar-ar-r-r—e-e-e—ooo—mmm—that awaken within self the abilities of drawing that love of the Father as shown to the children of men in the experiences of His own, through their activities in the earth.

Hence we will find that to many, and to this entity specifically, the attempts even—yea, the seeking for the harmonious expression—will bring that which only music alone as set can span; that concept between the finite and the Infinite in its relationships to those that seek to know His presence with them. 1158-10

With the return, and with the healing of the body for the greater activities, the entity arose in its thought and power through its application especially in the Temple Beautiful.

And from same comes that interest in harmony, and color—as does the sounding of that as was the call from the station of the third position in the Temple Beautiful over which the entity, as Omuna, presided—sound within self—O-oooo-ah-m-mmm-u-uuu-r-rrr-n—nn. These as they may be sounded within; not just the vocal box of the physical but as they rise along the centers from the bodily forces to unite the activities—the entity may bring greater harmony within the experience, as it did to many through the activities in that material sojourn. 1770-2

AFFIRMATION

These can be found in the section "prayers" (pages 160-163). Cayce suggested many of the previously mentioned prayers to be used as affirmations during meditation. However, he was once asked for the best time, prayer, and affirmation for meditation, and his answer was so good that I repeat it here:

Let all those who have signified their willingness to look to God for guidance know that God has remembered them. That they are conscious of being alive, with the abilities to hate and love, should indicate this to them.

Let each individual know that it came into life with a purpose from God. Let each individual know that it is as a harp upon which the breath of God would play.

While all may not be as prophets or as preachers, neither may all stand in the halls of learning as directors of men, know that you each have your part to do.

That God hath so willed that man should be free to choose should indicate for each individual his relationship to God, that may only be manifested in the manner the individual treats his fellow man.

All are aware that selfishness causes many to be downtrodden, living in hovels; that greed, as is being manifested, would make slaves of thy fellow man. Yet each individual as an individual, and as a group, may fulfill those words, "He stood between the living and the dead and the plague was stayed."

Thus each individual is alive unto God or dead unto self.

As to the periods—as near as practical, let there be unison of purpose. Early in the morning call unto thy God, and in the evening forget not His love nor His benefits.

Then, at that period when ye each are first aware, as ye awake, be *still* a moment and know that the Lord is God. Ask that ye be guided, *this* day, to so live that ye may stand between the living and the dead.

In the evening as ye sit at meat, be *still* a moment. For there is greater power in being still before thy God than in much speaking. Again give thanks for the day and its opportunities.

And so may ye, as seekers for divine guidance, be uplifted; and thus may ye hasten the day when war will be no more. 281-60

The ideals expressed in this reading make a wonderful foundation for developing many affirmations for our meditation sessions.

THE IMAGINATIVE FORCES

This is another fascinating concept in the Cayce volumes. Few would consider the imaginative forces as a powerful tool in spiritual development, but for Cayce they were essential. Here are two reading excerpts in which he expressed their importance:

(Q) What means are best for me to use to discover how I may keep the physical and mental forces in a condition which will permit the highest development of the spiritual forces?

(A) Keep that attunement in which the body-physical, imaginative, *and* spiritual, can visualize for each part of that that *develops* in the body *before* the mental, spiritual and imaginative forces of the body. Few people are able in the beginning to be as generally imaginative as the body! Hence the body should be able, with a little visualization of that as is *desired* by the self, to create for itself that atmosphere, that environ, for *that* being acted upon! This requires the necessary knowledge of the body, of the mind, of that as is desired by the body. Then *with* that knowledge and the proper visualization, the *understanding* comes. Knowledge is not power unless it is that that may be applied by the body *having* the knowledge—see? 1048-3

In the mental attributes of the body, we find there are *exceptional* abilities of the body, especially in those directions as tending towards the imaginative forces; the abilities to draw on the imagination for the visualization or picturization of conditions, places, circumstances, surroundings. These may be made into those conditions that may bring for a real *development* for the body, were these not so much as being condoned—or repressed, but rather as a *proper* reasoning with, encouragement of, the body mental to give expressions *to* such conditions as arise in the mental forces of the body. These may be turned into channels in which it will aid the body in its studies, especially along those lines that will enable it to vision forces as pertain to those of history or geography, or those as pertain to kindred subjects. These *should* be the ones in which the body should make for the greater expansion of self, as we find, for the advancement of the mental forces of the body.

In the spiritual attainments, these have often been questioned by others—for the body questions self as respecting same; yet with the finding of self in the *expressions* of self through the imaginative forces, or the intuitive forces—as they become with developments of the mental forces in the body here, [768]—we will find the *spirit* will be kept awake in that of the thorough, full, life-giving forces *to* the body, enabling the body not only to gain an insight into Life's forces, but to so give out to *others* that which will be of help, aid and strength to others. 768-1

Visualizing or *feeling imaginatively* the movement of energy, consciousness, and light through the body is very helpful. But Cayce also taught that we should visualize or feel the power, might, mercy, and grace of God and Christ flowing through us, transforming us, making us pure channels of Light and Love.

REBALANCING THE BODY

The concepts for rebalancing the body came from Edgar Cayce's own problems with headaches, dizziness, and feeling disoriented after one of his deep sessions, which he called his meditations. The guidance was that he, and presumably others doing similar sessions, were leaving supercharged energy in the upper portions of their bodies after meditations. This needed to be distributed throughout the body for normal functioning in this physical dimension. The basic method for rebalancing and redistributing the energy is to firmly direct the mind to move the energy throughout the body and strengthen this directive by seeing it, feeling it, and knowing that it is moving throughout the body equally.

SAME TIME, SAME PLACE

For best results with meditation, Cayce recommended going to the same location, chair, or area of your room, apartment, or house, at or near the same time each day. This will actually create rhythms and patterns conducive to gradual, but steady development. Many have found that if they don't follow their prayer and meditation schedule, then it takes several days of practice to get back to the levels of attunement and vibration that they had before the break in practice. Regular practice in the same place is the ideal, but, as Cayce would say, whatever you will and can do is better than no practice.

*   *   *

Endnotes

[1]You may recall from chapter 3 that Cayce said this was in the second and sixth chakras.

[2]See Hebrews 8-9.

[3]It can be found on p. 72 of Richard Wilhelm's translation.

7

DREAMS AND VISIONS

*H*e that dwelleth in the secret place of the Most High
shall abide under the shadow of the Almighty.

Psalms 91:1

Where is "the secret place of the Most High"? That's a very important
question to those of us seeking personal revelation. Are the inner "places" as
real as the outer? The ancient Egyptian Book of the Dead is literally titled,
The Book of the Master of the Hidden Places. Where are these hidden places,
and how do we find them so that we may dwell in the secret place of the
Most High? For our answers, we need only search the Old Testament.

In Job 33:14-16, we have an important clue, spoken by one of Job's
friends, Elihu: "God speaks . . . though man regards it not. In a dream, in
a vision of the night, when deep sleep falls upon men, in slumber upon the
bed; then He opens the ears of men . . . " In the "place" of sleep and dreams,
God has indeed met with humans many times in recorded history. One of
the first was Jacob. Genesis 28:10-17 recorded it this way:

And Jacob . . . lay down in that place to sleep. And he dreamed. And behold, a ladder set up on the earth, and the top of it reached to heaven. And behold, the angels of God ascending and descending on it. And, behold, Jehovah stood above it, and said, "I am Jehovah, the God of Abraham thy father, and the God of Isaac . . . And, behold, I am with thee, and will keep thee, whithersoever thou goest . . . For I will not leave thee, until I have done that which I have spoken to thee of." And Jacob awaked out of his sleep, and he said, "Surely Jehovah is in this place. And I knew it not." And he was afraid, and said, "How dreadful is this place! This is none other than the house of God and the gate of heaven."

Is the "place" where sleep and dreams occur "the house of God and the gate of heaven"? Most spiritual seekers who have been on the path for a while would say that it is, conceding that it is, nevertheless, a difficult place to know and explore—in Jacob's words, "How dreadful is this place!" All of us who have worked with dreams know exactly what he means.

Another great one who met God through sleep and dreams was Elijah. I Kings 19:5, 11-13 recorded it this way:

And he lay down and slept under a juniper-tree; and, behold, an angel touched him . . . And he said, Go forth, and stand upon the mount before Jehovah. And, behold, Jehovah passed by, and a great and strong wind rent the mountains, and brake in pieces the rocks before Jehovah; but Jehovah was not in the wind; and after the wind an earthquake; but Jehovah was not in the earthquake; and after the earthquake a fire; but Jehovah was not in the fire; and after the fire a still small voice. And it was so, when Elijah heard it, that he wrapped his face in his mantle, and went out, and stood in the entrance of the cave. And, behold, there came a voice unto him.

Note that the writer said that Elijah was standing "upon the mount before Jehovah," only to later tell us that he "went out, and stood in the entrance of the cave." Is this "mount" of God's *within* a cave in the realm of sleep and dreams? It is what the Taoist master Lao tsu was speaking of when he referred to the "square inch field of the square foot house,"[1] explaining that the square-foot house was the human head and the square-inch field was the place of heaven. How can a field be an inch and a house be a foot?

How can a mount be within a cave? Both teachers were trying to convey the invertedness of the inner world from the outer—mounts and fields in the mind. Lao tsu went on to guide us with, "In the middle of the square inch dwells the splendor."

Edgar Cayce taught that dreams were the "safest" way to the inner realms of consciousness. He even said that nothing occurs in our outer lives that was not already foreshadowed in our dreams—a hard concept to accept if one is purely physical. For those who have visited the place of deep slumber and dreams, however, it is easier to understand and believe. The sleep and dreams of a person developing spiritually can lead to the secret place of the Most High. The prophet Daniel described it by saying: "I saw in the night-visions, and, behold, there came with the clouds of heaven one like unto a son of man, and he came even to the ancient of days, and they brought him near before him." (Daniel 7:13)

As difficult as dreams are, they can be an invaluable source of help with life. Therefore, it is worth learning how to recall them, understand them, and apply them in our lives. Of course, the first problem is remembering them. The second problem is understanding or interpreting what you've remembered.

Tips for Remembering Dreams

1. *Presleep suggestion.* As we fall asleep, we move from the conscious mind to the subconscious, dreaming mind. The subconscious is amenable to suggestion. Therefore, give it the suggestion to *remember your dreams!*

2. *Don't move the body upon waking.* Moving the physical body often causes us to move out of the dreaming mind and into the conscious mind. We need to allow the subconscious sufficient time to give its content to the conscious mind gradually and completely. Lie still for this important transfer of data.

3. *Get the gist of the dream first, details second.* Feel the essence of the dream's meaning first, and don't let the details sway you from the fundamental essence or spirit of the dream.

4. *Use the essence of the dream in life.* Knowledge not applied is lost and becomes a stumbling block rather than a steppingstone.

5. *Keep a journal, but keep it simple.* Dream themes are developed over a series of dreams. Inner processing takes several dreams. Detailed guidance takes several dreams. Write your dreams down and read over them, but don't

let it become a burden. Keep it a dynamic, changing part of real life. The inner and outer are a team.

Steps for Interpreting Dreams

1. Identify the *mood*. Up, down, or neutral; scared or daring; sad or happy; worried or hopeful; and so on. Mood reveals your inner self's fundamental feelings.

2. Identify the *subject*. Refine this to the lowest common denominator: What is the subject that is being viewed? Not the action. Not the feeling. The subject. The matter under consideration.

3. Identify the *movement*. Watching, listening, waiting, reflecting, and the like; doing, acting, changing, making, running toward, and the like; or protecting, warning, retreating, running away, and the like. Movement reveals your inner self's basic call to action, further reflection, or retreat.

4. Identify the *nature* of the inner mind's activity. Is it reviewing, previewing, analyzing, processing, instructing, warning, encouraging, or experiencing? Determining the fundamental nature of the inner mind's activity helps us understand how to use the dream. In some cases, the dream is an experiencing, a processing, a reflecting, and calls for no action. In other cases, the dream is instructing, warning, or encouraging us, and action is clearly called for.

Let's review: As you awaken, take note of the overall *mood*, then the *subject*, then the *movement*, and finally the *nature* of the mind while in the dream. Remember, it is best to do this while still in or near the dreaming mind because the best interpreter of the dream is the dreamer. As we all quickly find out, the outer self is not the dreamer. Therefore, it is best to get the interpretation while still in or near the dreaming mind.

A significant aid to dreaming and dream interpretation is to go into sleep from meditation. Develop a brief meditation technique that you can do while lying in your bed ready for a night's sleep. The ancient Greeks referred to the sleep state as being "in the arms of Morpheus," their god of dreams and the son of Hypnos (yes, as in hypnosis). Movies and computer graphics have familiarized us with "morphing," shape-shifting from one form to another, as the poet Ovid referred to Morpheus's shifting forms in sleep.

Sleep is actually more than one condition. It is a series of conditions that begins by stilling the three-dimensional physical body, absorbing the normal three-dimensional mind into the deeper subconscious, and allowing the mind to gradually go through various transitions, which we can verify through changes in the brainwaves, from beta to alpha to theta, and so on. If the deepest type of sleep is achieved, then the inner being "morphs" from its normal ice-cubelike three-dimensional reality to a watery, flowing realm in which three-dimensional objects have the qualities of liquids and vapors—the realm of Morpheus. The inner mind and being enter an expansive state in which the mind, not the body, is the mover and doer. In this dimension, a three-dimensional cube would be an image. We could see it. We could even touch it—but not like we would a three-dimensional cube on Earth. This cube is the four-dimensional version of our three-dimensional solid. It is the thought form of the cube. Now we are perceiving beyond the three planes of the "real" cube. This is the four-dimensional thought form of the cube, the idea of the cube. It has all the characteristics of the three-dimensional cube, but is in an alternate reality to it. It is not matter. In this fourth dimension, we do not use the body's physical senses, yet we are sensing. The mind's sight, hearing, touch, taste, and smell are as real to the sleeper as the physical is to the three-dimensional self, but we are beyond the physical; we are in the next dimension.

To really enhance your consciousness in this other dimension, try meditating every night for a month before falling asleep. Your sleep state will come alive as your deeper, four-dimensional self takes conscious flight through the many realms beyond this little world of ours.

For protection and a right-guiding rudder, call for God's presence and purpose throughout the sleep experience. *See* them, *feel* them, *know* they are with you as you let go and fall into sleep.

As stated earlier, you must not move the three-dimensional body as you are waking, or you'll lose the experiences. Gently pass the dreams over to your outer mind. Once it has them firmly, get up and write them down. Otherwise, you'll forget them by 3 p.m.! Life here is just too consuming to retain the gossamerlike experiences of the realm of Morpheus.

Life is more than physical. As the poet William Wordsworth once noted, "The world is too much with us." Let's use the idle three-dimensional time of sleep for four-dimensional learning and growth.

Two of Cayce's best readings on dreams and the development of the sixth sense are 5754-2 and 5754-3, given in July 1932 at his home in Virginia Beach. Here they are in their entirety. I find it is best to read them slowly. After a while, you will get used to Cayce's syntax and style:

Now, with that as has just been given, that there is an active force within each individual that functions in the manner of a sense when the body-physical is in sleep, repose or rest, we would then outline as to what are the functions of this we have chosen to call a sixth sense.

What relation does it bear with the normal physical recognized five senses of a physical-aware body? If these are active, what relation do they bear to this sixth sense?

Many words have been used in attempting to describe what the spiritual entity of a body is, and what relations this spirit or soul bears with or to the active forces within a physical normal body. Some have chosen to call this the cosmic body, and the cosmic body as a sense in the universal consciousness, or that portion of same that is a part of, or that body with which the individual, or man, is clothed in his advent into the material plane.

These are correct in many respects, yet by their very classification, or by calling them by names to designate their faculties or function-ings, have been limited in many respects.

But what relation has this sixth sense (as has been termed in this presented) with this *soul* body, this cosmic consciousness? What rela-tion has it with the faculties and functionings of the normal physical mind? Which must be trained? The sixth sense? or must the body be trained in its other functionings to the dictates of the sixth sense?

In that as presented, we find this has been termed, that this ability or this functioning—that is so active when physical consciousness is laid aside—or, as has been termed by some poet, when the body rests in the arms of Morpheus—is nearer possibly to that as may be under-standable by or to many; for, as given, this activity—as is seen—of a mind, or an attribute of the mind in physical activity—*leaves* a *definite* impression. Upon what? The mental activities of the body, or upon the subconscious portion of the body (which, it has been termed that, it never forgets), upon the spiritual essence of the body, or upon the soul itself? These are questions, not statements!

In understanding, then, let's present illustrations as a pattern, that there may be comprehension of that which is being presented:

The activity, or this sixth sense activity, is the activating power or force of the other self. What other self? That which has been builded by the entity or body, or soul, through its experiences as a whole in the material and cosmic world, see? or is as a faculty of the soul-body itself. Hence, as the illustration given, does the subconscious make aware to this active force when the body is at rest, or this sixth sense, some action on the part of self or another that is in disagreement with that which has been builded by that other self, then *this* is the warring of conditions or emotions within an individual. Hence we may find that an individual may from sorrow *sleep* and wake with a feeling of elation. What has taken place? We possibly may then understand what we are speaking of. There has been, and ever when the physical consciousness is at rest, the other self communes with the *soul* of the body, see? or it goes *out* into that realm of experience in the relationships of all experiences of that entity that may have been throughout the *eons* of time, or in correlating *with* that as it, that entity, *has* accepted as its criterion or standard of judgments, or justice, within its sphere of activity.

Hence through such an association in sleep there may have come that peace, that understanding, that is accorded by that which has been correlated through that passage of the selves of a body in sleep. Hence we find the more spiritual-minded individuals are the more easily pacified, at peace, harmony, in normal active state as well as in sleep. Why? They have set before themselves (Now we are speaking of one individual!) that that *is* a criterion that may be wholly relied upon, for that from which an entity or soul sprang is its *concept*, its awareness of, the divine or creative forces within their experience. Hence they that have named the Name of the Son have put their trust in Him. He their standard, their model, their hope, their activity. Hence we see how that the action through such sleep, or such quieting as to enter the silence—What do we mean by entering the silence? Entering the presence of that which *is* the criterion of the selves of an entity!

On the other hand oft we find one may retire with a feeling of elation, or peace, and awaken with a feeling of depression, of aloofness, of being alone, of being without hope, or of fear entering, and the *body-physical* awakes with that depression that manifests itself as of low spirits, as is termed, or of coldness, gooseflesh over the body, in expressions of the forces. What has taken place? A comparison in that "arms of Morpheus," in that silence, in that relationship of the physical self being unawares of those comparisons between the soul and its experiences of that period with the experiences of itself throughout the ages, and the experience may not have been remembered as a dream—but it lives *on*—and on, and must find its expression in the relationships of all it has experienced in whatever sphere of activity it may have found itself. Hence we find oft individual circumstances of where a spiritual-minded individual in the material plane (that is, to outward appearances of individuals so viewing same) suffering oft under pain, sickness, sorrow, and the like. What takes place? The experiences of the soul are meeting that which it has merited, for the clarification for the associations of itself with that whatever has been set as its ideal. If one has set self in array against that of love as manifested by the Creator, in its activity brought into material plane, then there *must* be a continual—continual—*warring* of those elements. By the comparison we may find, then, how it was that, that energy of creation manifested in the Son—by the activities of the Son in the material plane, could say "He sleeps," while to the outward eye it was death; for He *was*—and *is*—and ever will be—Life and Death in one; for as we find ourselves *in* His presence, that we have builded in the soul makes for that condemnation or that pleasing of the presence of that in His presence. So, my son, let thine lights be in Him, for these are the *manners* through which all may come to an understanding of the activities; for, as was given, "I was in the Spirit on the Lord's day." "I was caught up to the seventh heaven. Whether I was in the body or out of the body I cannot tell." What was taking place? The subjugation of the physical attributes in accord and attune with its infinite force as set as its ideal brought to that soul, "Well done, thou good and faithful servant, enter into the joys of thy Lord." "He that would be the greatest among you—" Not as the Gentiles, not as the heathen, not as the scribes or Pharisees, but "He that would be the greatest will be the *servant* of all."

What, then, has this to do—you ask—with the subject of sleep? Sleep—that period when the soul takes stock of that it has acted upon during one rest period to another, making or drawing—as it were—the comparisons that make for Life itself in its *essence* as for harmony, peace, joy, love, long-suffering, patience, brotherly love, kindness—these are the fruits of the Spirit. Hate, harsh words, unkind thoughts, oppressions and the like, these are the fruits of the evil forces, or Satan and the soul either abhors that it has passed, or enters into the joy of its Lord. Hence we see the activities of same. This an *essence* of that which is intuitive in the active forces. Why should this be so in one portion, or one part of a body, rather than another? How received woman her awareness? Through the sleep of the man! Hence *intuition* is an attribute of that made aware through the suppression of those forces from that from which it sprang, yet endowed *with* all of those abilities and forces of its Maker that made for same its activity in an *aware* world, or—if we choose to term it such—a three dimensional world, a *material* world, where its beings must see a materialization to become aware of its existence in that plane; yet all are aware that the essence of Life itself as the air that is breathed—carries those elements that are not aware consciously of any existence to the body, yet the body subsists, lives upon such. In sleep all things become possible, as one finds self flying through space, lifting, or being chased, or what not, by those very things that make for a comparison of that which has been builded by the very soul of the body itself.

What, then, is the sixth sense? Not the soul, not the conscious mind, not the subconscious mind, not intuition alone, not any of those cosmic forces—but the very force or activity of the soul in its experience through *whatever* has been the experience of that soul itself. See? The same as we would say, is the mind of the body the body? No! Is the sixth sense, then, the soul? No! No more than the mind is the body! for the soul is the *body* of, or the spiritual essence of, an entity manifested in this material plane.

We are through for the present. 5754-2

Yes, we have that which has been given here. Now, as we have that condition that exists with the body and this functioning, or this sense, or this ability of sleep and sense, or a sixth sense, just what, how, may this knowledge be used to advantage for an individual's development towards that it would attain?

As to how it may be used, then, depends upon what is the ideal of that individual; for, as has been so well pointed out in Holy Writ, if the ideal of the individual is lost, then the abilities for that faculty or that sense of an individual to contact the spiritual forces are gradually lost, or barriers are builded that prevent this from being a sensing of the nearness of an individual to a spiritual development.

As to those who are nearer the spiritual realm, their visions, dreams, and the like, are more often—and are more often retained by the individual; for, as is seen as a first law, it is self-preservation. Then self rarely desires to condemn self, save when the selves are warring one with another, as are the elements within a body when eating of that which produces what is termed a nightmare—they are warring with the senses of the body, and partake either of those things that make afraid, or produce visions of the nature as partaking of the elements that are taken within the system, and active within same itself. These may be given as examples of what it is all about.

Then, how may this be used to develop a body in its relationship to the material, the mental, and the spiritual forces?

Whether the body desires or not, in sleep the consciousness physically is laid aside. As to what will be that it will seek, depends upon what has been builded as that it would associate itself with, physically, mentally, spiritually, and the closer the association in the mental mind in the physical forces, in the physical attributes, are with spiritual elements, then—as has been seen by even those attempting to produce a certain character of vision or dream—these follow much in that; for another law that is universal becomes active! Like begets like! That which is sown in honor is reaped in glory. That which is sown in corruption cannot be reaped in glory; and the likings are associations that are the companions of that which has been builded; for such experiences as dreams, visions and the like, are but the *activities* in the unseen world of the real self of an entity.

Ready for questions.

(Q) How may one train the sixth sense?

(A) This has just been given; that which is constantly associated in the mental visioning in the imaginative forces, that which is constantly associated with the senses of the body, that will it develop toward. What is that which is and may be sought? When under stress *many* an individual—There are *no* individuals who haven't at *some time* been warned as respecting that that may arise in their daily or physical experience! Have they heeded? Do they heed to that as may be given as advice? No! It must be experienced!

(Q) How may one be constantly guided by the accompanying entity on guard at the Throne?

(A) It is there! It's as to whether they desire or not! It doesn't leave but is the active force? As to its ability to *sense* the variations in the experiences that are seen, is as has been given in the illustration—"As to whether in the body or out of the body, I cannot tell." Hence this sense is that ability of the entity to associate its physical, mental or spiritual self to that realm that it, the entity, or the mind of the soul, seeks for its association during such periods—see? This might confuse some, for—as has been given—the subconscious and the abnormal, or the unconscious conscious, is the mind of the soul; that is, the sense that this is used, as being that subconscious or subliminal self that is on guard ever with the Throne itself; for has it not been said, "He has given his angels charge concerning thee, lest at any time thou dashest thy foot against a stone?" Have you heeded? Then He is near. Have you disregarded? He has withdrawn to thine own self, see? That self that has been builded, that that is as the companion, that must be presented—that *is* presented—*is* before the Throne itself! *Consciousness*—[physical] consciousness—see—man seeks this for his *own* diversion. In the sleep [the soul] seeks the *real* diversion, or the *real* activity of self.

(Q) What governs the experiences of the astral body while in the fourth dimensional plane during sleep?

(A) This is, as has been given, that upon which it has fed. That which it has builded; that which it seeks; that which the mental mind, the subconscious mind, the subliminal mind, *seeks!* That governs. Then we come to an understanding of that, "He that would find must seek." In the physical or material this we understand. That is a pattern of the subliminal or the spiritual self.

(Q) What state or trend of development is indicated if an individual does not remember dreams?

(A) The negligence of its associations, both physical, mental and spiritual. Indicates a very negligible personage!

(Q) Does one dream continually but simply fail to remember consciously?

(A) Continues an association or withdraws from that which *is* its right, or its ability to associate! There is no difference in the unseen world to that that is visible, save in the unseen so much greater expanse or space may be covered! Does one always desire to associate itself with others? Do individuals always seek companionship in this or that period of their experiences in each day? Do they withdraw themselves from? That desire lies or carries on! See? It's a *natural* experience! It's *not* an unnatural! Don't seek for unnatural or supernatural! It is the natural—it is nature—it is God's activity! His associations with man. His *desire* to make for man a way for an understanding! Is there seen or understood fully that illustration that was given of the Son of man, that while those in the ship were afraid because of the elements the Master of the sea, of the elements, slept? What associations may there have been with that sleep? Was it a natural withdrawing? yet when spoken to, the sea and the winds obeyed His voice. Thou may do even as He, wilt thou make thineself aware—whether that awareness through the ability of those forces within self to communicate with, understand, those elements of the spiritual life *in* the conscious and unconscious, these be one!

(Q) Is it possible for a conscious mind to dream while the astral or spirit body is absent?

(A) There may be dreams—(This is a division here) A conscious mind, while the body is absent, is as one's ability to divide self and do two things at once, as is seen by the activities of the mental mind.

The ability to read music and play is using different faculties of the same mind. Different portions of the same consciousness. Then, for one faculty to function while another is functioning in a different direction is not only possible but probable, dependent upon the ability of the individual to concentrate, or to centralize in their various places those functionings that are manifest of the spiritual forces in the material plane. *Beautiful* isn't it?

(Q) What connection is there between the physical or conscious mind and the spiritual body during sleep or during an astral experience?

(A) It's as has been given, that *sensing* With what? That separate sense, or the ability of sleep, that makes for acuteness with those forces in the physical being that are manifest in everything animate. As the unfolding of the rose, the quickening in the womb, of the grain as it buds forth, the awakening in all nature of that which has been set by the divine forces, to make the awareness of its presence in *matter*, or material things.

We are through for the present. 5754-3

* * *

Endnotes

[1]*The Secret of the Golden Flower*, translated by Richard Wilhelm, 1931, p. 22.

8

BALANCE, PATIENCE, AND APPLICATION

Balance

*T*o be divine and human and to remain sane, with enthusiasm for both the inner and outer life, require that we maintain a balance between our dual natures, our dual realities. If we are too much into the outer personality and outer life, we feel disconnected from our inner selves, and the outer activities consume us. If we are too much into the inner self and inner life, we feel disconnected from other people, and the inner activities cause us to "space out" on physical life and its importance to our soul's growth. The inner and the outer must be maintained in balance. We must budget our time to allow for both, just as we must balance sleep and wakefulness, eating and activity, work and recreation, companionship and solitude. Our inner nature and consciousness must be given their share of attention and opportunity; as well, we must give our outer nature and consciousness their share.

Let's examine some of the elements of these two natures and realities.

The inner reality is where God has promised to meet us. It is the realm of the infinite, universal oneness. It is the realm of dreams, visions, and imaginings. From out of it come intuitions, ideas, and inspirations. It is the yin, the night, the place of stillness and attunement. Prayer leads us there; stillness maintains us there. Deep, true knowing comes from within us. Deep, lasting companionship comes from within us. The "peace that passes understanding" (Philippians 4:7) comes from within us. In all our doing, we must stay "plugged in" to this portion of our nature and consciousness if we are to be truly whole and healthy.

The outer reality is where we interact with others, the second greatest commandment. It is the realm of the finite, the individual, and the multiplicity of the realm of "manyness." In this reality, we have the opportunity to love, give, do, and apply what we know and feel is best. It is the yang of life, the day, the realm of action and service. Guided by an ideal, we in this outer realm and consciousness manifest, or make real, our inner beliefs. Here we walk our talk. Here we test just how deeply we really mean what we think and say. Through this activity, our inner self finds truth in action: tested and proven. The peace that passes understanding may begin within, but its full realization comes only from outer application.

None of us maintains this balance all the time. Rather, life has cycles. Sometimes life provides more opportunity for inner attunement and development. At other times, it provides more opportunity for application and service. Even so, each day requires that we maintain some equilibrium between these two. Even during times of more focused inner work, our bodies require exercise, and our personalities require contact with others. Even during times of more focused outer work, our minds require some stillness and centering, and our souls require some contact with the Divine.

GOOD AND EVIL

When Edgar Cayce was asked, "In what form does the anti-Christ come . . . ?" he responded: "In the spirit of that opposed to the spirit of truth." He went on to explain that "The fruits of the spirit of the Christ are love, joy, obedience, long-suffering, brotherly love, kindness. Against such there is no law. The spirit of hate, the anti-Christ, is contention, strife, fault-finding, lovers of self, lovers of praise. Those are the anti-Christ, and take possession of groups, masses, and show themselves even in the lives of men." (281-16)

The dark forces are thus not ghosts or ghouls, but the attitude, the spirit of contention, strife, fault-finding in our everyday lives, which Cayce said take possession of not only individuals but also groups and masses. Touching again on this topic, Cayce identified the forces of darkness as "trouble, turmoil, strife, dissension, disorder, inharmony, and such—and *these* be the children of darkness . . . " (288-27)

Cayce said that the anti-Christ is given power by *us!* Individuals are the channels of light or darkness, depending upon which spirit we allow ourselves to be caught up with. If we give God a chance in our individual lives, then "the power of the Lord, may put the thousands [of dark influences] to flight." He went on to encourage each of us "to seek more and more for the strength, the direction, the might of that promised in 'If ye will call, I will hear.'" (3976-24)

Despite these strong statements about good and evil, Cayce frequently cautioned against judging who is good or evil, saying in one case, "Only a very thin veil [exists] between sublime and ridiculous, thinner between good and evil . . . " (3744-1) When judging one another, he encouraged us to: " . . . magnify the virtues . . . minimize the faults. It would be well for this to be thy policy, thy tenet. For there is none so bad nor yet so good that any can afford to judge or speak evil of the other. Ye may speak evil of evil things, but not of man. For he is in the image of his God and . . . man's soul is eternal. Then speak not evil of thy brother, lest ye condemn thine own self." (3509-1)

When asked how we can protect ourselves from evil influences, Cayce answered, "So surround thyself by thought, by deed, by act, *with* the consciousness of the Christ that *no man,* no group, no *thought,* may hurt thee." (531-9)

He went on: " . . . when others say, do, or act so that . . . depression comes, make self be *gentle,* be *kind,* be patient, be longsuffering, and if look *or* speech is made let it be in *gentleness,* in loving kindness, and not *stirring* up—either in self or without; for in so *doing* we *overcome* that as has been termed by some as karma . . . we *overcome* and put to rout the children of darkness that *prevent* the light." (288-27)

The powers against the dark forces are the fruits of the spirit. " . . . in the fruits of . . . the spirit—does man become aware of the infinite penetrating . . . into the finite—and the finite becomes conscious of same." (262-52)

Let's practice using the fruits of the spirit in our actions and reactions with one another each day. If we do this, we need to be prepared to face opportunities to avoid acting or reacting with judgment, contention, or "stirring up" (the dark forces) and to act instead with gentleness, kindness, patience, longsuffering, love, joy, and *with* Christ-consciousness (the light forces). The real Armageddon is every day in little acts, deeds, and thoughts.

Patience

Edgar Cayce had a fascinating perspective on patience. To him, patience was not just a virtue, but another dimension. "Time, space, and patience, then, are those channels through which man as a finite mind may become aware of the infinite," he explained in reading 3161-1. In the same reading, he went on to say, " . . . there is no time, there is no space, when patience becomes manifested in love." In 3161-1, he explained, "love unbounded is patience. Love manifested is patience." When patience becomes an active principle in our lives, we rise above the limitations of time and space. It is our finite mind, our human side, that holds us in the dimensions of time and space. But we have access to our infinite mind, our Christlike side, that can and will lift us beyond time and space:

> Self in the physical grows weary, because you are only human, because you are finite; you have a beginning, you have an end of your patience, your love, your hope, your fear, your desire . . . but when these problems arise know . . . you cannot walk the whole way alone, but He has promised in the Christ-Consciousness to give you strength, to give you life and that more abundant. 3161-1

> . . . in patience run the race that is set before thee, looking to Him, the author, the giver of light, truth and immortality. That should be the central theme in every individual. 262-24

Patience is not passive, enduring, and submissive. It is active, transforming, and filled with the power of God in action:

> Taking or enduring hardships, or censure, or idiosyncrasies of others, is not necessarily patience at all. 3161-1

> Patience is active rather than passive . . . 262-26

In one of his wonderful twists, Cayce asked us to consider the patience of God's relationship with us. How has God manifested His/Her patience with us? Has He/She taken away free will? Has He/She crushed evildoers? Banned nonbelievers? Cayce noted that, " . . . God is God of those who hate Him as well as of those who love Him. He is patient, He is kind, He is merciful." (254-115) Again, Cayce's statements expressed an active quality to patience:

" . . . love unbounded is patience. Love manifested is patience."
3161-1

"Remove self far from criticisms or fault-findings in others, and there comes then patience in word, deed and act." 262-24

Actively trying to resist finding fault or criticizing others is patience.
Actively trying to manifest love, when it hurts, is patience.

Where does tough love come into this philosophy? Cayce said, "Not in submissiveness alone, but in righteous wrath serve ye the living God . . . Be *mad*, but sin not!" (262-24) Here, William Shakespeare's suggestion that we judge the act, not the actor, is the better course to take. In this way, we may condemn the actions, the words, but withhold condemning the soul that committed them. These actions, these words are not tolerable, but the individual is. God tolerates even the evil ones—at least for a while longer.

In conclusion, patience requires that we loose the hold our finite mind and human side have upon us and open to our infinite mind, the Christ Consciousness, and our spiritual, godlike side. We should actively run the race set before us—loving, not condemning, those around us and walking the daily path with God. When we do this, we live in another dimension, one beyond the limitations of time and space. One that is eternal, filled with peace that passes all understanding. As Jesus taught, "In patience possess ye your soul." (Luke 21:19) Our souls are immortal. They are timeless and beyond the limitations of three-dimensional space. Let's actively apply patience in our lives and rise to a new level of understanding and life, life more abundant.

We are more than human. We are godlings of the infinite, omnipotent, omnipresent God. We need to begin using our godly faculties more frequently in order to become who we ultimately are: companions to and cocreators with God, a God who extends far beyond the dimensions of time and space. Active patience is a daily exercise that can help us get there.

APPLICATION

We come to what is without doubt one of the two or three most important precepts in the Cayce readings: Live your life in a manner that reflects your inner growth. Apply what you have gained. Find an outlet, find a way to bring some of this inner attunement to your outer life. Even if it simply means a different attitude that you are holding, a different way you are reacting, a different way you are listening to other people, perhaps a hobby or avocation that you are adding to your life that somehow fits with what's occurring within you, do so. I don't want to get too specific because there are so many ways we can initiate positive change, but I would like you to have your own freedom to let this concept manifest in the best way for you. It needs to be integrated and relevant to the outer life.

Since most of what Edgar Cayce said about application has to do with our relationships, let's look at reading 1000-19, which captures the essence of his approach:

(Q) I have given love and patience for three years and my brother Jack's promises have not been kept; in fact, he has become hostile. What is the cause of this, and how shall I proceed?

(A) Hold fast to that thou hast attained. This is the fault in the other, but do not look upon it as fault; and do not be hard or severe; do not criticize but continue to give the best.

Remember, as He, thy Master did, even for him who betrayed Him: He did not withhold the means of the material things given by others for the little group [Judas was in charge of the little band's money, even to the end]; neither was there a railing, neither a condemning—even with the kiss.

Though the fault was with this woman's brother, Cayce said that she should strive not to criticize, not be hard or severe, nor withhold trust, but continue to give the best. How hard this is to do, however, when family, friends, or associates are obviously wrong. The reading went on:

(Q) Can I hope for him to help my husband as promised? Or is it futile?

(A) Hold to the thought. Do not doubt. Creating doubts and fears or saying such things hinder the very activity. Just hold to that which is to the body the *right!*

Now here is a very important teaching for all of us. Cayce told her to "Hold to the thought." Her own doubt and fear about her brother's help hindered the very fruition of such hopes! *Hold to the thought to that which is being sought!* The reading continued:

(Q) Please give me further spiritual guidance that will enable me to meet the present trying situation.

(A) Just hold fast to that ye have known, and that ye know to be good. Do not condemn, ever, others. Do not rail on others.

This does not mean to be so passive as to become to the self that of self-condemnation; for this is even worse than condemning others.

Again, so important a teaching was being conveyed here: Worse than condemning others is condemning self. To abuse ourselves is to lose self-respect. We must first be able to live with ourselves, find a certain peace within our own heart, then act from that place. A delicate balance was being sought:

But it means doing day by day that which is *known* that which is proven, that which is experienced to be in keeping with what He would have thee do.

Thus ye will find that ye do the first things first; that is, the thought of self not so much as self-preservation from want, care, discouragements and the like, but rather as to just being gentle, just being kind.

For righteousness, which is taking time to be righteous, is just speaking gentle even when harsh words, harsh means are resorted to by others. This is what is meant by "Turn the other cheek," and know the *Lord* standeth with thee!

The only way we will know the real power of what is being taught in this reading is to *do it* in our daily lives, with those around us. Then we'll see just how amazing this approach is.

It helps to remember that on this plane, the earth plane, God manifests only in Nature and in the human heart. We came here, in part, to make that manifestation more real, more present:

Know that each entity enters the material sojourn not merely for the purpose of living an experience or a life, but as a part of the universal consciousness as would make the world, the earth, the individuals the entity meets from day to day, more hopeful, more patient, more longsuffering—yea, to make the world better for the entity having come in contact with the individuals the entity meets. 2550-1

Besides the benefits to our happiness, the application or giving out of Universal Consciousness also will deepen our meditations, by the principle that, as we apply what we have, more will be given:

(Q) How could I improve my meditations?
(A) By being, as given, more and more patient, more and more longsuffering, more and more tolerant, more and more *lovely* to everyone ye meet in *every* way ye act, in every word ye *speak* in every thought ye think. 272-9

After a while, we begin to feel the spirit of God, of Universal Consciousness, of Life itself, *flowing through us*, from meditations to situations to relationships, often with astonishing results. Love, patience, tolerance, and giving are all aspects of the Spirit of God. Doing them brings us into that Spirit. In the end, that is what our lives are all about:

In this period of man's experience in the earth there is the greater need that he, man, consider the purposes (and the needs) of God in his daily life. There is the need for such thought, such meditation on this universal consciousness, this field, to be manifested by man's love, man's activity towards his fellow man. 2262-129

Prayer, meditation, dreams, visions, and studying sacred teachings are all limited in their power to spiritualize and enlighten us. One also needs to be (1) living a balanced life; (2) discerning good and evil, and choosing good with our free wills; (3) making haste slowly, in patience and faith; (4) applying what we have learned; (5) giving of what we have received; (6) doing what we know to do; and (7) taking our attunement and spiritual growth and using them in service to humanity in cooperation with God. It is best to proceed step by step, day by day, here a little, there a little, until the whole loaf of our being (body, mind, soul) is leavened with the Spirit of God, bringing us into complete oneness and compatibility with our Mother/Father again:

Thus may you spiritualize desire, whether for those things that
bring the comforts or the necessities or the activities in thine experience in the earth. What is spiritualizing desire? Desire that the Lord
may use thee as a channel of blessings to all whom ye may contact day
by day; that there may come in thine experience whatever is necessary
that thou be cleansed every whit. For, when the soul shines forth in
thine daily walks, in thine conversation, in thine thoughts, in thine
meditation, and it is in that realm where the spirit of truth and life
may commune with same day by day, *then* indeed do ye spiritualize
desire in the earth. 262-65

PART 3

THE ORIGINAL MATERIAL

Illustration 1
The disciple John with the seven-star body.

Illustration 2
The Being with the seven churches.

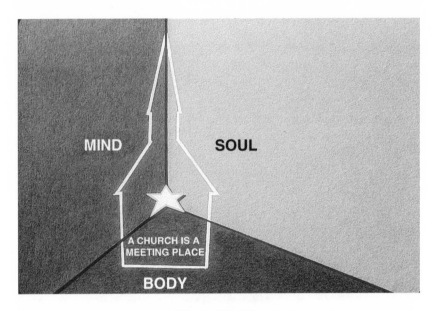

Illustration 3
Church: body, mind, and soul.

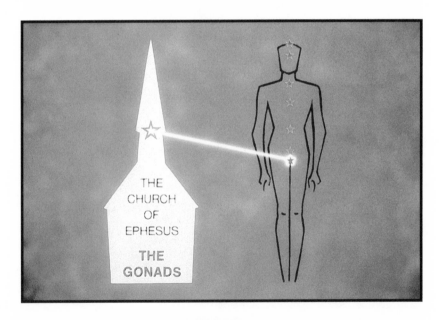

Illustration 4
The first spiritual center: gonads.

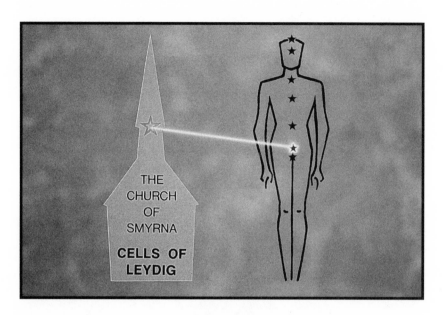

Illustration 5
Second spiritual center: cells of Leydig.

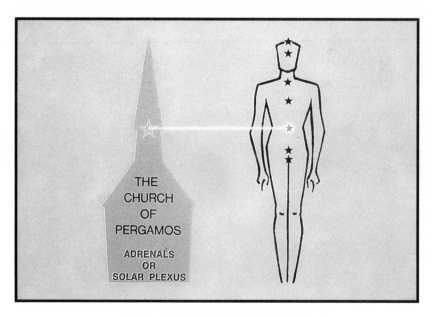

Illustration 6
Third spiritual center: adrenals.

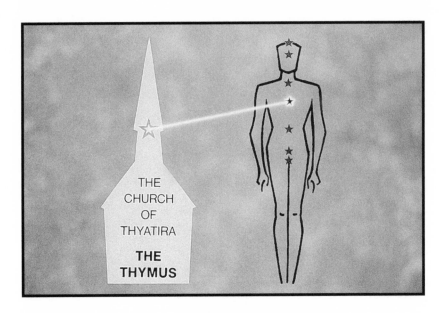

Illustration 7
Fourth spiritual center: thymus.

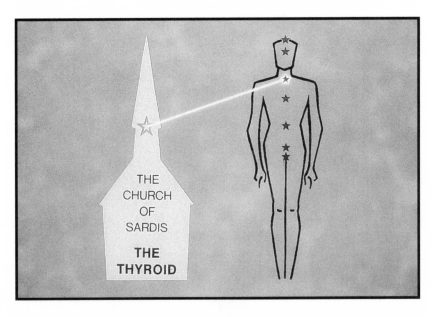

Illustration 8
Fifth spiritual center: thyroid.

Illustration 9
Sixth spiritual center: pineal.

Illustration 10
Seventh spiritual center: pituitary.

Illustration 11
Revelation 4: John visions the four beasts, seven lamps, twenty-four elders, sea of glass, and the stairway to heaven and the throne.

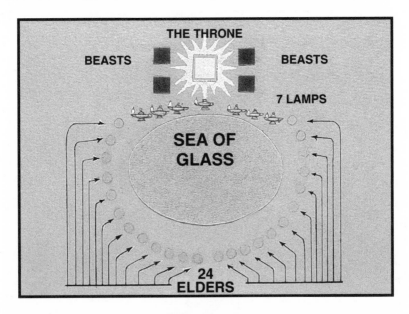

Illustration 12
Graphic arrangement of the throne, with the four beasts, seven lamps, twenty-four elders, and the sea of glass.

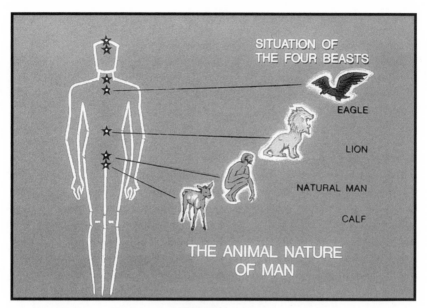

Illustration 13

The four lower centers or chakras in the body correspond to the four beasts or lower urges.

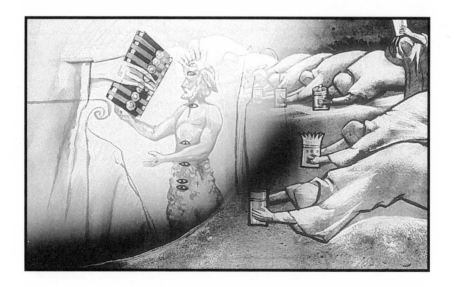

Illustration 14

He who sits upon the throne gives the book with the seven seals to the Lamb with the seven eyes, and the twenty-four elders bow to the worthiness of the Lamb of God who has earned the right to open the seals.

Illustration 15

Revelation 6: The Lamb opens the book of life with its seven seals, and out come the four horsemen.

Illustration 16

Revelation 7: Angels at the four corners stirring up the winds of

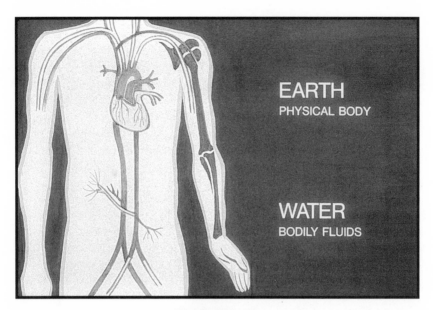

Illustration 17

The elements correspond to aspects of the body: water to bodily fluids and earth to physcial bone and tissue.

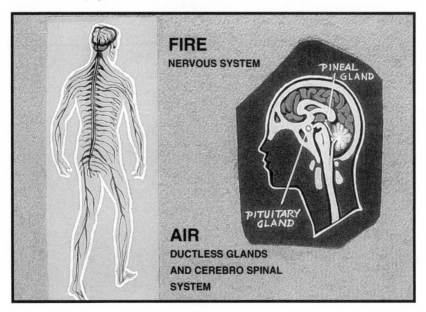

Illustration 18

The elements correspond to aspects of the body: air to the endocrine glands and cerebrospinal system, fire to the nervous system.

Illustration 19

Revelation 8: The sounding of the seven angels and their respective trumpets.

Illustration 20

Revelation 11: John is given a rod to measure the new temple, symbolic of him coming to a better understanding of the temple within him.

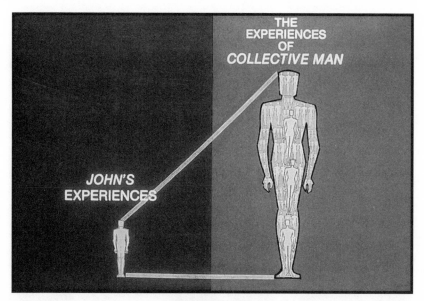

Illustration 21

The whole is reflected in the individual, the macrocosm in the microcosm, the collective humanity in an individual human. The individual's experiences add to the collective experiences of the whole.

Illustration 22

The beast and the number of the beast, representing the ultimate idol before God, self and self-centeredness.

Illustration 23

The new consciousness, in the form of a new baby, is being protected from the beastly urges represented by the seven-headed dragon.

Illustration 24

The divine feminine within each of us conceives the new consciousness that will overcome the lower urges of the dragon.

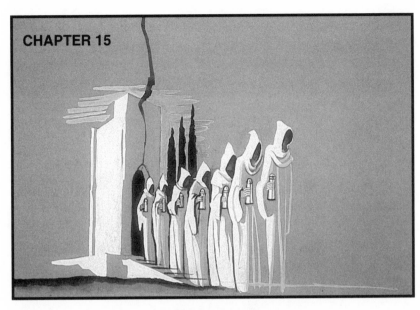

Illustration 25

Revelation 15: The purification of the body and mind continues with the seven vials or bowls.

Illustration 26

Revelation 16: Pouring out of the vials to cleanse a third of the earth.

Illustration 27

Our inner self learns from the things that our outer self suffers. Though it appears devastating to the outer self, the inner self lives on forever with the wisdom gained.

Illustration 28

Revelation 17: The whore of Babylon represents self: self-gratification, self-glorification, self-exaltation, self-satisfaction, and so on.

Illustration 29

Revelation 18: The angel of the Lord subdues the earth's influence upon us.

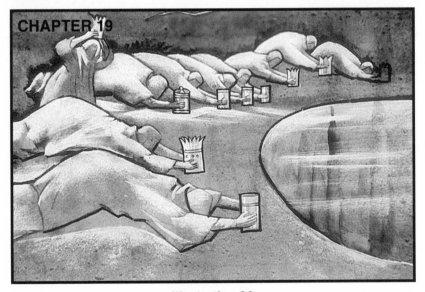

Illustration 30

Revelation 19: The twenty-four elders, representing the twelve paired cranial nerves within our brains, reverse their attention from earthly things to begin to give homage and attention to heavenly things. The sea of glass provides the calm necessary for this to happen.

Illustration 31

The divine feminine and the lamb reflect the gentleness and peace that are to come from this new consciousness.

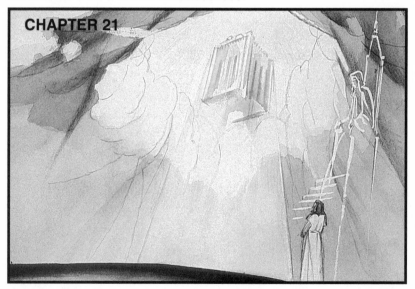

Illustration 32

Revelation 21: The New Jerusalem coming down from heaven represents the new state of consciousness that is gained from the purifications and elevations of body and mind to heavenly ways, subduing earthly influences.

The Temple of the Body
A Spiritual Attunement Device

7 Churches	7 Glands	7 Chakras	7 Plexuses	7 Influences
LAODICEA "Heaven" Silence (7 seals) Virtue ? (7 virtues) Lukewarm (7 faults)	Pituitary	Third Eye	Brain	Spirituality and Strength Violet *ti* Jupiter
PHILADELPHIA "Name" Earthquake Open Door No Faults—Remembers Everything	Pineal	Crown	Brain	Mind and Knowing Indigo *la* Mercury
SARDIS "Will" Souls Slain Not Defiled Imperfect	Thyroid	Throat	Cervical (C3)	Will and Psychic Ability Blue *so* Uranus (Grey)
THYATIRA "From Evil" Pale Horse—*to kill* Charity Fornication	Thymus	Heart	Cardiac (T4)	Love and Righteousness Green *fa* Venus Air—element Eagle—beast
PERGAMOS "Our Debts" Red Horse—*to war* Faithful Stumbling block	Adrenals	Navel	Solar (T9)	Madness and Forgiveness Yellow *mi* Mars Fire—element Lion—beast
SMYRNA "not into temptation" Black Horse—*to weigh in the balance* Suffering Insincerity	Lyden (Cells of Leydig)	Lower Abdomen	Pelvic (L4)	Mysticism and Guidance Orange *re* Neptune Water—element Like a man—beast
EPHESUS "Daily Bread" White Horse—*to conquer* Patience Left First Love	Ovaries or Testes	Root	Pelvic (L4)	Flesh and Bodily Needs Red *do* Saturn Earth—element Calf—beast

Illustration 33

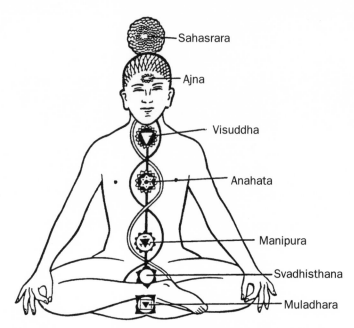

Illustration 34
The Chakra System.

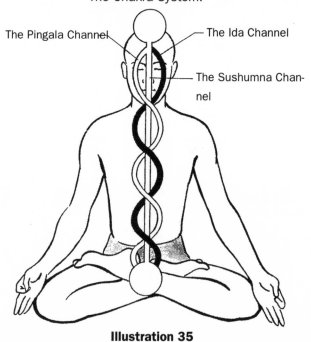

Illustration 35
The three channels of the kundalini energy.

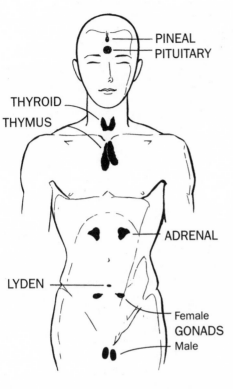

PINEAL
PITUITARY

THYROID
THYMUS

ADRENAL

LYDEN

Female
GONADS
Male

Illustration 36
The endocrine glands
of the human body.

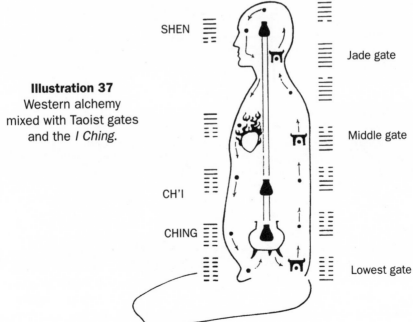

SHEN

Jade gate

Illustration 37
Western alchemy
mixed with Taoist gates
and the *I Ching*.

Middle gate

CH'I

CHING

Lowest gate

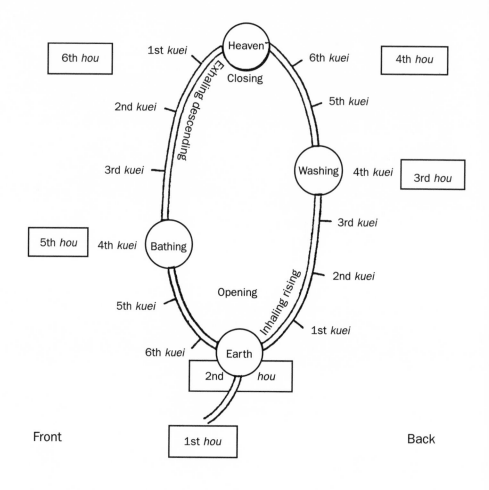

Illustration 38

The circulation of the light from the taoist text *The Secret of the Golden Flower*. Note how the energy is drawn up the body with inhalation and then moved down the body with exhalation. Getting the energy moving is the goal. The light results naturally from the circulation process.

Illustration 39
Conceiving and nourishing the spirit-body
in the womb of consciousness
during meditation (from the taoist text
The Secret of the Golden Flower).

Meditation, Stage 3: Separation of the spirit-body for independent exis-

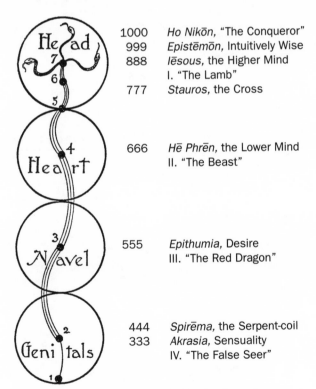

1000	*Ho Nikōn*, "The Conqueror"
999	*Epistēmōn*, Intuitively Wise
888	*Iēsous*, the Higher Mind
	I. "The Lamb"
777	*Stauros*, the Cross
666	*Hē Phrēn*, the Lower Mind
	II. "The Beast"
555	*Epithumia*, Desire
	III. "The Red Dragon"
444	*Spirēma*, the Serpent-coil
333	*Akrasia*, Sensuality
	IV. "The False Seer"

The Gnostic Chart Concealed in the Apocalypse

Illustration 40
A Gnostic chart that combines concepts from
the Cabala, the Revelation, and the chakra system.

Ancient Temples

As suggested by the Holy Bible and the A.R.E. video entitled *Entering the Temple Within* by John Van Auken (Version 0.1)

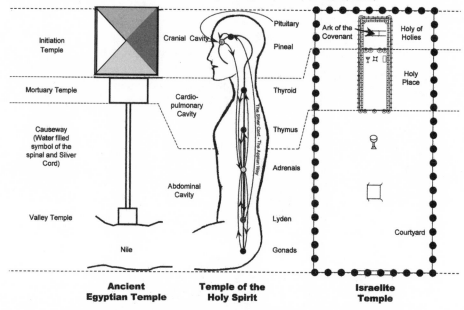

Ancient Egyptian Temple — **Temple of the Holy Spirit** — **Israelite Temple**

Illustration 41
Ancient temples correlate to the temple of the human body.

Ancient Temples & Consciousness Map

As suggested by the Edgar Cayce Readings and the A.R.E. audio tape entitled *Revelation and Cayce: A New Mind* by John Van Auken (Version 0.2)

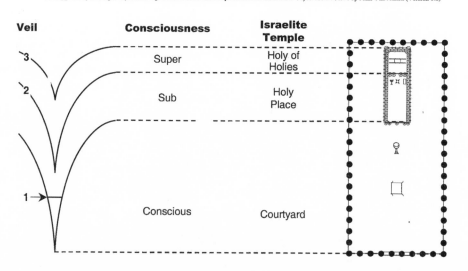

Illustration 42
Ancient Israelite temple and the levels of consciousness.

Illustration 43
The ark of the covenant.

Illustration 44
The ancient temple given to Moses from God. Notice the three areas: court, holy place, and holy of holies. In the court is the altar of sacrifice and the pool of washing. In the holy place is the seven-candled menorah on the left, the bread of the presence (sometimes called the showbread) on the right, and, in the far center, the incense altar. In the holy of holies is the ark of the covenant with the winged cherubim upon it.

Israelites' Wilderness Camp

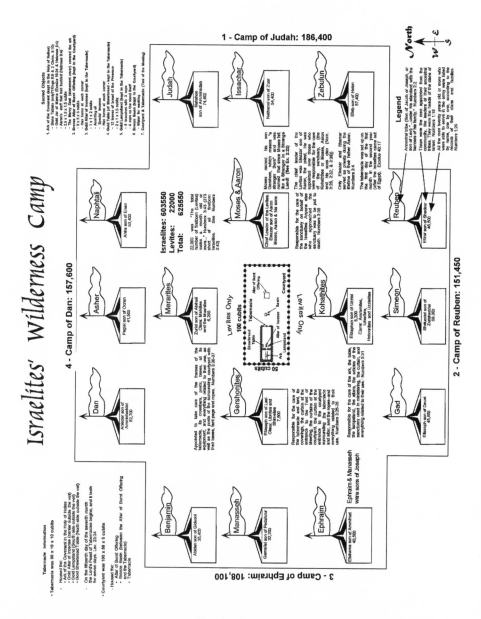

Illustration 45

The arrangement of the camp of the Israelites.

9

EDGAR CAYCE'S READINGS ON
THE REVELATION

*I*n this chapter are the original, verbatim readings given by Edgar Cayce concerning the Revelation. I have reproduced them from the Association for Research and Enlightenment's authorized edition of the CD-ROM, so that you can easily reference them. All the Edgar Cayce readings are copyrighted by the Edgar Cayce Foundation, 215 67th Street, Virginia Beach, VA 23451-2061. They are reprinted here by express, written permission of the Foundation.

The first group of readings are those given to the Glad Helpers prayer/ healing group and specifically related to the Revelation and the endocrine glands. Following these readings are various ones that I have found to be relevant to a study of Edgar Cayce's comments on the Revelation.

TEXT OF READING 281-16
March 13, 1933

GC: You will give at this time an interpretation of the Book of Revelation as recorded in the King James version of the bible, explaining the general plan and theme, the significance of the Book, and give such explanations of the symbols used as will make this book of personal value to those present seeking to awaken and develop the inner life. You will then answer the questions which will be asked regarding various parts of this Book.

EC: Yes, we have the text written in the Revelation, as recorded in the King James version of same.

In making this worth while in the experience of individuals who are seeking for the light, for the revelation that may be theirs as promised in the promises of same, it would be well that there be considered first the conditions which surrounded the writer, the apostle, the beloved, the last of those chosen; writing to a persecuted people, many despairing, many fallen away, yet, many seeking to hold to that which had been delivered to them through the efforts and activities of those upon whom the spirit had fallen by the very indwelling and the manifestations that had become the common knowledge of all.

Remember, then, that Peter—chosen as the rock, chosen to open the doors of that known today as the church—had said to this companion, "I will endeavor to keep thee in remembrance; even after my demise I will return to you." [II Peter 1:15]

The beloved, then, was banished to the isle, and was in meditation, in prayer, in communion with those saints who were in that position to see, to comprehend the greater needs of those that would carry on.

And, as given in the beginning, "I was in the Spirit on the Lord's day, and beheld, and heard, and saw, and was told to *write*."

Why, then, ye ask now, was this written (this vision) in such a manner that is hard to be interpreted, save in the experience of every soul who seeks to know, to walk in, a closer communion with Him?

For the visions, the experiences, the names, the churches, the places, the dragons, the cities, all are but emblems of those forces that may war within the individual in its journey through the material, or from the entering into the material manifestation to the entering into the glory, or the awakening in the spirit, in the inter-between, in the borderland, in the shadow.

Hence we find, as the churches are named, they are as the forces that are known as the senses, that must be spiritualized by the will of the individual made one in the very activities in a material world.

And the elders and the Lamb are the emblems, are the shadows of those acceptances or rejections that are made in the experiences of the individual.

As we find, in the various manners and forms that are presented as the vision or visions proceed, every force that is manifest is of one source; but the soul, the will of the individual, either makes such into a coordinating or cooperating influence in bringing about more and more manifestations in the material world of those experiences that are seen from the spiritual conditions, or the opposite.

Why, then, is it presented, ye ask, in the form of symbols? Why is there used those varied activities? These are for those that were, or will be, or may become, through the seeking, those initiated into an understanding of the glories that may be theirs if they will but put into work, into activity, that they know in the present.

In seeking, then, do individuals find from the beginning that there is presented, in every line, in every form, that good and bad (as termed) that arises from their activity, in what they do about that knowledge they have respecting law, the love, the mercy, the understanding of the wherefore of the Lamb's advent into the world that they, through His ensample set, may present themselves before that throne even as He, becoming—as given—heirs, joint heirs with Him, as the sons of God, to that *everlasting* glory that may be had in Him.

Then, seek to know what self is lacking, even as given in the first four chapters (as divided in the present).

What is lacking in self? Are ye cold? Are ye hot? Have ye been negligent of the knowledge that is thine? Are ye stiff-necked? Are ye adulterous in thought, in act, in the very glories that are thine?

Then, again—may ye not have had through the varied experiences those presentations before the throne, even as the elders twenty and four that are represented by the figures within thine own head, that which is shown in the physical forces of self? Has it not been given to thee, or has not the message come as the rider of the pale, the black, the white, or the red horses that are the figures of the messages that have come to thee in thine varied experiences? Or, art thou among the figures represented in the Babylon, or in the rivers of blood, or in the trees of life?

These we see, then, represent *self;* self's body-physical, self's body-mental, self's body-spiritual; with the attributes of the body-physical, attributes of the body-mental, attributes of the body-spiritual, and they are *one* in thee—even as the Father, the Son and the Holy Spirit is one in Him.

Then, dost thou seek to enter into the glories of the Father? Whosoever will may come, may take of the water of life freely—even as flows from the throne of the Lamb. For, the very leaves of the trees are for the healing of the nations, and—if ye will accept—the blood cleanses from all unrighteousness. How? From what? Saves self from what? To what are ye called? To know that only from the falling away of self may ye be saved. Unto the glorifying of self in Him may ye be saved.

Then, whosoever will, come!

Ready for Questions:

(Q) Please interpret the fall of Babylon as referred to in the 14th, 17th, and 18th chapters of Revelation.

(A) Babylon represented the individual; those periods through which every soul passes in its delving into the varied mysteries that are the experiences of the carnal-mental, the spiritual-mental forces of the body; and, as viewed from that presented, may come to the knowledge only through the *cleansing* that is shown must come to those that would be saved from the destructions that are given there.

(Q) What did the angel mean when he said: "I will tell thee the mystery of the woman, and of the beast that carrieth her"?

(A) That which is understood by those that follow in the way of the Lamb, that come to know how man separates himself through the desires to become as the procreator in the beasts; which made the necessity of the shedding of blood for redemption, for it brought sin *in* the shedding—and only through same may there be the fulfilling; and as given, the heavens and the earth may pass, but His law, His love, His mercy, His grace, endureth for those who *will* seek to know His will.

(Q) Where are the dead until Christ comes? Do they go direct to Him when they die?

(A) As visioned by the beloved, there are those of the saints making intercession always before the throne for those that are passing in and out of the inter-between; even as He, the Christ, is ever in the consciousness of those that are redeemed in Him.

The passing in, the passing out, is as but the summer, the fall, the spring; the birth into the interim, the birth into the material.

(Q) In what form does the anti-Christ come, spoken of in Revelation?

(A) In the spirit of that opposed to the spirit of truth. The fruits of the spirit of the Christ are love, joy, obedience, long-suffering, brotherly love, kindness. Against such there is no law. The spirit of hate, the anti-Christ, is contention strife, fault-finding, lovers of self, lovers of praise. Those are the anti-Christ, and take possession of groups, masses, and show themselves even in the lives of men.

(Q) Will we be punished by fire and brimstone?

(A) That as builded by self; as those emblematical influences are shown through the experiences of the beloved in that builded, that created. For, each soul is a portion of creation—and builds that in a portion of its experience that it, through its physical-mental or spiritual-mental, has builded for itself. And each entity's heaven or hell must, through *some* experience, be that which it has builded for itself.

Is thy hell one that is filled with fire or brimstone? But know, each and every soul is tried so as by fire; purified, purged; for He, though He were the Son, learned obedience through the things which He suffered. Ye also are known even as ye do, and have done.

(Q) Is this the period of the great tribulation spoken of in Revelation or just the beginning, and if so just how can we help ourselves and others to walk more closely with God?

(A) The great tribulation and periods of tribulation, as given, are the experiences of every soul, every entity. They arise from influences created by man through activity in the sphere of any sojourn. Man may become, with the people of the universe, ruler of any of the various spheres through which the soul passes in its experiences. Hence, as the cycles pass, as the cycles are passing, when there *is* come a time, a period of readjusting in the spheres (as well as in the little earth, the little soul)—seek, then, as known, to present self spotless before that throne; even as *all* are commanded to be circumspect, in thought, in act, to that which is held by self as that necessary for the closer walk with Him. In that manner only may each atom (as man is an atom, or corpuscle, in the body of the Father) become a helpmeet with Him in bringing that to pass that all may be one with Him.

(Q) What is meant by the four beasts?

(A) As given, the four destructive influences that make the greater desire for the carnal forces, that rise as the beasts within self to destroy. Even as man, in his desire to make for companionship, brought those elements within self's own experience. These must be met. Even as the dragon represents the one that separated self so far as to fight with, to destroy with, those that would make of themselves a kingdom of their own.

(Q) What is meant by "—a new heaven and a new earth"?

(A) Former things have passed away, when there is beheld within self that the whole will of the Creator, the Father, the place of abode the forces within and without, make for the *new* heaven, the *new* earth.

We are through.

TEXT OF READING 281-28
October 26, 1936

GC: You will have before you the Glad Helpers, members of which are present here. First you will give affirmations to be sent those on the prayer list; next you will consider the study which has been made by this group for several weeks on the Book of Revelation in attempting to follow the suggestions given through this channel that the references in this book should be applied to experiences in the physical, mental and spiritual bodies of individuals. You will answer the questions which will be presented on Revelation.

EC: Yes, we have the group as gathered here, as a group, as individuals; their work with others, which—first—we would commend. For there has been, is being and may be accomplished, a great deal of hope, of cheer, in the lives and in the experiences of individuals.

And in this manner may this group find within themselves that peace, that harmony, that is the promise from Him who hath given, "That as ye ask, as ye seek in my name, that may the Father do, that I may be glorified through you in the material world."

Be then faithful to that thou hast purposed in thy heart. For many there be who are weak, discouraged, troubled, that ye may aid. And as ye do it unto the least of thy brethren ye do it unto thy Maker. For as He hath given, "Ye that minister to the sick, to the disconsolate, to those in prison, to those in turmoils and strife, minister unto me."

The affirmations in the present are these:

Our Father, our God, hear the prayer of Thy servants; that we may know, that we may understand, that we may be what Thou would have us be.

Again: *Father of Mercy, of love, of patience, hear Thy humble servant. Thou knowest the needs of my body, my mind, my heart. Supply from Thy bounty. For we ask in the Christ name.*

Again: *Father, God, in humbleness of heart I seek. I pray Thy mercy, Thy love at this period: not only for myself but all that seek to know Thy ways.*

Again: *Father of mercy, of grace, let Thy protection be with all those that seek, in the name of the Christ.*

Again: *Father, who art in heaven, blessed be Thy name! May Thy love, Thy grace, Thy mercy, fill my life and make it that Thou, O God, would have it be!*

Again: *Father of love, of grace and mercy, keep my feet lest they falter in Thy ways. Keep my mind and my body that they go not in the way of doubt or despair.*

Again: *Father, God, in Thy Son Thou hast promised that what we ask we may receive. Make my body, my mind, of such an attitude and activity as to be worthy of those promises!*

Again: *Father who art in heaven, be Thou near to those that falter, to those that are afraid. Strengthen Thou through Thy love my purposes, that I may be a light, a help, a strength to many.*

Again: *Father, mercy! Mercy upon those that are wayward, that in their not understanding falter. Be patient, be kind with all!*

In considering then the studies that have been made with this group, in the understanding of the Revelation as given by the beloved of Him: These as we find have been well, and as you each become conscious in your own experience of the movement *of* the influences *through* the body upon the various stages of awareness, there comes a determination, a desire, a longing for the greater light. To him, to her that is faithful, there shall be given a *crown* of light. And His Name shall be above every name; For ye that have seen the light know in Whom thou hast believed, and know that in thine own body, thine own mind, there is set the temple of the living God, and that it may function in thy dealings with thy fellow man in such measures that ye become as rivers of light, as fountains of knowledge, as mountains of strength, as the pastures for the hungry, as the rest for the weary, as the strength for the weak. Keep the faith. Ready for questions.

(Q) Are we using the correct methods of breathing and intonation in our group meditations?

(A) As has been given in Meditation, to some, *this* then is the correct manner: As has been given so oft of old, purge ye your bodies, washing them with water, putting away those things of the mind and of the body; for tomorrow the Lord would speak with thee.

Hence in this group make thy mind, thy body, as a fit subject for a visit of thy Lord, thy God. Then as ye seek *ye know*, as He hath given, that the wedding feast is prepared and thou hast bid the guests, and that ye have come with the garments of the feast with thy Lord, thy Master, thy King, thy Savior.

For lowly as He was in His earthly ministry, He honored all such that gathered for the commemoration of a union of body, a union of mind, a union of strength for their worship, their sacrifice, their meeting with their God.

So do ye in thy meditation. For thy prayer is as a supplication or a plea to thy superior; yet thy meditation is that thou art meeting on *common* ground!

Then prepare thyself!

In breathing, take into the right nostril, *strength!* Exhale through thy mouth. Intake in thy left nostril, exhaling through the right; opening the centers of thy body—if it is first prepared to thine *own* understanding, thine *own* concept of what *ye* would have if ye would have a visitor, if ye would have a companion, if ye would have thy bridegroom!

Then, as ye begin with the incantation of the [Har-r-r-r-r-aum] Ar-ar-r-r-r—the e-e-e, the o-o-o, the m-m-m, *raise* these in thyself; and ye become close in the presence of thy Maker—as is *shown* in thyself! They that do such for selfish motives do so to their own undoing. Thus has it oft been said, the fear of the Lord is the beginning of wisdom.

Wisdom, then, is fear to misapply knowledge in thy dealings with thyself, thy fellow man.

For as ye are honest, as ye are patient, as ye are sincere with thyself in thy meeting with thy God, thy Savior, thy Christ, in thy meditation, ye will be in thy dealings with thy fellow man.

We are through for the present.

TEXT OF READING 281-29
October 28, 193 6

GC: You will have before you the Glad Helpers, members of which are present here. You will continue with answering questions which will be presented on Revelation.

EC: Yes, we have the Glad Helpers Group, as a group, as individuals; and the study that has been made by same on Revelation. In adding to *some* of those things as have been applied, let each consider how and why that such application would be made by the beloved in a message of the nature and character. First, the body of the Christ represented to the world a channel, a door, a mediation to the Father. Hence this then may become as the study of self in its relationship to the material world, the mental world, the spiritual world. And this is the manner that has been presented as the way through which each individual would make application of same, of the life of the Christ in his or her own experience.

(Q) Are we correct in interpreting the 7 churches as symbols of 7 spiritual centers in the physical body?

(A) Correct.

(Q) Do we have these correctly placed? As each is called, comment on each in relation to an individual's development and experiences in connection with these centers. Gonads—Ephesus; Lyden—Smyrna; Solar Plexus—Pergamos; Thymus—Thyatira; Thyroid—Sardis; Pineal—Philadelphia; Pituitary—Laodicea.

(A) Rather than the commenting, it is well that these are correctly placed, but each individual's *experience* in the application of that gained by each in his or her experience will be different. To give an interpretation that the opening or activity through a certain center raises or means or applies this or that, then would become rote. But know the way, then each may apply same as his or her environment, ability, experience, gives the opportunity. For know, in all and through all, the activity of self is only as a channel—and God giveth the understanding, the increase, to such; and in the manner as is best fitted for the individual. It is not then as a formula, that there are to be certain activities and certain results. These are true in the sense that they each represent or present the opportunity for the opening to the understanding of the individual. For, as has been given, man is free-willed. And only when this is entirely given, and actively given to the will of the Father may it be even as the life of the Christ.

(Q) Which is the highest gland in the body—the pineal or the pituitary?

(A) The pituitary!

(Q) Are we correct in interpreting the 24 elders as the 24 cranial nerves of the head especially related to the 5 senses?

(A) Correct.

(Q) Is the frequent reference to the throne indicating the head in which are found the higher gland centers?

(A) Correct.

(Q) Are we correct in interpreting the 4 beasts as the 4 fundamental physical natures (desires) of man which must be overcome? Give us more light on each of these.

(A) Correct.

In all of these, let this be understood: These are symbolized; they are as in these representing the elemental forces—as the body is of the earth, is of the elements. For as has so oft been given, and as may be found in man, every element or every influence that is outside of man is found in the *living* man—not a dead one but a *living* man! For the *living* force is that *of* which all that is *was* brought into being. Hence all the influences, all the forces, all the activities are in that. And in man, man's experience, there never has been, never will be found in material activity an instrument, an action, that is not shown as a replica or expression or manifestation of that in a living man; whether it be in this, that or the other of the forces of nature, of activity. For when such is active, unless found in man—or an answer to some thing within, it would not be cognizable by man.

(Q) Do we have these 4 beasts placed correctly in relation to the centers in the body and the ancient elementals? Air—Eagle—Thymus?

(A) These are *relatively,* yes. Relatively correct.

(Q) Fire—Lion—Solar Plexus?

(A) Correct.

(Q) Water—Man—Lyden?

(A) Yes.

(Q) Earth—Calf—Gonads?

(A) Yes.

(Q) Is the book with the 7 seals the human body with the 7 spiritual centers?

(A) This is correct.

(Q) Do we have the opening of the seals correctly placed in our chart? As each is called, give advice that will help us in properly opening these centers.

(A) (Interrupting) First, let's give as this: Do not attempt to open any of the centers of the book until self has been tried in the balance of self's own conscious relationship to the Creative Forces and not found wanting by the spiritual answer in self to that rather as is seen in the manner in which the book itself becomes as that in the whole body which may be assimilated by the body, when taken properly. In these then there has been set as ye have in thine outline. These are well. *Do not* misuse them!

(Q) Gonads—White Horse?

(A) Yes.

(Q) Lyden—Black Horse?

(A) Yes.

(Q) Solar Plexus—Red Horse?

(A) Yes.

(Q) Thymus—Pale Horse?

(A) Yes.

For a reference to these, let each in your study of these, as in relation to the centers themselves, consider the effect of the color itself upon thine own body as ye attempt to apply same by either concentration, dedication or meditating upon these. For as has been given, color is but vibration. Vibration is movement. Movement is activity of a positive and negative force. Is the activity of self as in relationship to these then positive? Proceed.

(Q) Thyroid—Souls slain for Word of God?

(A) Correct.

(Q) What color here?

(A) Gray.

(Q) Pineal—Upheavals?

(A) Correct, but this would have to be *relatively* so. For these are at those periods when, in the colors that these arise to—which are of the purple, they become rather such that there *must* be the *disseminating* or the giving away of the egotism of self. Consider as an example in thy study of same, the servant Moses. For these become as may be found even for and from that record as ye have, the stumblingblock at Meribah.

(Q) Pituitary—Silence?

(A) Silence, golden; the forces upon which the greater expression has been set of all the influences of might and power as may be seen in man's experience—*silence* if ye would hear the Voice of thy Maker!

(Q) Do the planets as placed in our chart have proper relation and significance? Pituitary—Jupiter; Pineal—Mercury; Thyroid—Uranus; Thymus—Venus; Solar Plexus—Mars; Lyden—Neptune; Gonads—Saturn?

(A) These are very well done. These vary, to be sure, according to the variation of an *experience*. For these are the variable forces in the very nature of man himself, for he partakes of all and from all the influences and forces. For remember as has been given, it is not that the planets rule the man; rather has man, as man of God, ruled the planets! For he's a portion of same.

Then these are as we have given; only relative. Relatively, these are correct. At times these are represented by others. It is here the application of these influences in the experience of the individual rather than there being set, as it were, a blanket to cover each and every individual.

(Q) Does the outline of the Lord's Prayer as placed on our chart have any bearing on the opening of the centers?

(A) Here is indicated the manner in which it was given as to the purpose for which it was given; not as an *only* way but as a way that would answer for those that sought to be—as others—seekers for *a* way, *an* understanding, to the relationships to the Creative Forces. It bears in relationships to this, then, the proper place.

(Q) Pituitary—Heaven?

(A) Correct. In all of its activities these open, for the upward lift of the thoughts of man as in relationships to that which becomes—how has it been given?—"He is alpha, omega, the beginning and the end." Hence as we find in its relationships to man, it becomes then the beginnings, the endings, of all things.

(Q) Pineal—Name?

(A) Relatively, yes.

(Q) Thyroid—Will?

(A) Correct.

(Q) Thymus—Evil?

(A) Correct.

(Q) Solar Plexus—Debts?

(A) Yes.

(Q) Lyden—Temptation?

(A) Correct.

(Q) Gonads—Bread?

(A) Right.

(Q) How should the Lord's Prayer be used in this connection?

(A) As in feeling, as it were, the flow of the meanings of each portion of same throughout the body-physical. For as there is the response to the mental representations of all of these in the *mental* body, it may build into the physical body in the manner as He, thy Lord, thy Brother, so well expressed in, "I have bread ye know not of."

(Q) What is meant by the 7 lamps of fire burning before the throne, described as the 7 spirits of God—Ch. 4:5?

(A) Those influences or forces which in their activity in the natures of man are without, that stand ever before the throne of grace—or God, to become the messengers, the aiders, the destructions of hindrances; as the ways of dividing man's knowledge of or between—good and evil. Hence they work ever as those influences that stand between, as it were; being the helpful influences that become as the powers of activity in the very nature or force of man.

(Q) What is meant by the angels at the 4 corners of the earth as given in Ch. 7?

(A) These are only as from the body-forces ever. There are those four influences or forces in the natures of man from his source; as in environment, heredity as of the earth and as of the mental and spiritual. These are as the four corners that become represented here as the very natures or forces to which all approaches to all these influences are made in the very nature of man.

(Q) Are we correct in interpreting the 144,000 who were sealed as being spiritualized cellular structure of the 12 major divisions of the body?

(A) Correct. And this is as of a man, and the name of same.

(Q) Are the zodiacal divisions of the body proper and do they have any relation to this?

(A) Only relatively. For this is as we have given again and again in reference to same; for as they have been set as the zodiacal signs, correct. As they have moved in their orb or their sphere about the earth, these have just recently passed and have become—as has been indicated—a very different nature to them.

(Q) Is the multitude before the throne as described in Ch. 7 the rest of the cellular structure in process of spiritualization?

(A) This is correct.

(Q) Are we correct in interpreting the sounding of the 7 angels as the experience during physical purification?

(A) Correct.

We are through for the present.

TEXT OF READING 281-30
February 17, 1937

GC: You will have before you the Glad Helpers of the Ass'n for Research & Enlightenment, Inc., members of which are present here; and their study of the Book of Revelation together with the information given them through this channel on Oct. 26, 1936, and Oct. 28, 1936, in connection with this study. You will answer the questions regarding this study which will be asked.

EC: Yes, we have the work of the Glad Helpers, together with their study of Revelation, and the information which has been given respecting same. In the beginning again we would give this, that it may be clarified in the minds of those who seek to have the interpretation of *the* Revelation in their own experience:

Know first that the knowledge of God is a growing thing, for ye grow in grace, in knowledge, in understanding *as* ye apply that ye *know*. But remember, as has been given by Him, to know to do good and do it not is sin.

In the interpretation then of the Revelation as given by John in Patmos: This was John's revelation of *his* experience, and interpreted in the individual by the application of the body of self as a pattern with the attributes physically, mentally, spiritually, in their respective spheres for thine *own* revelation.

For this to be practical, to be applicable in the experience of each soul, it must be an individual experience; and the varied experiences or activities of an entity in its relationship to the study of self are planned, builded, workable in the pattern as John has given in the Revelation.

Each attribute of the body, whether organ or functioning or the expression of same, becomes then in the experience of each soul as a seeker first. Seek and ye shall find, knock and it shall be opened unto you!

Then in thy study, for those who would become Glad Helpers, in the physical, in the moral, in the mental, in the spiritual life of each soul: Condemn no one. Love all. Do good. And ye may experience it all.

Ready for questions.

(Q) Please discuss more fully the relation of colors to the seven major glandular centers. Do the colors vary for each center with different individuals, or may definite colors be associated with each center?

(A) Both. For to each—remember, to study each of these in the light not only of what has just been given but that as is a practical experience in the material world; as is known, vibration is the essence or the basis of color. As color and vibration then become to the consciousness along the various centers in an individual's experience in meditation made aware, they come to mean definite experiences. Just as anger is red, or as something depressing is blue; yet in their shades, their tones, their activities, to each they begin with the use of same in the experience to mean those various stages. For instance, while red is anger, rosy to most souls means delight and joy—yet to others, as they are formed in their transmission from center to center, come to mean or to express what *manner* of joy; whether that as would arise from a material, a mental or a spiritual experience. Just as may be seen in the common interpretation of white, but with all manner of rays from same begins or comes to mean that above the aura of all in its vibration from the body and from the activity of the mental experience when the various centers are vibrating to color.

(Q) If so, give color for: (1) Gonads (2) Lyden (3) Solar Plexus (4) Thymus (5) Thyroid (6) Pineal (7) Pituitary.

(A) These come from the leaden, going on through to the highest—to that as is the halo. To each they become the various forces as active throughout, and will go in the regular order of the prism.

(Q) What is the significance of the color of the four horses associated with 4 lower centers; pale horse for Thymus; red for Solar Plexus; black for Lyden; white for Gonads?

(A) That comes as has just been given as the illustration of same from the *emotions* or physical forces that ride forth to their expression in the higher forces of the activity.

(Q) Please explain what was meant in Reading of Oct. 28, regarding the "relative" connection of Name in the Lord's Prayer with the Pineal gland?

(A) This might occupy a whole period of several hours, if the full conclusion were to be given; but each must reach this. There is a Name to each soul. For He hath called His own *by name!* What name? All the names that may have been as a material experience through an earthly sojourn, or all the names that may have been through the experience of an entity in that environ or those relative associations of Venus, Mars, Jupiter, Uranus, Saturn, Sun, Moon, or what! Or a Name that is above *every* name!

Then as has been indicated this becomes relative, as is signified in the indication as given to the number, which is of John's own. But as has been given, every influence—you see—is *relative!* Hence the name is relative to that which *is* accomplished by the soul *in* its sojourn throughout its whole experience; whether in those environs about this individual sphere or another—this individual sphere meaning thine own sun, thine own planets with all of their attributes (Does an earth mind comprehend such?) and it carried through with what is its *relative* force to that which has been or is the activity of the entity-soul (not a body now at all!) toward Constructive

Force or God, or God's infinite force to that integral activity of the soul in its sojourn. Hence it becomes *relative.* And for the finite mind to say Jane, John, Joe, James or Jude would mean only as the *vibrations* of those bring the *relative* force or influence to which, through which an entity's sojourns have brought the concrete experience in any one given or definite period of activity!

Was one named John by chance? Was one named Joe or Llewellyn by chance? No; they are relative! While it may be truly in the material plane relative because you have a rich aunt by that name, or relative because an uncle might be named that—but these carry then the vibrations of same; and in the end the name is the sum total of what the soul-entity in all of its vibratory forces has borne toward the Creative Force itself.

Hence each soul has a definite influence upon the experiences through which it may be passing. This ye have illustrated in thine own secret organizations, in thy papal activities in the religious associations, and in each vibration. For when ye have set a vibration by the activity of thy *soul's* force, ye are then either in parallel, in direct accord, or in opposition to constructive force—whatever may be the position or activity of the soul in infinity. For ye *are* gods! But you are becoming devils or real gods!

(Q) What was meant in the Reading of Oct. 28, in connection with 144,000 who were sealed as being spiritualized cellular structure of the 12 major divisions of the body, when the Reading gave, "Correct, and this is as of a man, and the name of same." Please explain.

(A) Just as has been illustrated or given, as to the relative force of the vibratory forces of the individual; which is shown in an individual soul or entity by its name and its activity in all the influences or environs through which it passes in that which is a shadow in man (active, living) to those influences that are relative to the infinitive position of a soul's activity in a universe.

(Q) In connection with the symbols of Revelation, what are the 12 major divisions of the body?

(A) Those that are of the general construction and those that are of the keeping alive physical, and those that are in keeping with the influences to the mental, to the material, to the spiritual; and the illustrations are shown in the bodily forces that are opened for those activities in a material plane.

(Q) What is meant by the symbol of the angel with the golden censer and the incense described in Rev. 8:3-5?

(A) As the influence is visualized in the experience of each soul by the name as implied in "angel," or the good that goes out from the individual soul in its relationships to the influences or forces about same, so is it called or given as the angel with the censer of the activities that emanate from each individual. And as has been given in other illustrations, that ye are—that of good—rises ever as an incense, sweet before the throne of mercy. Or to take the back track, as it were, and take the angel with the censer, with the incense that is before the image of a soul seeking to become one with the Creative Forces or God—that which has been kind, gentle, patient, merciful, longsuffering in self's experience during a day, rises before the throne of the mercy seat within self to that of an incense of satisfaction. Why? Hate, unkindness, harshness, all such become as base in thine own experience, and as usual one condemns self by saying, "Why can't I do this or that?" And, "What is the use?" Well—and the censer is broken!

(Q) Do the 7 angels described in Rev. 8-9 represent spiritual forces governing the various dimensional planes through which souls pass between incarnations on the earth? Please explain.

(A) This is a very good interpretation. Yes. While this explanation becomes a portion of another group's study and activity in the lesson just being approached on *Happiness*, it may be best explained in this; as to how this must indeed be interpreted in the experience of each soul, whether considered in a material plane in which there is found the real essence of happiness or that in the interim when ye are looked over, or when the promises become more and more as has been interpreted from that given by others—to be absent from the body-physical is to be present in the grace and glory and presence of divinity; or to be those influences that make for an activity in an influence without self. Now ye are studying yourself! Do not confuse the interpretation with that outside of thyself, by Happiness is love of something outside of self! It may never be obtained, may never be known by loving only things within self or self's own domain!

Then the expression that has been given by an entity in a sojourn in the earth becomes as a portion of that activity as has been given, "He hath given His angels charge concerning thee, least at any time ye dash thy foot against a stone."

Hence we find that in the expression then of those interims where there are the guiding influences of that we have loved, we have love—for this becomes then very definite.

If ye have loved self-glory, if ye have loved the honor of the people more than those thoughts of the mental and spiritual and moral welfare, what manner of angels will direct thee between thy interims?

Think on the study then of *self,* in thy body—but let it all become as has been *so oft* given:

Study to show thyself approved unto God, the God in self, the God in thine own consciousness—that *is* creative in its essence; rightly divining and dividing the words of truth and light; keeping self unspotted from the world. And ye become lights to those that sit in darkness, to those that wander.

Though ye may be reviled, revile not again. Though ye may be spoken of harshly, smile—*smile!* For it is upon the river of Life that smiles are made. Not grins! No Cheshire cat activities bring other than those that are of the earth, of such natures that create in the minds and the experiences those things that becomes repulsive. But the smile of understanding cheers on the hearts of those who are discouraged, who are disheartened.

It costs so little! It does thee so much good, and lifts the burdens of so many!

We are through for the present.

TEXT OF READING 281-31
March 12, 1932

GC: You will have before you the Glad Helpers of the Ass'n for Research & Enlightenment, Inc., members of which are present here; and their study of the Book of Revelation together with the information already given them through this channel in connections with this study. You will continue answering the questions which have been prepared.

EC: Yes, we have the Glad Helpers Group, and their study of Revelation; and the information that has been given here respecting same.

Ready for questions.

(Q) Please interpret the 2nd Chapter, 17th verse of Revelation. "To him that overcometh will I give to eat of the hidden manna, and will give him a white stone, and in the stone a new name written, which no man knoweth saving he that receiveth it."

(A) In giving the interpretation of this particular portion of the Revelation, it must all be kept in mind that, as has been indicated, while many of the references—or all—refer to the physical body as the pattern, there is that as may be said to be the literal and the spiritual and the metaphysical interpretation of almost all portions of the Scripture, and especially of the Revelation as given by John.

Yet all of these to be true, to be practical, to be applicable in the experiences of individuals, *must* coordinate: or be as one, even as the Father, the Son and the Holy Spirit.

In the interpretation of the Name, then: Each entity, each soul, is known—in all the experiences through its activities—as a name to designate it from another. It is not only then a material convenience, but it implies—as has been given, unless it is for material gain—a definite period in the evolution of the experience of the entity in the material plane.

Then as each entity under a given name makes its correlating of that it does about the Creative Forces in its experience, it is coming under those influences that are being fed by the manna—which is a representation of the universality as well as the stability of purposes in the Creative Forces as manifested to a group or a nation of peoples.

So it becomes that as the Master gave, "Ye shall not live by bread alone but by every word that proceedeth from the mouth of the Father."

That indeed is the holy manna which each entity, each soul in each experience must make a part of its mental and spiritual self. Thus it becomes as is indicated, in that the name—as in each experience—bears a relative relationship to the development of the individual entity in each experience.

Then in the end, or in those periods as indicated, it is when each entity, each soul has so manifested, so acted in its relationships as to become then as the new name; white, clear, known only to him that hath overcome. Overcome what? The world, even as He.

For what meaneth a name? John, Jane, Peter, Andrew, Bartholomew, Thaddeus, Rhoda, Hannah? All of these have not only the attunement of vibration but of color, harmony; and all those relative relationships as one to another.

Then as has been asked, and has been indicated in another portion of Revelation, all those that bear the mark, those that have the name, those that have the stone—these are representatives then of the same experience in the various phases of an individual experience for its activity.

Then the interpretation is that they *have* overcome, they *have* the new name, they *have* the manna, they *have* the understanding, they *have* their relationships as secure in the blood of the Lamb!

(Q) Continuing with the references to the 7 angels described in Rev. 8:9, are we correct in interpreting the sounding of these 7 angels as the influence of spiritual development in these other planes becoming active through the vibrating centers of the physical body during the process of purification?

(A) Correct. But these are not always interpreted in individual experiences as the true sound, true tone.

Now, this is not to confuse but rather to clarify for those who are studying these, in the relationships to what takes place as the various centers in the body are opened, that are represented by the Spirit's activative forces upon same; that these may be the more perfectly understood:

Just as the individual who has by practical application gained the correct pitch, correct tone in a musical composition. This may be as a soul-expression or a mechanical expression; and only when it is in the true accord, as from the soul, is it perfectly understood. See?

(Q) Do the 7 angels govern in order the major glanular centers of the physical body?

(A) In their order, as they have been set.

(Q) Please explain the meaning of some of the symbols in the sounding of the 7 angels: 1. Hail and fire, blood and ⅓ of earth burned. What is the earth in this connection?

(A) As has been intimated or given in the first interpretations of what the elements represent, that are apparent or a portion of the First Cause; as the Earth, Air, Water and the like. These are then as has just been given, ever to represent or be symbolical of the same influences or forces throughout; else we may become confused as to their place. Earth—that as we represent as being in a state of transition, or as earthy. Not necessarily lowly or unduly a condition that would belie development. But as Fire is purifying, as Hail is the crystallization of the Water, the Air and the temperaments, so all of these then represent those as figuratives of that as may be purified by the fires of Nature; as may be represented by the earth when they are met and conquered and used for the development—as in the Hail and the like becoming purifying in their natures for the crystallization and the oneness of the individual's purposes and desires.

For to go back just a bit, that we may ever keep what is the purpose of the Revelation: Was it for the purpose of confusing, of being mysterious? (This has been gone over before, to be sure.) Rather was it not to present it that each entity, each soul, might find within itself that which answers to that within, that makes the real answer to that as was before stated, "My Spirit beareth witness with thy spirit"? And until the answer is in accord, in attune, is there the consciousness of the prompting of the ability in a manifested material world to make same practical?

Then as the progress is made, as the understanding comes more and more, *never, never* does it make the manifested individual entity other than the more humble, the more meek, the more longsuffering, the more patient. Of this ye may be sure.

Then in all of the experiences of the opening of the centers as are represented, and those vibrations that find expression in the various temperaments of individual souls, these come not as justifications in *self* but justification in the Lamb of God!

(Q) 2. Mountain of fire in sea, sea becomes blood.

(A) Again as the body elements that becomes conflicting one with another, which shows the overcoming within the individual activities of the influences that are constantly warring within.

How has it been said? "O today there is life and death, good and evil— Choose thou." This may be said to be symbolical then of these conflicting forces within the influences that are ever present, or as given by another, "The Spirit is willing, the flesh is weak." These are symbolical then, one interpreting the other.

(Q) 3. Great star falls from heaven. What are the ⅓ part of the rivers and fountains that it falls upon?

(A) The star signifies simply the coming of the influence from without to the influences from within, as is signified by "His Star have we seen." Then this becomes that as falls upon the 3rd, or that is a 3rd portion of the bodily activities—and as interpreted in the experience of the individual, ye have made so many steps as it were along the way.

(Q) ⅓ part of sun smitten and ⅓ of stars.

(A) These are symbolical and represent in the experience of the individual that of life and heat, beauty and that as given in another portion, "The stars declare the glory of God, the firmament showeth His handiwork." These then represent in the experiences the vibrations of the emotions that are being aroused, as has just been given. Again less and less then is it of self, and more and more unto the glory of the Father.

(Q) Star from heaven, Key to bottomless pit. What are the locusts as described in this sounding? King Apollyon in this connection?

(A) As has been given as to how each of these vibratory forces arises from the lower portion, or as has been put in another setting—that which represents in the bodily forces the most uncomely, or that from the depths of the bottomless pit, or from out the presence of God, again has the spirit of man arosen to the glory of the star as in the Son (not sun, but Son), to those glories that become as the natures of the bodily forces, and every influence as comes through the earthly natures becomes lost in that beauty in the Son.

(Q) Voice from 4 horns before the throne.

(A) As indicated by the horns of the altar, as indicated by the 4 forces in nature, as indicated by the 4 influences in the experiences of the individual soul which cry then in the voice raised as a sweet incense, or as the essence of the purifying that has come to the individual entity or soul to arise before the Throne of Him who is Lord of Lords and King of Kings, for His love as given, as shown in that as accomplished in the raising of self in the Christ, the Son, in Jesus.

We are through for the present.

TEXT OF READING 281-32
Date: March 24, 1937

GC: You will have before you the Glad Helpers, members of which are present here, who come seeking at this time further light and understanding on the Book of Revelation. You will continue to answer the questions which will be presented on this study.

EC: Yes, we have the group, the Glad Helpers, and their study and their seeking in the study and understanding of Revelation; together with that which has been given respecting this. Ready for questions.

(Q) What is meant by the 4 angels bound in the river Euphrates in connection with the sounding of the 6th angel? [Gen. 2:14; Rev. 9:14; 16:12]

(A) As has been given, each reference in the Revelation is to some portion of the body as in its relative position to the emotions physical, mental, material; and their activities through portions of the system, as places that represent conditions in some phase of manifestation or development of the entity. Or the whole (to be put in another way and manner) is an experience of an entity (individual) through its relationships, its study, its application in the material world; and illustrated by influences or forces in the body and by places or conditions in the experience of man as known to those who were being spoken to by the writer.

Then we find, as in the beginning, the Euphrates—or *the good river* [Frat], or *the river* of the fiat [covenant Gen. 15:18]—is being represented as being sounded now for the beginnings of the changes which have been affected by the activities of those who have preceded, who have acted upon the various influences or forces by the opening of centers and the emotions and the understandings and the conditions of the individual entity.

Hence it represents now, as it were, to the individual—that ye now begin to again to make practical or applicable, mentally, spiritually, materially, with that which has been thus far attained.

(Q) What are the 4 angels that are bound in the river Euphrates?

(A) As has been indicated, the four influences that are as the Air, the Earth, the Fire, the Water; being influences now that are—as understood by the entity, the soul, the individual—as a portion of itself again.

(Q) What is meant by the symbol of the Euphrates in relation to the body, if it may be connected?

(A) As just been given, it represents that as a boundary of its beginnings, or a beginning, or an end, from the material standpoint.

(Q) What is meant by the symbols of the horsemen who were to kill ⅓ part of men, in connection with the sounding of the 6th angel?

(A) That as a place, as a condition, an experience through which the influences are acted upon by the emotions in which the changes are wrought by the application of those very forces or conditions that have been spoken of in the experience of the individual, see?

Or, as put by another, "When I was a child I did as a child, when I was a man I did as a man," the same as in the beginning and the same as in the activities, or the same as in the relationships to all of these then as has been given heretofore—they must be as one, they must be compatible, they must be coordinant, they must be in the relative relationships one to another. These then become as destroying influences within the individual, a third portion of that which has been set as such a necessary force for a material body. How hath it been given throughout? The Father, the Son, the Holy Spirit—which is the third. They are all one, and yet a third. The same as the death of those influences or forces or activities within the emotional, the physical, the material forces. All of these then are as representatives of these, or the activities from the four-fold elements that are activative in the experience of each entity, each soul.

(Q) Do we interpret correctly the angel described in Rev. 10, with the little book, as a guardian of the book of knowledge?

(A) This is a very good interpretation; or we come to that point in the experience of each soul—know ye have passed through the experiences of attaining to the understanding of thine emotions, the understanding of the needs of thy physical body, the understanding of thy relationships to the spiritual forces; and know ye come to that which is to be—what will ye do with that knowledge?

It might be set or interpreted as the guardian force, for as is understood by each and every one that have studied in these influences or forces, all force, all power, all knowledge (constructive) is from a one source—is it not?

Then the guardian force is that ability to use or abuse that which has been combined in the book; or the *body*, see, as an illustration of that, as a parallel of that. Know ye have gained these, know ye are to use these in thine own experience.

(Q) Is the little book described in Rev. 10—Power of Creative Thought?

(A) As has just been given, it may be that of the whole influence or that of the body itself, or—yes—that of creative through itself; for these are one.

(Q) What is the significance of John eating it up and of the verse, "Thou must prophesy again before many peoples, and nations, and tongues, and kings."

(A) As illustrated in that as indicated, and as from the use of same. Know ye have it—what will ye do with it? It becomes part and parcel, by the eating up. It is very beautiful to look upon, very beautiful to be desired; but in the application of same at times very bitter.

As is seen in the very manner in which—How did the Son in the earth become as an intermediator between sinful man and an All-Wise, All-Merciful God? By going through or experiencing, or in giving to, through the very sufferings in the body, the right, the purpose, the aim to be in that position!

Now, man having attained same by this study must prophesy—apply —prophesy *is* apply—before many in many experiences, in many ways, in many environs, in many lands. All of these are a part and parcel of same. How did He put it as He gave, "I will bring to your remembrance *all* things, from the foundations of the world."

Then as it has been experienced by those who have taken hold of, who have combined the book (that is the book of Life), into the experience, it becomes within its body then a part and parcel of—and is to be expended in its relationships to the environs in that of prophecy, yes; in experiences before kings, yes; yea as beggars; ye as rulers; yea as those in authority; yea as those authoritative over.

Think of how this is shown in the life of the Master Himself; He that made man, yet under the authority and the will of man by the mere giving of self in the experience of passing through same. Not that these were needed other than that it might be fulfilled, what? Prophecy, as had been given in man's search for God.

Then as this has been found, as is illustrated here by John, in the taking of the book and in becoming these, each then must pass in its experience through the same sources.

(Q) What is meant by the symbol of the "reed like unto a rod" with which John was told to measure the temple? Rev. 11. Please explain.

(A) How again has it been given by Him? "With what measure ye mete it shall be measured to thee again." Know that he had acceded to the point wherein he is to set the metes and bounds (John as an individual). Ye, your own souls as individuals, who will you put in your heaven? Ye of a denomination, ye of a certain creed, ye of a certain measurement, with what measure ye mete it is measured to thee again.

This then is an illustration that to each there is given, what? All power to set that as the metes and bounds of what heaven in itself shall be to those who would gather these, or those, or the self. What would be heaven to a soul that built it for its individual self? Heaven, yes—but alone!

Those that will measure then, those that will set metes and bounds—how has it been given oft? When ye name a name, or when ye give metes and bounds, ye forget that God's force, God's power is *infinite!* and this is beyond the comprehension of the finite mind. Yet as is illustrated here to John, as is illustrated to thee, thou art given—with the understanding—as to what the metes and bounds shall be. As to the numbers as seen, as understood, these become as parts of its own understanding.

(Q) Is the temple here the physical body?

(A) Rather the *mental* in which is the pattern as of the tabernacle; or the holy mount—or that as set by a *unified* service of the body-mind, the body-physical, the body-spiritual; that vehicle that is without nails (as was the tabernacle as a pattern), not bound together, yet a covering, a place, an understanding for a *unified* activity with Creative Forces, or the power of God. The veil without, the holy within, and the holy of holies—knowing that there must be the cleansing, there must be the purifying, there must be the consecration. All of these are as patterns, they are as conditions, they are as experiences for each and every soul.

(Q) Is the court referred to the body apart from the spiritual centers?

(A) As indicated, rather is it as the environ without—the body-physical and mental within for its sacrificial forces, and then to the spiritual force within as to the holy of holies.

(Q) Are the Gentiles here those not seeking spiritual development?

(A) Rather do the Gentiles here refer to that without the court. Not necessarily not seeking, but—remember the measuring rod He hath set. These do not change because if thou art worthy, Christ-like in the material, ye are Christ-like in the broader sense in the mental—and how much greater in the spiritual! The same as in those who are very devout without—as a Catholic, as a Protestant—as of such and such creed or faith; how much smaller have they grown within!

We are through for the present.

TEXT OF READING 281-33
March 31, 1937

GC: You will have before you the Glad Helpers, members of which are present here, and their study of the Book of Revelation. You will continue to answer the questions which have been prepared.

EC: Yes, we have the Glad Helpers, as a group, as individuals; and their study of Revelation, with that which has been given as respecting same.

In considering the study, the seeking of the Group as here, and that as has been given: The Book thus far, as has been given, is the study of the body, the mind, the soul; the physical body, its attributes; the mental body, its associations and attributes; the soul body and its attributes.

Now we have reached the point as implied by the book as eaten, the rod as given to John; that these understandings are now to be, and are, applied in the experience of the individual *entity*—in its relationships to its fellow man. [Rev. 10:10, Rev. 11:1]

Hence we see in the symbolized form that as now gives place to the references as to the influences from without, that have had, do have, their influences upon these activative forces in the human experience—or the individual experience in this material life.

Now: In the study of the rest or the last half of the Revelation, we find this is referring to the application, the effect, the influence—and, as in the end, "Whosoever will may come, drink of the water of life and be whole in Him."

Ready for questions.

(Q) What is meant by the 2 witnesses mentioned in Rev. 11:3? Are they the mental and emotional bodies of the soul of man?

(A) As has been made reference, now—the Book of Life has been eaten.

It is in the mouth, sweet; in the belly (or the body), bitter.

This may be the interpretation then: the mental or the subconscious; but rather is it the *conscious physical* lives, or the attributes and the consciousness in the *experience* of the soul in the attributes of a physical consciousness!

Do not confuse self; and many of you are wondering just what it is. Then, as has been so oft given, all of this was recognized by John. Hence all of this is given in form, ritual, the emblems, what we may term numerology, astrology, and all the forms of the ancient wisdoms; yet it is represented by the activities of same upon a physical being.

As has so oft been given, an individual experience in the earth plane is motivated by that which arises from its sojourns in the influences of the consciousnesses outside of the physical being—or as ye would say astrologically the sojourn in the environ of Venus, Jupiter, Mars, Neptune, Saturn, Uranus, Sun, Moon, and the constellations and those effects upon same—emotionally from the *innate* forces; *and* by the *emotional* effect from sojourns in the earth. Both of these are witnesses.

As the Book of Life then is opened, there is seen the effect of that which now has been attained by the opening of the system, the body, the mind; all of those effects that have been created by the ability of the entity to, in the physical being, attune self to the consciousness of being at-one with the divine within.

Now we see those in the material world using these influences for self-exaltation, self-indulgence, self-glorification; and yet we see those using same for the glory, the understanding, the knowledge, the wisdom of the Father.

These then are the witnesses. The innate and the emotional; or the spiritual-mental, the physical-mental; the subconscious, the superconscious.

(Q) Explain the symbol of the death of the 2 witnesses.

(A) As in the symbol of—Does the individual, unless—Let's illustrate by what has been given: The Master gave, "Before the world was, I AM! Now if ye abide in me and I in the Father, then I will bring to thy remembrance *all things*—from the foundations of the world!"

Yet these are as dead, or the only consciousness that arises from same is that which is fanned into life or activity by the application of the laws concerning same. Hence they are as dead, yet become alive again by remembrance, by the application of thought. In what? The light of that which has been attained by the entity or soul that has applied the former lessons in its experience.

(Q) What is meant by the "great city which is called Sodom and Egypt, where also our Lord was crucified"?

(A) As has been so oft given, all places—as Egypt or Sodom or the Crucifixion, or the Lord—are conditions, circumstances, experiences, as well as individual places. Then in the minds of those who would attempt or that would seek knowledge, they represent their own experiences. Thus these to the people represent—Egypt, the release from bondage; Gomorrah, as a reckoning with sin—as the Lord was crucified there. As has been given, there has never been an experience when His Christ-mas, His death, His birth, wasn't an experience of the age, the people. Though it may go under many names, as an individual may be under many names, in many environs, there is one—*one* that ever comes as is shown in that later given as to those who have the name in the hand, in the head or in the forehead and the like; that is, what is the intent and purpose. Just as the Savior of the world, as Lord, as Christ—what do these as names indicate? That which is as a help in a time of trouble alone? or that to glory in, in thy joy, thy gladness, thy happiness? How many, O how many have there been that have laughed with God, that have wept with Jesus, that have gloried with the Christ! or rather has it been, "My happiness and my joy is of myself"?

No condemnation; but rather is there the pattern pointed to as was set by Him. He was *all* things to *all* men; rejoiced with those that did rejoice; He wept with those that wept. He was glad, He was happy, He was sorry, He kept the faith.

(Q) What is signified by the revival of these witnesses?

(A) How hath He given? "If ye meditate on these things, I will bring to thy remembrance all things." The reviving, the renewing, by the abilities of the soul to take hold upon the witnesses of the life itself! And what is life? God!

(Q) What is meant by the sounding of the 7th angel? How should time be interpreted as given?

(A) Remember, as has been given to him that was given a measure, as a mete, as a rod to measure heaven—as to how large his heaven would be. All right! Then we have as to how much time—What is time? Is it a record merely of the events of self or of the glory of God? What is the extent of the glory of thy heaven or of thy God? This is as a reckoning. Yet as is shown by the indication of so many days, so many weeks, it is the *inclination* of the individual mind in materiality to set (as was said of John) metes and bounds; and we judge from—How many days or years have ye set? Nineteen thirty-seven (1937) is what? And thy Lord has been continuous! yet ye say only 1937!

(Q) In Rev. 12 we find the symbols of the Woman, Dragon and Child. Do these represent the part played by souls in the creation and fall of man? Please explain the reference of these symbols.

(A) Rather is the reference given to show to the individual entity that from which or through which the soul in the earth has passed in its creation, its activity in the earthly sojourn, see?

For as we go on or interpret further we find: The war was in heaven, see? The woman—or the mother—earth; the source from which all materiality is to become a conscious thing—and these are brought forth.

Now, as is given, ye have reached to that understanding of thy perfection with God; how in materiality ye may attune the attributes of self.

Now, from what have ye arisen? These are emblems, significant of that as given as the name of Satan, the Devil, the Dragon or the like, through which man's rebellious forces arise, even though he has attained to the Book even itself in his body! And these are the experiences then to be met.

(Q) What is meant here by the war in heaven between Michael and the Devil?

(A) As has just been given, as is understood by those here, there is first— as is the spiritual concept—the spiritual rebellion, before it takes mental or physical form. This warring is illustrated there by the war between the Lord of the Way and the Lord of Darkness—or the Lord of Rebellion.

(Q) What is meant by the symbols of the wings of eagle given to the woman for escape and "the time and times and half a time"?

(A) This is as the entrance into or the flight from materiality into those influences through which the body may rest within itself; as physical, or the mental flight, or that to the astral forces as about its various changes. It is figurative of the transitions from the various spheres of mental experience; by the mind, the spiritual influences as arise—and are as the use of same. Remember, all of these should be then in accord with that ye have attained to, that the Book of Life is given thee. What is the Book of Life?

The record of God, of thee, thy soul within and the knowledge of same.

We are through for the present.

TEXT OF READING 281-34
April 21, 1937

GC: You will have before you the Glad Helpers, members of which are present here, and their work in studying the Book of Revelation. You will continue to answer the questions which have been prepared on this book.

EC: Yes, we have the group as gathered here and the work of the Glad Helpers with their study of the Revelation; and that which has been given.

In continuing the interpretations of the symbols, and the experiences of John as written to those in the various churches in Revelation, these portions—or the last half of same, as has been indicated—are the application of what is gained by the analyzing of self and the emotions and the affects of activities through the physical being—as is applied by and to the individuals in the application of the truths gained in their material, their mental, their spiritual relations.

Ready for questions.

(Q) What is meant by the symbol of the child in Rev. 12?

(A) That which is the outgrowth of the application of the Word, or the Book, upon self. For as the child it is born of application of the elements in the body (physical, mental and spiritual) of the individual.

(Q) Explain the flood as caused by the serpent to destroy the woman and the help given by the earth? Rev. 12:15-16.

(A) The flood is the emotions upon the influences of the body in all of its relationships to the activities in its relationships to others; and destroys the baser forces—aided by the application in the earth; which represents the elements of material manifestations in the experiences of the individual.

For, how hath He given? The children of earth are wiser in their generation than the children of light, or from the very growth of what is the experience of the individual in the earth in its seeking for light. Or as He gave in the parable, for impunity's sake or for custom's sake, or for the help that the influence may bring, He will arise and give.

So in the experience of the individual, know that there constantly arises within the sojourn in the life or in an experience in the earth the flood of emotions that make for doubt, fears, tribulation, disturbances, anxieties. For the very sake of that as becometh then impunity, the earth aids in the quieting of the influence as is illustrated here.

(Q) Please explain the symbol of the beast like a leopard with 7 heads and 10 horns. Rev. 13.

(A) As has been described in the Revelation as to how the influences of the knowledge as gained arise through the various forces and centers of the body. Now we find them visualized by John the revelatory as representing the beast, or by the beast that makes for the fears as given in the minds of many by the representing of same in the forms as given, working as it were upon those very forces that have been aroused by the application in the seeking for the understanding of the book, or of the body, or of the relationship of the individual, to the relationships borne by the individual. For it is all as individual, yet is applicable to every force or influence that is in the earth in an individual experience.

(Q) Explain what is meant by those whose names are not written in the book of life.

(A) Those not written are those who have climbed up some other way, or have only for impunity's sake or only for the momentary conscience's sake, as form the influence about them, acknowledged the Way. For as we see later more definitely given, whosoever *will* may take of the water of life.

But as has been given, there are those who from the first—as he that is last to be bound—had the import to do evil. Then those who have followed closely after the flesh, or the indulgences of the emotions of the body alone, without the considerations of others, without, other than self's own interest—as is shown by the beast that is loosened—these are they whose names are not written, and these are they who are easily led about by every wind that bloweth, unstable as it were in those as represented in a portion or one of the churches; not hot, not cold, but allowing today, tomorrow, the circumstance of the moment to sway—without purpose, without direction, without the Name. For there is only given under heaven that Name whereby men may be saved, by their belief, their faith, their trust, their works in Him. Hence those who do them not, those who are seen about the individuals striving, are not to be by the individual lamented so much as that the individual loses his own way, but rather knowing that God, the merciful Father, the loving Father of the Christ, in His own time, His own way, will bring those necessary influences.

Be *ye* then, as is given, in the same association by the promptings of that ye have gained. Having tasted of the tree of life, the knowledge of God, make thyself and thy calling and thy election *sure* in that ye faint not when ye see these troubles, these disturbances that are only of the earth-earthy, that only the emotions of the desires of self's own show coming to pass in thine experience.

(Q) Explain the symbol of the 2nd beast with 2 horns, having the power to perform miracles. Rev. 13.

(A) As has been given by Him, the power as attained by the study that has been shown in the first portions is to be applied, or may be applied unworthily—as is shown by the beast with two ways, two horns. Then here, how hath it been given? One Lord, one faith, one God, one baptism, one way! Yet in the experiences as ye watch about you there are constantly shown the influences by the very forces of the beast with the double-mindedness, as showing wonders in the earth yet they must come even as He hath given, "though ye may have done this or that, though ye may have healed the sick, though ye may have cast out demons in my name, I know ye not; for ye have followed rather as the beast of self-aggrandizement, self-indulgence, self-glorification," even as the beast shown here.

(Q) Do these two beasts as described in Rev. 13 have relation to the subconscious and conscious mind of man?

(A) They work in and through these influences, to be sure; the subconscious forces that become as a portion, and the consciousness that works through the elements—for self or for God. They work *through* these but not as directing, as being the beast.

(Q) What is meant by the mark of the beast in the right hand, or forehead?

(A) These are as signs or symbols of this or that grouping, or of the organizations that become as a part of the vows or obligations to those who have joined in with the work of the beast.

Hence the warning that if these come to mean more in the experience they stand as that which condemns, rather than that which is the helpful experience.

For having the mark of the beast and the mark of the Lamb becomes the difference between the consciousness of the indwelling presence of the Christ and the hoped for yet not seen or known.

(Q) What is meant by the number of the beast is the number of a man, 666?

(A) Just as has been given, that when it is taken on as being the exercise of the man without reference to or realizing the influence which has brought same—though it may be in an organization, in a group, in any influence that becomes the work of man's hands—then it is the number of a man and is numbered as may be the days of man, but lacks that consciousness of God and God alone directing.

For as in each organized work or each association, or each group—it should never be as is said of any man, but how hath He given? God that worketh in and through Him. Thus is the mark of the beast effaced from the workings of the hand or the activities of the head, and it becomes not as the name or the number of a man but the trust alone in God.

(Q) Explain "Here is wisdom" mentioned in this connection?

(A) That as ye have gained by the analysis or the study of the activity and influence of the spirit of truth throughout the whole members of thy body, physical, mental and spiritual, and have come to the knowledge of that which has first been given, that there is only *one* God, *one* Christ, one faith, one baptism; or as Christ hath given—this is the whole law; to love the Lord thy God with all thy mind, thy body, thy soul; thy neighbor as thyself. This is the whole law. This is wisdom. This is knowledge. Knowing that those things which have been put on through the activities of the elements within thine own forces of thy body and mind are but as the stepping-stones to the knowledge that God is in and through *all* and in Him ye live and move and have thy being. When this is fully comprehended, fully understood, ye have the working knowledge of God in the earth.

We are through for the present.

TEXT OF READING 281-36
July 28, 1937

GC: You will have before you the Glad Helpers, members of which are present here, and their work in studying the Book of Revelation. You will continue to answer the questions prepared on this Book.

EC: Yes, we have the group as gathered here, as a group and as individuals, with the information that has been given the group respecting the Revelation—and its application in the experience of the individual.

In continuing, as has been given, the portions now begin with that assurance to the individual having put on the whole armor, with the full understanding of what is meant by the various activities that are given as emblematical experiences in the affairs and conditions of the earth, of which each material entity then is a part.

These assurances become rather as the great help in those periods of temptation or trial.

Ready for questions.

(Q) In Rev. 14 do the harpers as mentioned symbolize the souls or spiritual beings that took part in the early attempts to stop the fall of man, but who have not entered the earth plane?

(A) These have entered the earth plane but were those that in the beginning were as the sons of God *in* the earth plane; and hence are referred to as the *first* of those redeemed.

(Q) What is the meaning of the new song of the harpers?

(A) The new experience that comes to each soul. Let's keep it individual, see? The new experience that comes to each soul, as to the assurance of that help when necessary of the saints of the Father.

(Q) Please explain the symbols of the angels mentioned in Rev. 14. What is meant by the symbols of the sickles and reaping?

(A) That those individuals who have and are a part of the active force in a material world are to work, to give forth, to give out of their strength, theirselves in active service and not as those that would rest (from the material angle); but as the reapers, as the harvesters—which to the individual mind means labors for a definite purpose and service.

(Q) What is meant by "Blessed are the dead which are in the Lord from henceforth, yea, saith the spirit, that they may rest from their labors, and their works do follow them." Rev. 14:13?

(A) As referred to or given, the changes that have come and the assurance that has come to each individual who has recognized that the Lamb (or the Christ), or the activities of Jesus becoming the Christ are the assurance of the activity of the Christ in the passage from the material plane to the celestial. For as He preached to those bound even in the shadows of death, loosened that which made it possible for them to become again conscious of the opportunities for reconstructing of themselves in the experiences through which error had come, so blessed then are they who die in the Lord—for the body alone is bound.

(Q) What is meant by the angels with the 7 last plagues, in Rev. 15?

(A) These are the activities that come to those who have begun and have found and have known the experiences of the activities and influences as indicated, and even have put on and become a part of—or are still in the active forces in the materiality—these see the pouring out of that which is the meeting of self in individuals yet in the earth, see? that is, the angels are the figures of that influence as of the wrath; that is, then the law, see? and this becomes necessary for the fulfilling of that "He hath not willed that any soul shall perish but hath with every ill provided a means, a way." Hence the pouring out, the meeting—and the great work or service that those may render who have named the Name, those who have known the song, those that are one with Him.

(Q) Is the temple or tabernacle of testimony, Rev. 15:5, referring to Akashic Records?

(A) That as you may term the Akashic Record, or the Book of Life, or the Book of Revelation; that is, of the individual, see?

(Q) What is meant by the temple filled with smoke, Rev. 15:8? Is the temple the body and are these final steps in the process of spiritualization of the body?

(A) These are the final steps in the abilities of the individuals for their effective service, or filled with the smoke as the glory of the Father, see? This is the temple of the body, and—as such—where the Lord hath promised to meet those that are faithful and true.

(Q) What is meant by the angels with the 7 vials, Rev. 16?

(A) This again is that fulfilling of the law. This is as the carrying forth in the earth of those influences that bring the wrath in the active forces, in the experience of the individuals.

(Q) What is the symbol of the 1st vial and the pouring of it?

(A) These all are as the same, through are represented as the effective activity upon the various conditions that have become a part of the errors in those that have the mark of the beast.

(Q) In Rev. 17 does the woman here symbolize the cause of the fall of spiritual man? Please explain with reference to Creation.

(A) It represents rather that which made for the projecting of man into matter through the associations that brought carnal relationships in those very activities. Not as a spiritual but as a material giving or bringing spiritual activity in the desire of the individual or soul.

(Q) Do the 7 heads and mountains have any reference to the spiritual centers of the body, Rev. 17:9?

(A) These have reference to the spiritual centers, as has been indicated; and indicate and show in the latter portion of same as to how these have become purified in the redeeming forces of the Lamb.

(Q) Does Babylon symbolize self?

(A) Babylon symbolizes self.

(Q) Does Rev. 18 give some idea in symbols of the effect of the fall of self—selfishness?

(A) It does.

(Q) Does the marriage of the Lamb symbolize the complete spiritualization of the body? Please explain.

(A) As there has been given through the whole portion of Revelation; first how the symbols of the activity of the body mentally, spiritually, physically, are affected by influences in the earth—and as to how now the body has been raised to the realizations of the associations with spirit and matter through mind, the builder, and comes now to that as represented by the Lamb—or the mind, spiritual—that has now so raised the body as to become as a new being; or as was given by Him—the body is the church, the Christ-Consciousness is that activity which motivates same within the individual.

We are through for the present.

TEXT OF READING 281-37
September 8, 1937

GC: You will have before you the Glad Helpers, members of which are present here, and their work in studying the Book of Revelation. You will continue to answer the questions they have prepared on the last few chapters.

EC: Yes, we have the group as gathered here; as a group, as individuals, and their work on the study of Revelation.

In continuing with that which has been given, well that you each here review within yourselves the experiences of the Revelation as related to your individual lives.

In this manner may you each attune yourselves to the more comprehensive understanding of the latter portion of same.

For the latter portion becomes again the invitation to all for all to partake of the life that is theirs, so living same in such a manner that each individual they contact in each experience of their associations may find every one different—and closer in accord with those teachings that are so a part of the Revelation; the body-Christ, the body-self, that may be one with Him.

Ready for questions.

(Q) Explain Rev. 19:9-10. To whom is John talking here? Is it Peter?

(A) That which is represented by Peter. What did Peter represent? That as had been given, "Flesh and blood hath not revealed this unto thee, but my father in heaven."

All then who have taken, who do take that which had been given as the example, as the pattern, as the manner of expression, as the acknowledgement of the activities within self, are in that position—that they have touched, do touch as it were the knowledge of God in that His ways, His laws, His love are not only a part of their individual lives but are by them manifested in their daily life, their daily conversation, as one to another.

Yes, then—to the Peter in every experience of the body, the mind, the soul.

(Q) Explain the symbols of the white horse and rider in Rev. 19. Is this the Christ?

(A) This is the Christ in that it, as the horse, in the experiences of the awakening is the symbol of the messenger; and this is Christ, Jesus, the messenger.

(Q) Explain what is meant by the first and second resurrections.

(A) The first is of those who have not tasted death in the sense of the dread of same. The second is of those who have *gained* the understanding that in Him there *is* no death.

(Q) What is the meaning of one thousand years that Satan is bound?

(A) Is banished. That, as there are the activities of the forty and four thousand—in the same manner that the prayer of ten just should save a city, the deeds, the prayers of the faithful will allow that period when the incarnation of those only that are in the Lord shall rule the earth, and the period is as a thousand years.

Thus is Satan bound, thus is Satan banished from the earth. The desire to do evil is only of him. And when there are—as the symbols—those only whose desire and purpose of their heart is to glorify the Father, these will be those periods when this shall come to pass.

Be *ye all determined* within thy minds, thy hearts, thy purposes, to be of that number!

(Q) In Rev. 21:1 what is the meaning of "a new heaven and a new earth: for the first heaven and the first earth were passed away; and there was no more sea"?

(A) When the foundations of the earth are broken up by those very disturbances. Can the mind of man comprehend no desire to sin, no purpose but that the glory of the Son may be manifested in his life? Is this not a new heaven, a new earth? For the former things would have passed away. For as the desires, the purposes, the aims are to bring about the whole change physically, so does it create in the experience of each soul a new vision, a new comprehension.

For as has been given, it hath not entered the heart of man to know the glories that have been prepared, that are a part of the experiences of those that love *only* the Lord and His ways.

(Q) Please explain 2nd thru 4th verse of Chapter 21—the new Jerusalem and no more death.

(A) Those then that are come into the new life, the new understanding, the new regeneration, there *is* then the new Jerusalem. For as has been given, the place is not as a place alone but as a condition, as an experience of the soul.

Jerusalem has figuratively, symbolically, meant the holy place, the holy city—for there the ark of the covenant, the ark of the covenant in the minds, the hearts, the understandings, the comprehensions of those who have put away earthly desires and become as the *new* purposes in their experience, become the new Jerusalem, the new undertakings, the new desires.

(Q) What is meant by the second death in Rev. 21:8?

(A) Those that have passed into the understanding and then fall away, become minded of the earthly desires for self-exaltation, know the second death.

(Q) What is meant by the Holy Jerusalem Rev. 21:12?

(A) As indicated, that purpose, that estate to which there is the attaining of those who through the purifying—as has been indicated in the earlier portion—now come to the holy purpose—as the Holy Jerusalem; the Holy of Holies becomes the dwelling as it were of those.

(Q) What is meant by the 12 gates?

(A) The twelve manners, the twelve ways, the twelve openings, the twelve experiences of the physical to all, and those that have all been purified in purpose for the activities with same.

(Q) What is the significance of the 12 angels?

(A) The twelve purposes as represented by the activities of the openings to the bodily forces for their activities in the experiences of expression in the phases of the activities of the individual.

(Q) Please explain the 12 names which represent the 12 tribes of the children of Israel.

(A) The same as the twelve gates, the twelve angels, the twelve ways, the twelve understandings; or the approach to *Israel* the seeker—all seeking not then as the expression of self but as *one* in the Holy One!!

(Q) Rev. 21:15: Please interpret—What is the golden reed to measure the city? and what is the significance of the stones of the new Jerusalem and their colors?

(A) The new understanding, the reed to measure the city, the abilities of each. Not unto all is it given to be ministers, not unto all to be interpreters, not unto all to be this or that; but measured according to that whereunto they have purposed in their hearts. Though all are as one, remember it has been given that the purpose of the heart is to know *yourself* to *be* yourself and yet one with God even as Jesus, even as is represented in God the Father, Christ the Son, and the Holy Spirit; each knowing themselves to be themselves yet *one!*

So the measurements for those that make the vibrations within themselves that become attuned to the new purpose, the new desire, the new hopes, the new Revelation, the new understandings to do the will of the Father with the will of that made perfect in the Christ.

(Q) Rev. 22:1: Please interpret. And he showed me a pure river of water of life, clear as crystal proceeding out of the throne of God and of the Lamb?

(A) As the river, the water, the life represents the active flow of the purpose of the souls of men made pure in same. Then they flow with that purpose from the throne of God Itself, made pure in the blood of the Lamb—which is in Jesus, the Christ, to those who seek to know His ways.

(Q) Rev. 22:2: What is meant by the tree of life with its twelve kinds of fruit that yielded her fruit every month and the leaves of the tree for the healing of the nations?

(A) That as the tree planted by the water of life; that is, as the sturdiness of the purpose of the individual in its sureness in the Christ; and the leaves represent the activities that are as for the healing of all that the individual activities may contact, even in material life. And that it is *continuous,* as by the month, as for purpose, as for the activities.

(Q) Rev. 22-10, 11: Seal not the sayings of the prophecy, etc. and He that is unjust, let him be unjust still; and he which is filthy be filthy still, etc.

(A) As that period approaches when there shall be those influences of the power of those incarnated in the activities of the earth, then the purposes become set as in that indicated by the activities of each being in that to which they have then given themselves.

(Q) Just how should this material be presented so as to be the most helpful and readable? Comment on the following:

(A) Rather than commenting (for these touch upon the same), we would give this: First let there be not one but *all* who would purpose, who have purposed to be among that number that are called of God to give to those that seek the interpretation, compare and prepare the messages that have been given; and then choose ye they that would write—and let them—yea, by day and night—find themselves even as John, moved only by the spirit of truth. Thus preparing the message.

Then when prepared, in one *sitting* read the whole *to* your source of information and receive the rejections or acceptations!

We are through for the present.

TEXT OF READING 281-38
October 27, 1937

GC: You will give at this time a discourse on the endocrine glands of the human organism, discussing their functions in relation to physical body and their relations to the mental and spiritual forces.

EC: Yes, we have the activity of the endocrine system, as may be described from this body here. A discourse, to be of help or aid, may not be finished under fifteen or twenty series; for this is the system whereby or in which dispositions, characters, natures and races all have their source.

Little of course is as yet known or recorded as to the activities of same. For these are being discovered, or rediscovered by man in his search for the anatomical structure of the human body; and are continuing to be found. Hence, as is the natural thing, they are not present in a dead body.

Hence those influences or opportunities that have been given to man under varied circumstances from the study of the anatomical structure in a way or means or manner in which they may be observed; namely, through the Digestive System (and even about this very little is known). For only this one portion in the animal kingdom and in the history of medicine has been studied by observation.

So in the study of the glandular systems that work within the glands or the organs, or the active forces of a physical body, these become then only those that may be seen or observed as from an *individual* activity; and thus are only *relative*—or may be correlated to others as they may be observed in that which is produced within same.

For as has been indicated in some manners, some activities, there is an activity within the system produced by anger, fear, mirth, joy, or any of those active forces, that produces through the glandular secretion those activities that flow into the whole of the system. Such an activity then is of this endocrine system, and only has been observed in very remote manners, or just here and there. Only the more recently has this activity received that consideration from the specialist in *any* activity in the relationships to the human body.

And as has been indicated by those who are possibly leading the whole of the revolutionary activities as related to these, in making for the visibility even of the circulatory system, there is to be considered ever the whole activity; not as separating them one from another but the whole anatomical structure must be considered *ever* as a whole.

Then we would give—to be as brief as possible in this short period, though for you to be aware or gain much it will take eight to ten to fifteen such periods for a really *instructive* influence:

What are the activities of the glands? Most every organ of the body may be considered a gland, or at least there must be within the functioning activity of each portion—as the eye, the ear, the nose, the brain itself, the neck, the trachea, the bronchi, the lungs, the heart, the liver, the spleen, the pancreas—that which enables it to perform its duty in taking *from* the system that which enables it to *reproduce* itself! That is the functioning of the glands!

Not as a whole only, but as individual well as the whole.

Hence there is then in the system that activity of the soul, that is the gift of the Creator to man. It may be easily seen, then, how very closely the glands are associated with reproduction, degeneration, regeneration; and this throughout—not only the physical forces of the body but the mental body and the soul body.

The glandular forces then are ever akin to the sources from which, through which, the soul dwells within the body.

As an illustration—for this may be very brief for this particular period, but that you may grasp an inkling even of what you have begun:

Let us consider the Race question. Why in the mixture of races is there in the third and then the tenth generation a reverting to first principles? (Remember, we are speaking only from the physical reaction.)

Because that period is required for the cycle of activity in the glandular force of reproduction to reassert itself. How is it given in our Word? That the sins of the fathers are visited unto the children of the third and fourth generation, even to the tenth. This is not saying that the results are seen only in the bodily functions of the descendants, as is ordinarily implied; but that the essence of the message is given to the individual respecting the activity of which he may or must eventually be well aware in his own being. That is, what effect does it have upon you to even get mad, to laugh, to cry, to be sorrowful? All of these activities affect not only yourself, your relationships to your fellow man, but your next experience in the earth!

This is indicated in this particular body which lies here, through which the information is being given—you call him Cayce; John would be better!

There are those very influences as used or manifested in those periods of activity in indulgences, as we have indicated, which have magnified such activity of the glandular system. Hence in the present actions as related to the physical forces of the body these make for a continual warring—against those influences or activities within the system.

This same reverting to first causes may be seen in others, when there has been the self-indulgence in any manner. Hence as you may see about you, and which is coming to pass: Why is the race of the people in America growing taller and taller. The exercising of the glandular forces as related to the activity that produces within the system the extension of the physical structural forces of the body! Fast rather than thinking! The glories of self rather than the glories of God!

Monstrosities or giants or such active forces are the results from the glandular secretions produced in the system—and these show themselves again and again.

This does not necessitate, as you see from viewing of same, that the parents of such be monstrosities themselves, but that they have in their union made possible the expression of that which *has* made for the extravagant use of the individual's influences in his own experiences in the earth!

Then we find the endocrine system—not glands but system—is that which is disseminated throughout the whole of the body, as related to the physical forces of same; and may be studied or may be followed in their relationship not only to the physical structural forces of the body but to what we call hereditary and environmental forces and how they may be expected to react upon the system.

And if these are considered in their proper relationships at those periods during conception and during those formative periods, the application of these may be made in such a way and manner as to make—as the Romans did—a beautiful, lovely body; yet the life may be as of Satan itself!

We are through for the present.

TEXT OF READING 281-46
September 25, 1940

GC: You will have before you the members of the Glad Helpers gathered here. You will give at this time the first of a series of discourses on the endocrine system in the human body, presenting this information in such a way as will aid us in understanding the functions of each of the seven major glandular centers in relation to other glands in the system; heredity, temperament, character, environment, physical, mental and spiritual growth and expression. You will answer the questions, as I ask them:

EC: Yes, we have the group as gathered here; their purposes, their desires. In giving that as may be understandable in the study of man—man then as the inception and conception into that *from* the purpose, desire, and its relationships to the universe and universal consciousness—it will be well to follow—in the first—what the happenings are in conception; the growth and the determining factors as to that growth—spiritually, mentally, physically—by and through the word of that Creator.

Man was given the ability to create through self a channel through which the manifestations of spirit might be made manifest in a material world. As is observed in such, there needs be first that of desire, purpose. It is known as a fact that this may be wholly of the carnal or animal nature on the part of even one, and yet conception may take place; and the end of that physical activity is written in that purpose and desire.

Then it is evident that there is the ideal, as well as the partial or whole carnal force, that may be manifested or exercised in and through such activities—as to bring a channel of mental, spiritual and material expression in the earth.

The ideal manner, first, is that there may be a channel through which the spirit of truth, hope, divine knowledge and purpose, may be made manifest.

What then, ye may ask, are the spiritual, mental and physical variations that may take place under the physical activities for varied expressions?

It may be seen that from the same source, even at the same period of conception, there may come quite varied expressions or characteristics in the *individual* expression manifested.

Desire, first, creates certain forces about which there is a physical nucleus that is the pattern of the universe; with a number. Thence it is given by some sages that each entity, each expression in a material experience has its number. Yet the more often there is the "guess" or mistake as to what physically caused there to be a number for an individual entity. There may be all the variations possible represented in thy digits from one to nine. This means the variations of the positive and negative influences or the neurones or electrons, or forces that form that vibration upon which that individual entity *will* or *does* vibrate at its period or source of conception. And each relationship of its vibration to the universe is relative, according to its number, in relationships to influences and environs, heredity as well as those influences which are a part of its conscious experience.

Thus the greater unison of purpose, of desire, at a period of conception brings the more universal consciousness—or being—for a perfect or equalized vibration for that conception.

As an illustration of such (that this may be wholly—or in part, by some—understood): When Hannah desired that there be an expression that God, the Universal Consciousness, had not forgotten that there were prayers and alms offered, was there wholly the lack of selfishness? or was there the shadow of jealousy?

Then we find there was the promise of the dedication and the purposes, that this expression would be wholly given the Lord, ever. Yet it brought into being an entity, though dedicated as few—yea, as none other individually—to the Lord, unable of himself to give that expression which would keep his own offspring in the *same* vibration!

Thus we see the *relative* relationships of the electrons, the neurones, the positive and negative forces brought into being at the period when there begins the *opportunity* of conception.

Then, when such takes place—no matter as to what may be the vibrations that are set by the union of body, of mind and of purpose or spirit at such a period (for, to be sure, these are as varied as the individual)—there remains the *ideal* manner.

But—ye are asking—what physically takes place? Is it a physical activity of a gland, an impulse, a heartbeat, that becomes an influence for activity through the body so conceived?

The cord that is eventually known or classified as the pineal is the first movement that takes place of a physical nature through the act of conception; determining eventually—as we shall see—not only the physical stature of the individual entity but the *mental* capacity also, and the spiritual attributes.

We would rest for the period.

TEXT OF READING 281-47
October 2, 1940

GC: You will have before you the members of the Glad Helpers gathered here. You will continue with the discourse on the endocrine system in the human body.

EC: Yes.

As the nucleus forms, there begins that activity which becomes the motivating force of the mental, the physical and the spiritual influences as related to *growth.*

It has been indicated, by the sage, the manner of growth in the womb is not understood by man; yet here ye may find a concept of that development.

That gland [pineal?] a nucleus extending in the shape or form of a moving atom, gathers from its surroundings physical nourishment; and from the mind of the body it takes its *physical* characteristics, or the moulding as it were of its features as related to the external expression of same.

Then as the mind of the bearer binds those forces that are its natures in itself, its purposes, its desires, its hopes, its fears, these begin gradually to extend themselves through the nucleus; so that as the shape or form begins to find expression, there are also the channels through which the growth of the spiritual being gives its expression.

It is centered first, then about that known as the cranial center; next the 9th dorsal, or that which is the motivative force to other portions through the umbilical cord, that begins then in the third week to give material manifestations in physical development.

Then the centers of the heart, liver and kidney areas begin their expression.

Thus we have first the pineal, the aerial, the adrenals, the thymus—or the pump gland of the heart itself.

Each organ as it materializes in its development forms its own nucleus for the production of that which enables it in itself, from its own glandular system, to reproduce itself.

With the production of itself, the blood system begins its flow—then—in the second month of conception.

Then there begins the growth of the glands that forms eyes, ears, nasal passages; and those areas begin their formations.

The seeking here is for that area, that center, in which the system makes its relative relationships or associations with spiritual, mental and physical being.

These areas indicated, that have come through growth into being in relation to the mental, spiritual and physical attitude of the mother, are constantly dependent upon that one from which the body draws its *physical* sustenance; but purpose, desire and hope are through the mental. Thus these centers are opposite the umbilical cord, or those areas through which *all* messages of desire, or of the mental nature, pass; not only to the brain in its reflexes but along the cords to the pineal—that has been and is the extenuation of is first cause.

In those glands that are eventually known as the genital, or in the lyden, and the inner centers of the thyroid through and from which the exterior forces are indicated in their activity, there begins then the formation of the superficial circulation; that leads or connects between its spiritual import, its mental purpose, and its physical development—for their coordination.

Thus we find, as indicated in the bodily expressions, there comes in these areas—or from those centers of the areas given—the disturbances of a physical nature to which the young are more susceptible; which are of a glandular nature, finding expressions in the various forms in the physical to the superficial and the deeper circulation, between the cerebrospinal and sympathetic, or to the organs that are under the direction of same. We refer to such as measles, mumps, conditions of throat, the head and eyes. All of these are glandular centers.

That is why in portions of the Scripture the extenuating activities that take place in the spiritual being are described by the expressions through those body centers.

These follow through, throughout the periods of gestation, and are dependent still upon the environs, the mental attributes and activities, the purposes and aims of that individual *bearing* the entity.

Thus it comes into the material world with that held to by *that* parent, with the *characteristics* that are the sum of spiritual, mental *and* material purposes of the *first* cause, as combined with its age and era or period of development.

We rest here.

TEXT OF READING 281-48
October 16, 1940

GC: You will have before you the members of the Glad Helpers gathered here. You will continue with the discourse on the endocrine system of the human body.

EC: Yes, we have the group as gathered here; and their study of the endocrine system.

It has been indicated as to what takes place at the time of conception, and the manner, and the influences which regulate activities spiritually, mentally, physically, through the period of gestation. It will possibly be well to illustrate same; that there may be drawn, by those studying same, the experience as in the life of individuals.

We begin then with the seers or sages of old, from that period indicated as to how influences affected the offspring:

When Abraham and Sarah were given the promise of an heir through which the nations of the earth would be blessed, there were many years of preparation of these individuals, of the physical, mental and spiritual natures. Again and again it is indicated as to how they each in their material concept (watch the words here, please, if you would understand) attempted to offer a plan, or way, through which this material blessing from a spiritual source might be made manifest.

Hence we find as to how the material or mental self-misunderstanding, misconstruing the spiritual promises—offered or *effected* channels through which quite a different individual entity was made manifest; and through same brought confusion, distress, disturbance one to another in the material manifestations.

Yet, when the last promise was given, that even in their old age there would be given an heir, we find that when Sarah thus conceived there was the development of a body physically, mentally and spiritually so well balanced as to be almost etheric in his relationships to the world about him, when the material manifestation had grown to maturity.

Here we find, then, that mind and matter are coordinated into bringing a channel for spiritual activity that is not exceeded in any of the characters depicted in Holy Writ.

What, then, were the characteristics, the activity of the glandular system as related to that individual entity? We find that there was a perfect coordination in and through the whole period of gestation, and the fulfilling of the time according to the law set in motion by the divine influence that was the directing force of both parents through the period.

We find also that throughout the period of gestation the activities about the entity, the mother, were such as to *influence* the entity yet unborn, in patience to a degree not manifested in any other of the patriarchs. While the physical conditions made manifest in the body during the growth into manhood were affected by *material* laws, there was not the changing or deviating whatsoever from the spiritual through the mental.

Hence we have that illustration of what may be termed the individual ideally conceived, ideally cherished and nourished through the periods of gestation. As to the care afterward—these vary, as we shall see from other illustrations.

What, then, were the developments of that ideally conceived entity as related to the study here of the endocrine system?

First—the individual was one conceived in promise; with the desire, the purpose, the hope—in the act *of* conception—to bring forth that which had *been* promised. Hence the ideal attitude of both parents in that individual case.

Hence as given, first the pineal, the cranial, the thymus; then the aerial, then the gradual development of those influences which brought a goodly child; one subject to the care of both parents—by natural tendencies from conception; bringing into materialization that one worthy of being accepted and of *receiving* the promise beyond *many* of those who were of the seed of Abraham.

Then we have that illustration in the sons of Isaac, when there were those periods in which there was to be the fulfilling of the promise to Isaac and Rebekah. We find that their *minds* differed as to the nature or character of channel through which there would come this promise; when, as we understand, there must be the cooperation spiritually, mentally, in order for the physical result to be the same. *Here* we find a different situation taking place at the time of conception, for *both* attitudes found expression. Hence twins were found to be the result of this long preparation, and yet two minds, two opinions, two ideas, two ideals. Hence we find that *here* it became necessary that even the *Divine* indicate to the mother that channel which was to be the ruler, or that one upon whom would be bestowed the rightful heritage through which the greater blessings were to be indicated to the world, to humanity, to mankind as a whole.

Hence we find two natures, two characteristics—physically, mentally, spiritually. Here we find what might be termed a perfect channel again, and with same a testing—not only of the parents themselves but of the individuals that were begotten under those conditions in which the promise was as clear to them as it had been to Abraham.

What, then, were the physical and mental attitudes which contributed to this condition which existed in that period, and that may be used as an illustration of those ideas being presented here for the study of man, his nature, his characteristics, his spirituality, his weakness in physical being?

Here we find, as indicated, there was *not* a union of purpose in those periods of conception. Hence we find both characteristics, or both purposes of the individuals, were made materially manifest.

What then, ye may well ask, made this difference in the characteristics of the individuals; conceived of the same parents, under the environ or the law from the body of the one; with such a different characteristic made manifest as they grew to maturity?

As indicated, the first cause—that purpose with which the individuals performed the act for conception to take place, or under which it did take place. *That* is the First Cause! And the growth of that conceived under the same environ, through the same circulation, through the same impulse, was such that—when gestation was finished—one was of the nature or characteristic of the mother, the other was of the nature of indifference with the determination of the father; one smooth as the mother, the other hairy, red, as the father in maturity; and their characteristics made manifest were just those examples of the variations. Though conceived at once, born together, they were far separated in their purposes, their aims, their hopes; one holding to that which made body, mind and soul coordinant; the other satisfying, gratifying the appetites of the physical and mental without coordinating same through its spiritual relationships to the progenitor or those conditions and environs from which they each drew their desires, their hopes, their wishes.

Do ye think that one received a different instruction from the other? Each received the same, yet their reaction, their choice of that in the environment made physical characteristics that varied in their activity.

Why were the characteristics such that one desired or loved the chase, the hunt or the like, while the other chose rather the home, the mother, the environ about same? Were these depicted in the very physiognomy of each individual? When they had reached that period when the *choices* were made, these were manifested. But when did they begin? What gland developed this characteristic in one and not in the other? The cranial and the thymus receiving the varied vibration, one brought harmony—not fear, but harmony—with caution; the other brought just the opposite, by this "stepping up" in the rate of vibration. Or, if we were to study these by numbers, we would find one a three, the other a five; yet conceived together.

What do we mean here by the vibration of the number? One had the nucleus, the structure about same, three to one of its spiritual import; the other five to one of the material import, see?

Hence we find there the various forms or manners in which there is illustrated those characteristics that made for individual activity, that *prompted* the carrying on of that through which the channel of hope might be made manifest.

Let's change these then to those illustrations of quite varied forms, in which more of the characteristics became manifested of the environmental nature; for the illustrations we have just used show how the characteristics of the individuals responded to the environment as each grew to maturity and became active in relationships and dealings with others.

Then, with Jacob and Rachel we have the material love, and those natures in which the characteristics of material love were athwarted. Yet, in the very conception of same—though under stress (for there is held here by the mother the desire to outshine, as it might be poorly said)—we find a goodly child, one with all the attributes of the spiritual-minded individual; partaking of both the father and the mother in the seeking for a channel through which God might be manifested in the earth. And yet the entity had those physical attributes that brought into the experience of individuals those things that were reflected in the mind, in the movements and activities of the mother throughout the periods of gestation—when the entity had grown to manhood.

Also from the same attitude taken by those parents when the second son, Benjamin, was conceived—what were the varying characteristics here? The material love was just as great, the satisfying of material desire was completely fulfilled; yet it lacked that desire to *bring* such as was wholly a channel through which the *spiritual* was to be made manifest. But it was a channel that *eventually* brought the material made manifest in Saul, an incarnation of Benjamin.

Hence we find the varied characteristics illustrated not only by the attitude of the pair as the channel being made manifest, but the attitude of that channel which was given from the beginning.

Now, conceive first what the variations are in the sexes, as given in the beginning in the creating of same; one to be a channel of material and mental satisfaction to the other; the other to be a channel, a manner, through which there was to be the alleviation of desire when spiritualized in the purpose toward the mate.

Hence we may find again and again here, in the Word, that which *is* the connection between man and his Maker; that finds its final concept in the manner which John presents to the elect—in which all the varied attributes of the human development—in body, in mind, in spirit, with each phase of man's development—are also chosen as channels through which expressions of same are given.

We would rest with the illustrations; for there are others that need to be given.

We are through for the present.

TEXT OF READING 281-49
October 23, 1940

GC: You will have before you the members of the Glad Helpers gathered here. You will continue with the discourse on the endocrine system of the human body.

EC: Yes, we have the group as gathered here, and their study of the endocrine system.

In that which has been given there is the attempt to show the necessary coordination of the mental with the physical and spiritual; or, to be exact, the coordinating of the mental with the spiritual that so alters the characteristics, the purposes, the hopes of the individual entity materialized and manifested. That entity, however, is altered by choices made under its own impulse.

But to further demonstrate or illustrate those phases of the emotions, and that necessary in the union of purpose for the channels, we find that—as indicated—other illustrations are needed.

From the patriarchs there may be taken others—as first indicated in Samson; and also that which has been referred to in those relationships borne by Kish and Methulabah (?), when there were the preparations for the individual entity that was to be king over that chosen people. We find that the preparation of the parents, mentally and physically, was such that there was an elongation of activity in the endocrine system of the pineal; so that the stature of the entity then was of a different type, a different nature, and the mental and spiritual so balanced and coordinated that through the experience of the entity there was a physical and mental development equaled and surpassed by few. Yet the *application* of the entity *of* those opportunities was personal; so that what was individually personified of the mental and spiritual of the entity's sojourn was then of self in its *latter* analysis.

But the activities of the glands—what has this to do with those activities or choices that the entity or individual makes after the periods of gestation are completed, either during the period when the entity is under the direction or counsel of the parents, or tutors or friends and associates? What have the glands to do with the choices the individual makes? This depends upon whether or not the activity has been such that there is kept the coordinating of the glands of the body as related *to* the activity of the organs being directed.

Then, it is not that the entire life experience is laid out for an individual when there has been received that imprint as of the first breath, or the spirit entering the body as prepared for activity in the material world. For, again, choice is left to the individual, and the personality—as to whether it is the laudation of the ego or cooperation with its fellow men, or as a consecration to the service of the Creative Forces in its material environs.

All of these are to be taken into consideration, then; just as they are indicated in the study that first prompted this search for the *beginnings* of individuality and personality in an entity entering and becoming active in the material complacency of a changing world.

Further illustrations we may find, of both a physical and a mental nature.

When Manoah sought with his whole desire and purpose that there might be the blight taken from his associations among his fellows, he with his companion, prayed oft; and then the visitation come.

Here we find a consideration also to be taken, when one studies even the anatomical structure of the channel for expression of body, mind and soul. In the material world, in the anatomy books that have been written by some, attempted by many, there is considered only the physical channel, and not the mental and spiritual attributes and activities. But if ye are studying these in the light that they are to be applied in the interpreting of Revelation, then the mental and spiritual must also be taken into consideration.

The prayer of Manoah and his companion was answered by the visitation of a heavenly figure, in the form of a man; which was not conceivable by the husband—yet when satisfied of same, and the wife—Mahoa [?]—conceived, the entity physically—*physically*—was the greater tower of strength. Yet as indicated that strength lay in the hair of the head of the individual. What *gland* caused that activity of such a physical nature, as to be the determining factor in that development?

As is indicated, the thyroid is within the body so placed as to have that influence. There are only a few of these that are not within the organs themselves.

It has been given at first that as each organ develops in the foetus there is the development of the gland within itself to give it the ability to *reproduce* itself. Yet there are those outside, or they are centers from and through which pass the emotions, the activities from the organs of other portions of the body; and become so influenced as to produce a definite *physical* effect.

If they produce the definite mental effect, if they produce through same definite spiritual attributes or abilities, and if these are coordinated by the individual into personality—what are the results?

Here this is illustrated in Samson—a lad who grew to manhood with the unusual strength and power, the ability to cope with exterior forces and influences that were beyond the understanding and comprehension of his associates. Yet his ability to say no to the opposite sex was nil—his ability not to be influenced by the opposite sex was nil—because of the desire for the gratification of those activities which were of a glandular nature within the body.

What are the lessons to be gained or understood, then, from the illustrations here given?

We will begin, then, with the various glands that act independent of the organs, and yet *affect* them through *their* glandular force or source that lies within the functioning of the organ itself.

We are through for the present.

TEXT OF READING 281-51
January 15, 1941

HLC: You will have before you the Glad Helpers Prayer Group, members of which are present in this room, and their study of the endocrine system in the human body. You will continue with the discourse on this subject.

EC: Yes, we have the group as gathered here; as a group, as individuals; and the information which has been indicated through this channel. In continuing with the subject, and as we come to the application of that which has been indicated, let that which is given here and now *not* become confusing. For, it will require deep meditation upon such, that ye may get the correct insight; which ye will not be able to put into words at first, and will *know* when ye know, but by the experience of coordinating physical, mental and spiritual attributes into one.

For, as given, few have conceived of—or attempted to analyze—the effect created in a physical body through the *mental* impressions received, or conceded that there is an activity spiritually that may go on in active force within the human body.

For, so oft we see contradictory effects produced in the activities of the individuality and personality of persons.

Also it has been and is hard for individuals to conceive of Adam sinning in a material world—as a man, a son, made by the hands of God.

Neither is it easy to understand the illustrations used from the life of Kish, who conceived through righteous desire a son, a channel chosen for a manifestation of material power in a material world; given through the choice of the Maker Himself, and yet the *individual* in his personal relationships defied even that which had been prophesied by himself!

Few can conceive of the body through which the Prince of Peace manifested—the Son, the first and the last Adam—as having been a channel for material desire, when considered as a body so purified as to bear that perfect One.

Yet, all of these facts are demonstrated in the life of each individual.

There has long been sought, by a few, the interpretation of the seven centers; and many have in various stages of awareness, or development, placed the association or connection between physical, mental and spiritual in varied portions of the body. Some have interpreted as of the mind, motivated by impulse; and thus called the center from which mind acts.

This is only relatively so, as will be understood by those who analyze those conditions presented through these interpretations; for in fact the body, the mind and the soul are *one,* in the material manifestation. Yet in analyzing them, as given through the Revelation by John, they are active in the various influences that are a part of each living organism conceived in the forces making up that known as man; that power able to conceive—in mind—of God, and to demonstrate same in relationships to others; that in mind able to conceive of manners for the destruction of its fellow man, little realizing that it is *self* being destroyed by that very activity!

Then, why are there such contradictions within those very influences? As is said, in the heart love finds its way. Love is conceived as of God, as of all pleasant, as all giving; given in that great expression—indicating to what power it may arise—"God so loved the world as to give His only begotten son; that through Him we might have eternal life."

Yet the other side, or the reverse of love, is suffering, hate, malice, injustice. It is the reverse. Why?

What is that about man's activity in body, as an individual, that causes such?

This has been indicated through those patterns which have been used as illustrations of what took place in the *union* of bodies that through desire, hope, conceived or prepared in conception a channel through which *all* this contradiction might be made manifest.

Is the First Cause, then, that the separation of God in the desire for companionship with Himself, that as created or brought into a material manifestation the reverse of love, of hope, of patience, of all the attributes that are the spirit of activity, the moving influence or force?

This we see manifested in a physical body through the glandular system—as the activity of conception, the dividing of the activity of the gland itself, that brings conception.

Thus, this is the first of the centers from which arises all that is movement, to bring into being both the face and the preface—or the back, or the reverse—in the experience. It carries with it, what? That *mind!* For, remember, ever, the pattern is ever the same—Mind the Builder!

Conceived, then the first movement is along that center or gland which either fades or becomes a channel along which there may move the power and might to find expression through the very activities of the organs of the body itself. [Leydig?]

Then the next is the pineal, through which the brain forces make manifest—either in its determining factor there of becoming mighty in stature physically or dwarfed; as may be understood by the face, as may be said, that is held to by the *individual* separation and *combination* of the activity of the glands in that period of conception. Hence there arises the race condition or contour, or the figure of that beheld by that choice in its activity as it has separated itself from the first cause, or first premise; by the very will of the Father-God in the beginning.

Then there is the third, that is ever of the feeding or building nature—or the basic cord through which during the period of gestation there is fed the imaginations, as well as the latent response of the body to those conditions external—or that center from which there is drawn the growth in the physical.

Then there becomes the first indication of individuality being established in that movement which has come about in its growth, its evolvement; or the gland of the solar plexus, or that *ye* misinterpret and call the adrenals—as they act with the emotions and the growth and unfoldment of the body itself.

There begins then the gland—the heart—through which courses begin to flow; and then the gland—the liver—its counterpart; and then the spleen (as a balance); the thyroid—as the outer individual begins to show activities for self-protection, or the first laws of nature as would be made manifest in the material associations.

Then there are the general, or the whole of the activities through the system, as in the thymus, all of the centers of activity through which spirit first moves from the lyden [Leydigian?]—the center of the spiritual forces; the brain, or the highest force individually or personally; then the others in their order as they control themselves.

Then within each of the organs themselves (though they each are, in the main, glands) the functioning is stimulated by the activity of each organ's ability to assimilate that needed from the environs, as well as from that upon which it is fed, to grow *into* that direction given *by* the mental purpose, the mental desire of the *personality—as* it, as an individual, makes itself manifest in a material environ.

Hence we find—as has been interpreted for those who would interpret—the seven centers, the seven churches, the seven activities to which an individual physical activity is prompted.

We would rest for the present.

TEXT OF READING 281-52
February 5, 1941

HLC: You will have before you the Glad Helpers Prayer Group, members of which are present in this room. You will consider their work and study on the endocrine system of the human body, and continue the discourse on this subject.

EC: Yes, we have the work of the Glad Helpers Prayer Group, members present in this room, and their study of the endocrine system as indicated through this channel.

As we find, with the information that has been given, now there should be rather those agreements—by the study of that given; and thus from same form the questions as *might* be expressed in "Is it false or is it true?" Else, the group may become burdened with knowledge and have little of wisdom—in making application of such knowledge as to become helpful or beneficial to them.

For, in their study and in the work of the prayer group, this must be a practical thing; that it may be used by them as individuals in aiding others to dismiss error from their consciousness, and in its place to put not merely the wishful thinking but activities of such a nature as to be helpful in same.

Let the approach be made by not other than the question, then, "Is it true or false?"

We are through for the present.

TEXT OF READING 281-53
April 2, 1941

HLC: You will have before you the Glad Helpers Prayer Group, members of which are present in this room. You will consider their work and study on the endocrine system of the human body, answering the questions they submit, as I ask them:

EC: Yes, we have the group gathered here; as a group and as individuals, also their work and study of the endocrine system in the human body, with the information which has been indicated through this channel—that was to be analyzed in the mind of each.

Ready for questions.

(Q) Are the following statements true or false? Comment on each as I read it: The life force rises directly from the Leydig gland through the Gonads, thence to Pineal, and then to the other centers.

(A) This is correct; though, to be sure, as it rises and is distributed through the other centers it returns to the solar plexus area for its impulse through the system.

For the moment, let's consider the variation here in this life force—or as respecting this life force. The question is asked not in relation to the life alone as manifested in the human body, but as to the process through which coordination is attained or gained in and through meditation, see?

Hence physically, as we have indicated, there is first the nucleus—or the union of the first activities; and then the pineal as the long thread activity to the center of the brain, see? Then from there, as development progresses, there are those activities through reflexes to the growth or the developing of the body.

Interpret that variation, then, as being indicated here. One life force is the body-growth, as just described. The other is the impulse that arises, from the life center, in meditation.

(Q) As the life force passes through the glands it illuminates them.

(A) In meditation, yes. In the life growth, yes and no; it illuminates them in their own activity in life growth.

(Q) The leydig gland is the same as that we have called the lyden, and is located in the gonads.

(A) It is in and above, or the activity passes through the gonads. Lyden is the meaning—or the seal, see? while Leydig is the name of the individual who indicated this was the activity. You can call it either of these that you want to.

(Q) The life force crosses the solar plexus each time it passes to another center.

(A) In growth, yes. In meditation, yes and no; if there remains the balance as of the attunement, yes.

When we are considering these various phases, the questions should be prepared so that they would not crisscross, or so that there would not be a confusion or a misinterpretation as to what is meant.

You see, what takes place in the developing body, or in life growth (which we have used as a demonstration, or have illustrated), may be different from that which takes place as one attempts to meditate and to distribute the life force in order to aid another—or to control the influence as in healing, or to attain to an attunement in self for a deeper or better understanding. These questions or statements are such that they will be confusing to some; but if they are asked properly there will not be confusion.

(Q) The solar plexus is the aerial gland.

(A) No. By the term aerial we mean that impulse or activity that flows in an upward, lifting, raising or rising movement. It is an activity in itself, you see; not as a gland but as an activity *upon* glands as it flows in, through, from or to the various centers of activity in the system itself. It is a function.

Let's illustrate—possibly this will give an interpretation such that you may understand:

In your radio you have what you call an aerial for communications that are without any visible connection. This is not a part of that making up the framework, yet it is necessary for certain characters of reception or for the better distribution of that which takes place in the instrument as related to communication itself.

So in the physical body the aerial activity is the flow through the pineal, to and through all the centers. It aids the individual, or is an effective activity for the individual who may consciously attempt to attune, coordinate, or to bring about perfect accord, or to keep a balance in that attempting to be reached or attained through the process.

As the process begins in the physical body, it is along the pineal; or it is the same movement that is the controlling or attuning influence from the mother with the developing forces of the body through the period of gestation.

That is the manner, or the process, or the way in which the impressions are made. So, if there is beauty about the body of the mother through such periods, there are those influences to bring about accord. It may be indicated in contour of face. It may be indicated in the process of change in the activity of the thyroid as related to all the forces—even to the color of hair or eyes, or the skin's activity; the nails, or more toes than should be—or less, or such activities. Or, the influences existent through such processes might make for a lacking of something in the body itself, pathologically; by the attempt to create a normal balance without the necessary influences being available.

All of this is what we have referred to as the aerial activity, see?

HLC: I see.

EC: Don't say you see if you don't see! You only had a portion of it! Let's illustrate it in this way, so you will comprehend:

Understand the processes of activity through which there are the needs of the aerial in reception. For, of course, it is a matter of vibration in the body, as well as that illustrated in the physical condition. Thus there are activities about a body that is supplying the needs physically and mentally for a developing body, that become a part of the process, see?

(Q) The entity preparing to be born into the earth has an influence upon the mother in building its own body.

(A) No. That would be the same as saying that an atom had an influence upon that to which it could be attracted! See the variation?

As in the realms outside of the material body, we have influences that are sympathetic one to another and we have influences that have an antipathy one for another—as in fire and water, yet they are much alike. There are other forces that are active in the same manner, or that are of the same nature.

But in the physical world there is builded a body, by the process of a physical law, see? Now: There is builded also a mental body, see?

God breathed into man the breath of life and he became a *living* soul.

Then, with the first breath of the infant there comes into being in the flesh a soul—that has been attracted, that has been called for, by all the influences and activities that have gone to make up the process through the period of gestation, see?

Many souls are seeking to enter, but not all are attracted. Some may be repelled. Some are attracted and then suddenly repelled, so that the life in the earth is only a few days. Oft the passing of such a soul is accredited to, and *is* because of disease, neglect or the like, but *still* there was the attraction, was there not?

Hence to say that the body is in any way builded by an entity from the other side is incorrect. *But* those mental and physical forces that *are* builded *are* those influences needed *for* that soul that does enter!

(Q) The entity desiring to enter governs the change in sex, which may occur as late as the third month.

(A) It may occur even nineteen years after the body is born! So, it doesn't change in that direction!

(Q) The physical development of the child is wholly dependent upon the mother from whom it draws physical sustenance, but its purpose, desire and hope are built up or influenced by the minds of all concerned.

(A) That's the first question you've asked correctly. *Correct!*

We are through for the present.

TEXT OF READING 281-54
May 28, 1941

GC: You will have before you the Glad Helpers Prayer Group, members of which are present in this room. You will consider their work and study on the endocrine system of the human body, answering the questions they submit, as I ask them:

EC: Yes, we have the group as gathered here, as a group and as individuals; also their work and study on the endocrine system.

As we have indicated—much study, much meditation is needed here. Much has been given. As it is better understood, papers may be prepared on same which would prove not only interesting but most beneficial.

Continue with the study of same.

Ready for questions.

(Q) Are the following statements true or false: First—Saul, the son of righteous Kish, in the latter part of his life chose evil. It was the exercising of his own choice rather than environmental or hereditary conditions.

(A) Correct.

(Q) God made the mineral, vegetable and animal kingdoms, then out of these He made man and breathed into him the breath of life. Adam, who at that period was devoid of any of the spiritualized cells of the physical body, had a stronger urge to revert to physical desires.

(A) Yes and no. Consider that, whether it is mineral, vegetable or animal, these are spiritualized in that ability of using, doing, being all that the Creator had given them to do.

Hence man was given that which is *not* a part of mineral, vegetable or animal kingdoms; though man, by man, is considered of the animal kingdom. *Will*—with the environmental forces and the spiritual negative in the serpent—acceded to desire, to become and to experience IN that kingdom of influence. This brought the acceptance, by man's own will.

(Q) The mother of Jesus in being a channel for material desires was making practical her spiritual activities.

(A) Correct.

(Q) It would be well for prospective parents to learn the lessons illustrated by the lives of Samuel, Saul, Samson, Joseph, Jesus, etc.

(A) It would be well.

(Q) Instruction regarding the endocrine glands should be given to the parents of coming generations.

(A) Correct.

(Q) It is the spiritual activity within the body of the parents, or the lack of it that determines the influence predominant in the life of their child.

(A) This is true.

(Q) Anger causes poisons to be secreted from the glands. Joy has the opposite effect. The adrenal glands are principally involved, reacting through the solar plexus to all parts of the body.

(A) The adrenals principally, but *all* of the glands are involved; as: A nursing mother would find that anger would affect the mammary glands. One pregnant would find the digestive glands affected. The liver, the kidneys and *all* glands are affected; though it is correct that the reaction is *principally* through the adrenals.

(Q) As the shape or form of the embryo begins to find expression, the growth of the spiritual being gives its expression through the channels of the aerial.

(A) It gives *expression* through the channels of the aerial, but arises from the lyden [Leydig?]—to be sure.

(Q) Medical Science calls the glands at the base of the brain Pituitary and 3rd eye Pineal. Why have these names been reversed? Please explain.

(A) Their activity indicates that, from the angles of this study, these should be reversed.

(Q) Meaning we should reverse ours, or that Medical Science should?

(A) To understand what is being given, reverse them! We are not telling Medical Science what to do! We are telling *you* what to do!

We are through for the present.

TEXT OF READING 281-55
June 7, 1941

GC: You will have before you the Glad Helpers Prayer Group, members of which are present in this room. You will consider their work and study on the endocrine system of the human body, answering the questions they submit, as I ask them:

EC: Yes, we have the work of the Glad Helpers, and their work on the endocrine system—as a group, as individuals, and those present in this room.

In answering questions, it is well that all members of the group, as well as those present, analyze their own experiences in the light of that which has been, may be or will be given respecting the manners in which they each may use such information as a helpful influence—first in their *own* experience, and then in assisting others to understand their purposes, their desires—physically, mentally, spiritually—in human relationships.

Ready for questions.

(Q) Are the following statements true or false: Inception is the aerial activity to the nucleus.

(A) This is correct, if there is the understanding that there is the physical, the mental *and* the spiritual aspect also.

(Q) Conception is the physical activity.

(A) Not necessarily. For, aerial activity produces conception. It is that movement by which the parts of the activity become one. *That* is conception.

(Q) In giving that as may be understandable in the study of man, it is necessary to understand that purpose for which an entity decided to enter the earth plane from the first creation of that entity.

(A) This is too far-reaching to be answered Yes or No. For, each experience of a soul-entity in materiality is part of the whole experience of the entity. Each inception, each conception upon which the soul depends for its period of manifestation is as but a moment, a day, a year in the activity of the *entity* itself. Thus it could not be said that an individual conception is a beginning. It is a part of a whole—from those activities first conceived in mind—and there is no time in spirit, see?

(Q) There may be wholly the carnal or animal nature on the part of both and yet conception may take place.

(A) Correct. But there is also the physical law that is active under such conditions. There are also laws of the mental and the spiritual being that are also active. As it were, it is an individual using a life-giving and a death-dealing influence without happening to be destroyed.

(Q) Comment on the following: Considered from the physical—when conception takes place only the physical body is limited.

(A) And this relatively so. For, when conception takes place there is also to be considered the form or manner in which the environmental conditions are to influence the relative physical stature, the relative physical beauty, the relative physical activity as to whether it is to become male or female—by the motivative force of the nucleus about which the positive and negative forces are vibrating. This is not determined at conception but is a development—the sex, see?

(Q) Considered from the mental, when conception takes place the mental capacity is limited to the highest positive count of the soul number.

(A) Yes and No. For, again, there are those relative relationships with the environmental forces. For, it is or has been conceded that in the Grecian experience the beauty and the stature and the symmetrical figure were all wrought by the environment. So, also, the environment of the mental force may be such as to bring those vibrations that may alter or attune, or confuse or hinder, that mental expansion. For, within the nucleus at conception is the pattern of all that is possible. And remember, man—the soul of man, the body of man, the mind of man—is nearer to limitlessness than anything in creation.

Hence those who consider the manner of being channels through which souls may enter are taking hold upon God-Force itself; and it is not the same as an animal, insect or any of the rest of creation—which is limited always.

This statement would be true, then, of *any* conception below man.

(Q) Considered from the spiritual—when conception takes place the spiritual attributes are limited to the highest positive count of the soul number.

(A) Here you are accrediting again those conditions to material things, and yet you are dealing with the infinite. Then, this is not true.

(Q) Conception can only take place when the spiritual ideal set by both is met.

(A) *True* conception, spiritual conception, *mental* conception only takes place under such; but, as we have just stated above, physical conception may take place from purely carnal influences!

(Q) Conception can take place when the spiritual ideal set by one is met.

(A) Conception may take place under *any* circumstances—physical, mental or spiritual!

(Q) When twins are conceived the ideal of each parent is expressed.

(A) This may or may not be true.

(Q) When triplets or more are conceived it is the result of confusing ideals in each parent.

(A) Remember, it is physical first, mental next, and spiritual next. All are dependent one upon the other.

(Q) An individual entity is attracted to the soul number which is determined at conception.

(A) Again you are confusing signs for reality. Yes, it may be; but how many two's are there in your mind? How many of *any* number, or how many combinations of same? It is true that there are certain set numbers, but as to the *capacity* of that number—how many times may there be three's, five's, eight's, nine's? These are limitless! So are the abilities, spiritual, of an entity's conception in activity.

(Q) The changing of the positive and negative forces by the mind of the mother determines the entity that enters.

(A) Yes and No.

(Q) An entity only has a soul number when in the earth plane.

(A) Yes.

(Q) Through other planetary sojourns an entity has the opportunity to change its rate of vibration so as to be attracted in the earth plane under another soul number.

(A) Each planetary influence vibrates at a different rate of vibration. An entity entering that influence enters that vibration; not necessary that he change, but it is the grace of God that he may! It is part of the universal consciousness, the universal law.

(Q) Numbers are indications of abilities, as the astrological influence indicates urges.

(A) Correct from a physical standpoint only. These have nothing to do with *will*, that is the controlling factor of an individual entity or soul. They are merely signs! Do not dwell upon signs and become a sign reader, and believe in signs and not in the *truth!*

(Q) The number is parallel to the incarnation, which is relative to the universal consciousness.

(A) Yes and No.

We are through for the present.

TEXT OF READING 281-57
August 27, 1941

GC: You will have before you the Glad Helpers Prayer Group, members of which are present in this room. You will consider their work and study on the endocrine system of the human body, and continue the discourse on this subject; answering the questions that may be submitted, as I ask them:

EC: Yes, we have the work of the prayer group; its purposes, its aims and desires, and the studies thus far made of the endocrine system.

In continuing a discourse, or in giving information regarding same, it would be well—before too much *information* becomes burdensome—that what has already been given be better understood; either by the attempts of individuals to discuss same or by the compilers setting in order those activities that are related to the physical, the mental and spiritual development.

As may be easily indicated, some of the activities of the glands relate to the purely physical functioning; yet the physical functioning in a life-giving body must of its very nature be empowered with mind and spirit.

Ye have interpreted, and have data indicating what, where, when there are the various stations or centers in the body-function physically, and how these also are analyzed as to their activity in a physical sense, and how they each are related to the mental body, and the relation its relative activity bears with the spiritual forces of the body.

Thus this group should be able to answer—to self, at least—that question which has not been answered since man began to think: Where is the dwelling place of the soul in the physical body? What is the connection or center through which the mind and the soul function, that makes one individual a devil and another a saint?

These should be the studies. Then, they may be applied to that purpose for which this group came into being: aiding seekers to find health, understanding and prosperity in their own environs.

Then, find the answers to these in that ye have attained, in that which has been given. Ye comprehend that though there may be the complete development to manhood or womanhood, the foetus in its activities, the gland of reproduction becomes the source from and through which impulse acts. Thus it is the source of propagation throughout the experience.

Ye have gained that the first movement of same physically reaches out and becomes the brain, through which the pineal in its activity brings its physical development; and that it is related to the mind of the body and the environs of the body supplying physical activities to that developing physical entity. Ye know that it reverts then to the brain of the nervous system, to the solar plexus center, and then reflexes through its own *mental* activity to the physical forces of the still developing body. Ye know that when such a body has developed, when gestation has been completed and it becomes an entity in itself—because of its center through which all physical and mental impulse has passed—it is then cut asunder—and yet functions on. Why? How?

These are not merely pathological questions, but mental and spiritual also.

We are through for the present.

TEXT OF READING 281-58
October 1, 1941

GC: You will have before you the Glad Helpers Prayer Group, members of which are present in this room, and their study of the endocrine system of the human body. You will answer the questions they submit, as I ask them.

EC: Yes, we have the group as gathered here, as a group, as individuals, and their study of the endocrine system. Ready for questions.

(Q) Please consider the outlines, copy of which I hold in my hand, and make such corrections and additions that may be necessary.

(A) These—corrections or the activities—are not to be from here. This is the work of the group as individuals, from that they have gained that has proven helpful in their *own* minds and may prove helpful to others!

(Q) Please give a discourse on each of the seven major glandular centers, as I call them, that will help us and others to have a better understanding of their functions physically and mentally during the adolescent period, the adult period and the changing period; also mentally and spiritually during meditation, opening of the door, the baptism of the Holy Spirit: First—Pituitary.

(A) This, as has been indicated, is the way along the system. (This is going backward—we should begin with the first cause, if an understanding is to be maintained!) These, they pass along the way; that has to do with the correlating of physical, mental and spiritual understanding. It is the growth of body and mind, the opening of which is the arousing in the adolescent to the disputations that become the conflicting influences in the experience of the individual entity.

It is the door, as interpreted by some, through which physically all of the reflex actions respond through the various forces of the nerve system.

It is that to and through which the mental activities come that produce the influences in the imaginative system as well as the racial prejudices as termed the predominating influences—or the blood force itself.

In the spiritual, it is that to which the singleness in the adult brings the awakening to its capabilities, its possibilities, its ultimate hope and desire.

It is that which in the change period brings the physical influence in which there is the correlating by experience, through the changing influences in body as related to its *own* findings and its individual intent and purpose. Or, as may be termed, it is physically the ripening of the fruit of the experience of the body; as to whether it has been material-mindedness or of spiritual import.

And in the mental it is that which gives judgement and understanding, tolerance *and* relationships to the determining factors. Hence we find some grow old gracefully, some tolerantly, some fussily and some very meanly. All of these, then, are the expressions of that which has been the dominant force that began from its first active influence that passed from its innate to the animate, to its full completion in the individual experience of the entity.

This is the influence also, or the activities spoken of, as the door upon and through which the old men may dream dreams, the young men may see visions.

All of these are the expressions of this activity in its relationships, correlated with other influences and glands that are of the physical as well as the mental natures in the body.

We are through for the present.

TEXT OF READING 281-63
March 6, 1943

GC: You will have before you the enquiring minds of those present in this room who are studying the Book of Revelation in relation to the human body; also the information already compiled and that which may be acquired, including the chart which I hold in my hand. These individuals seek an understanding of all the attributes and influences that go to make up a living, moving, human body. You will answer the questions they submit, as I ask them:

EC: Yes, we have the enquiring minds of those present in this room, those seen and unseen; the information that has been given respecting the application of the study of Revelation in reference to the human body.

Ready for questions.

(Q) Comment on the chart [see chart on page 207], give corrections and value of it as a key to this study.

(A) As interpreted in the minds of those who have put the chart together, this in the main is very good. As to the varied centers, their reactions and activities, these—to be sure—become more individual. But as we have indicated, and as will be the experience of individuals in the study of this chart, these will necessarily respond to that consciousness or awareness that has been attained by the student—or the individual entity. And these should be a helpful influence in the minds of those as they attempt to apply same in their own experience and relationships.

To be sure, as given, and as may be the experience of those as they study the outline indicated from the chart—there will be times when individuals will interpret correctly. There will be times when there will be doubts—until a practical application of same is made in the experience of the individual entity.

Revelation—Chart prepared by Helen Ellington and Gladys Davis, based on their study of [281] series, Bible dictionary (Smith's) 1895 edition Holman & Co.] meditation, etc. [See 281-63, Par. R1-R4.]

281-29, Par. 33-A; Rev. 7, Rdg. 10/28/36, Par. 33-A:

281-30, Par. 14-A; Rev. 7, Gen. 49, Rdg. 2/17/37, Par. 14-A:

4 Corners of the Earth (Body-Jacob) (Influences)
12 Tribes: 12 Major divisions:

SPIRITUAL (Hail-Water-Sea):
3 Attributes

Light	Zabulon	Digestive
Soul (Love)	Joseph	Covering
Will	Benjamin	Bone Structure

MENTAL (Fire-Heat):
3 Attributes

Desire	Simeon	Organs
Choice	Levi	Glands
Conscious	Issachar	Membranes

HEREDITY (Air-Blood):
3 Attributes

Life (Sensation)	Aser	Lymph
Opportunity	Nepthalim	Nerves
Power	Manasses	Elimination

ENVIRONMENT (Earth-Physical):
3 Attributes

Preservation	Juda	Assimilation
	(To Mental Material-Spiritual)	
Perpetuation	Reuben	Blood Circulation
	(Keeping Alive)	
Attraction	Gad	Cells
	(Construction)	

(Q) What attribute dominates the X and Y chromosomes found in the spermatozoa and ovum?

(A) This is dependent upon purpose and attitude of individual entities that produce or bring about the uniting of same. If this is from those conditions that have had those activities which cause any deteriorating effect, it produces then that value of the cycle about the center of the positive and negative forces. What produce same? Attitude!

(Q) What influence dominates the activity of each of the 3 distinct divisions in the cell that produces the sperm?

(A) The life experience of the individual entity, as a whole; as related to the spiritual ideal of that entity—which may be indicated in that He gave, "Ye do not gather grapes from thistles."

(Q) The ovum?

(A) The same.

(Q) Why are the divisions unequal in the breaking down process of the cell producing ovum?

(A) That is the activity of the negative and positive force as related one to another. Just as in the current in electrical energies the electrons by activity are broken down, as dissipation takes place; unless there are boosters in the connections in same. So, in the production of the cell in its unity, if there is activity upon same by an ideal or purpose in the act itself, then there becomes variations in its centers about which the vibration begins.

(Q) What influence does the individuality of each of the polar bodies have on fertilization of the ovum, and development in the nucleus?

(A) Each supplies that individuality which in its union produces a personality. This then would come to this: What is personality and individuality, as related to the sex relationship in the act itself? These determine, then, much of that activity that is the dominating influence in that brought about, by the contact of or the piercing of the ovum.

(Q) How are the chromosomes from each of the polar bodies used in cooperation with the 24 from the sperm and 24 from the ovum to bring into manifestation the 3 types of cell layers—ectoderm, entoderm, mesoderm—in development of embryo?

(A) These are as the factors in that of anatomical rebuilding of influences or force upon the body produced. These each, then, have their relationship to each layer as related to that which brings about the individuality or the sex activity of the body, in the activity of the ovum in this relationship.

(Q) What power does the centrosome have, and what is it relative to in a living, human body?

(A) The emotions as related to the *central* forces in the eventual activity within the lyden gland itself, or that ability to reproduce within its own self.

(Q) How many genes are contained in the chromosome, and what is their relative activity to various portions of the human body?

(A) These are varied in their activity in the body building force, by the relationship of the individual entity that has the controlling force upon the developing of the foetus in its activity, see? For, as the first activity is the reaching out by the very force of the numbers of the cellular force in the various layer in that activity, these bring their relative relationships upon each center from and through which impulses arise in the body forces themselves. One is active upon emotions, one upon the reflexes, one upon the centralization—or coordination of the reflexes with this activity in itself.

(Q) Why are the Y chromosomes found in some of the spermatozoa and are lacking in all ova and their polar bodies?

(A) This is the variation in the very nature or character in the spermatozoa and the ovum activity itself. These are the natures of this. For, one was created first and the other came out *from* same.

(Q) What is the difference in quality between an ovum fertilized by a sperm containing an X chromosome and one containing a Y chromosome?

(A) The ability of the reflexes, as just indicated, as the nature or the activities of same in their relationships to one another.

(Q) Is our chart valuable in tracing disease from result to cause? Please give an example using chart.

(A) This as a tracing of heredity in disease may be valuable. As for that of other natures, not so good. These would give, as by the very nature of the chart activity, how the activity of the chromosome upon the ovum shows whether the body would be susceptible to one or another character of disease.

(Q) Please give a pattern outlining how the 12 major divisions of the body are set up through the endocrine system in the nucleus? [See also 281-29 and 281-30.]

(A) This has been given, as to how they pass from one influence to another, in manner in which the mother in its application of thought, of food, of mind, carries those activities to the various centers making the body-building, the nerve and blood building, the emotions, and the very natures to which the pattern will be formed in its relationship to that with which contact is made.

For, oft—as may be demonstrated in individualities—there are those who are geniuses and yet are so very close to the border that an emotional shock may make a demon of a genius. There are those activities in which a spiritualized cell, by environment, may make of the demon a saint.

(Q) Would the history of the Jewish race from Abraham to Jesus parallel the development of the embryo from conception to birth?

(A) Rather would the history of man from Noah to Abraham; while that from Abraham to Christ would be the mental unfoldment of the body. For, that which leads to the Christ is the mind. And the mind's unfoldment may be that indicated from Abraham to the Christ.

(Q) Please give others we may parallel.

(A) Such activities as just indicated give the parallel or pattern through which it may be indicated at the birth of an individual entity as to the direction it will take.

(Q) Please give definite direction to [2175] present in this room, for future study and fuller understanding.

(A) As indicated, knowledge without the practical ability to apply same may become sin. For, it is knowledge misapplied that was the fall—or the confusion—in Eve.

In the application and study, then, of all influences that go to make up the developments—as the entity may find, as indicated to the entity in that just stated, the unfoldment of the mind as may be paralleled by the history of the communication of spirit, or God, with individual entities from Abraham to Christ, may be seen in thine own children. For, this is the manner to make same practical—that knowledge ye have gained in not only watching but aiding in the unfoldment of their minds. Do not put off questions asked too long to be answered. And have an answer when the question is asked.

We are through for the present.

This concludes the collection of readings given to the Glad Helpers group specifically relating to the Revelation and the endocrine glands.

OTHER EXCERPTS

The following are various readings that I have either quoted in this book or simply found to be relevant to a study of Edgar Cayce's comments on the Revelation. In many of these cases, the entire reading is not relevant, so I included only that comment, sentence, or paragraph that is. Again, they are in the same format as A.R.E.'s database and library. The reading number appears at the beginning of each selection.

Numbers in brackets, such as the following [69], replace the individual's name, for privacy purposes. Therefore, in this reading, Ms. [69] asked the question.

262-20

(Q) [69]: Please explain what was meant by the spiritual eye, or third eye, in relation to psychic development. Should we today seek to develop this particular facility? If so, how?

(A) As has been given, there is ever a channel or manner in which the expressions of a force may manifest in a material world. Hence the term, "Angels took form," that there might be the expression of, or vehicle for, the activity of an individual force manifestation in the *material* plane. In the psychic forces, or spiritual forces (which are psychic forces), there has ever then been a vehicle, or portion of the anatomical forces of the body, through which the expressions come to individual activity, and these may find various forms of manifestations, or *movements* of—as has been given, that finds its seat in the creative energies and forces of the body. In the eye, "Let thine eye be *single*" may be the interpretation of same, or vehicles, or channels, or glands through which man has lost his vision, or the ability of seeing the self-expression in same in the pituitary forces, as in the lyden and the others—we find expressions in various forms of the body. These become, as has been seen or given, in the feminine body more manifested than ordinarily in the male, in man forces, in that called intuition, or that which is active in that portion of the system. These are but one expression of that portion of the body, for these may be added to by the feeding of same, that partake of other forces of the body in such quantities, or such character of development, as to produce other conditions in the body, as the growing of portions of the body that have become lax, or lacking in their activity in the system, but development in the spiritual sense—by meditation, prayer—dependent upon the external forces, or the creative energies, for its food, rather than upon that which is wholly of the material, develops that as may be termed the psychic development of individuals. Well that psychic forces and occult influences be developed in the individuals that so

find within their individual selves that which makes for a closer relationship
with that they individually worship as their ideal! That does not indicate that
every individual should make of themselves a psychic channel that may be
used to their own destruction; for, as has been given, there be many things
hard to be understood that many wrest with to their own destruction, but
that which gives more understanding of the relationships of self with the
creative forces of a universal experience, rather than individual, makes for
a closer walk with God, that from which the essence of life itself has its
emanation. In the body we find that which connects the pineal, the pituitary,
the lyden, may be truly called the silver cord, or the golden cup that may be
filled with a closer walk with that which is the creative essence in physical,
mental and spiritual life; for the destruction wholly of either will make for
the disintegration of the soul from its house of clay. To be purely material
minded, were an anatomical or pathological study made for a period of seven
years (which is a cycle of change in all the body-elements) of one that is
acted upon through the third eye alone, we will find one fed upon spiritual
things becomes a light that may shine from and in the darkest corner. One
fed upon the purely material will become a Frankenstein that is without a
concept of any influence other than material or mental.

264-19

(Q) In what respects can The Book of Revelation be applied to Gray's
Anatomy in aiding this body to become a scientific analyst?

(A) In that as the anatomical condition of the body is understood, the
various references to portions of the Book of Revelation, there is a better
understanding of that as occurs in the body when the vibrations are raised
within the body through meditation, or through that of fasting and prayer.
As is seen by most of the illustrations that are used by John in Revelation,
this is speaking of the physical, the mental, and the spiritual body, as are
manifested in the various organs of a physical body. Hence an analysis of
an individual's experiences as in emotions, as in inability to raise vibrations, comes from and of an overloading, or an aggrandizing of, portions
of the *organic* forces within a physical body. For, as from the beginning, we
find—as has been outlined—the body has rather that ability to *project* itself
in that direction that was *willed* by the body, so that it—in its assimila-
tion—*absorbed,* or folded *over,* as it were, that which would be assimilated

by that body; and, as these began then to take more of the personality, came into the form of a *physical* body much as is seen, or was seen, about them in the various forms as were the inhabitants of that portion of the sphere in which that body or being itself developed. Hence they partook *of,* and became a portion of, absorbing all *within* themselves so that every element *without* a human body is—or finds an expression within some form, or some activity of a *living* organism. Hence the various activities as are manifested without find a response within the physical organism. A very crude illustration may be seen, as the effect certain pollens have upon individuals of certain vibrations or attunements, and produce irritations in portions of the system at certain periods of the year. Or there may be another seen, as to how that individuals of certain attunements are affected by odors, colors, noises, or the like, dependent upon their vibration to which they have become attuned by the use of that they have applied through their experience in the earth's sphere. Hence we find in Revelation, that the revelation is to the *imaginative* and spiritual *body*—as is expressed, or finds expression through an *individuality.* Now get the difference between the personality and the individuality! The individuality of those who would know themselves before the Lord!

262-51

(Q) [993]: Why am I called to read Revelation and the prophets during this lesson?

(A) For, as has been presented, opportunity is of the spirit presented or manifesting itself in the activity of individual souls. As is shown in the prophets, *these* were also called to present truths that came into the experience of those to whom the prophets spoke.

So, in Revelation is there seen, in the activities of those that name the name, those that are called, those that would harken—hence, as in water the face answereth to the face, so in thine consciousness does the spirit of truth in the prophets, in the Revelation, answer to the consciousness in self.

Know that those who spoke there spoke even as is spoken to thee in thine experiences, in meeting the spirits of truth in revealed activity in thy meditation.

262-87

(Q) Why did Jesus say, "Touch me not," when He first appeared to Mary after the resurrection?

(A) For the vibrations to which the glorified body was raised would have been the same as a physical body touching a high power current. Why do you say not touch the wire? If ye are in accord, or not in touch with the earth, it doesn't harm; otherwise, it's too bad!

262-117

GC: You will have before you Group #1, members of which are present here, and their study of the lesson *Spirit*. You will answer the questions that have been prepared on this.

EC: Yes, we have the group as gathered here; and their work on the lesson Spirit.

There has not been the completion of that which has been outlined for the group study, nor for their work on same.

This then should be very much more complete, for you have only gotten the effects and are questioning these rather than the cause or the conception of that which moves the individuals in the activity of the study and presentation of that as may be helpful in the preparation to others.

Rather would we question those here, than be questioned:

What is *spirit?* God of heaven, of the universe, of the state, of the nation, of the home, of thyself?

Are these one in thy conception? Then *why* do ye not act like that?

What is thy relation to thy home, thy community, thy county, thy state; thy church, thy nation; thy God? Are these one? Then *why* is there not better cooperation in thy home, in thy relations to thy home, thy church, thy country, thy state?

What is that spirit that moves thee to find fault with thy brother, thy neighbor? Is that in keeping with what ye believe? Is that how ye will spend eternity? Is that what ye would have thy Savior, thy God, be? Then *why* is not thy life more in accord with that ye profess that ye believe? *god is!* Thy spirit is in the Maker. Then what are ye doing about that in thy daily conversation, in thy daily proclaiming of this or that as comes into thy experience?

Ye believe that good and right and justice live *on,* and are continuous in thy experience. Yet ye find fault with what this or that person may have said, may have done, may have looked; or may have failed to say or do.

What manner of spirit, then, hast thou directing thy life? Look within. See thyself, that which has motivated thee in thy dealings with thy fellow man; or as to what ye have proclaimed is thy concept, thy thought of thy Creator.

Have ye opened thy heart, thy desires to Him? Are they in keeping with that thou would have meted to thee, to thy fellow man, to thy Maker, to thy Savior?

Does the Spirit of the Master and the Father abide with thee? This is His promise. "If ye love me, I will come and abide with thee." Have ye driven Him from thy home, thy church, thy state? yea, from thine own consciousness?

Have ye not rather entertained the anti-Christ?

Have ye considered as to *who* is the author of thy activities day by day? yea, in thy dealings with those in thy home, in thy neighborhood, in thy city, in thy state? Have ye not preferred one above another?

Is that the spirit of truth? Is that the consciousness with which He that is the author of thy faith ministered to those He met day by day?

Has He changed? Have the circumstances, the environs, the times changed? Are not Time, Space and Patience in thy consciousness a manifestation rather of His love, His patience, His longsuffering, His activities with the children of men?

Art thou wiser in thy own conceit than He?

Do ye day by day, in *every* way, say *"Thy will, not mine, be done"?* Rather do ye not say, "Bless me and my house, my son, my children, my kinfolks; for we are a little better and we do a little better"? Do ye not excuse thyself?

Be these in keeping with Spirit as ye now conceive, as ye now understand?

Then gather together, even as He gave; "Let not your hearts be troubled; ye believe in God, believe also in me. And I go to the Father, and if ye love me ye will keep my commandments. For my commandments are not grievous, but are *living* and *doing* day by day those things that ye *know* to do!"

Patience, love, gentleness! Not gainsaying, not finding fault!

These be the little things, yet bespeak that fact that ye have known, ye do know, and ye entertain the Spirit of the Christ!

If ye do these, then, there is no question as to whether "I shall do this

or that," for the Spirit of the Christ will and does direct thee! if ye live the
Christ-life!

281-12

(Q) [288]: Please explain the pumping sensation I experience in the
lower part of my spine during meditation, and what I should understand
from it?

(A) As has been given, as to how those forces in the system are the
channels through which the activating sensations arise through those forces
of the body for transmission to those portions of the physical body from
which sensations are sent out for the activating forces *in* the physical bodies, then these are but the samples, or the attempts of those forces to rise
to their activities in the consciousness of the body. Do not force same, but
so conduct the mind's trend, the body's activities, as to leave self a channel
for such expression.

294-142

(Q) What other glands in the body, if any, besides the Leydigian, pineal,
and glands of reproduction, are directly connected with psychic development?

(A) These three are the ducts, or glands. In some developments these
have reached a stage where they do not function as ducts or glands, but
are rather dormant; yet much passes through same, especially for the various stages of a psychical sojourn or development. These, as we find—the
genitive organism is as the motor, and the Leydig as a sealed or open door,
dependent upon the development or the use same has been put to by the
entity in its mental, its spiritual, activity. The mental may have been misused,
or used aright. The spiritual activity goes on just the same. It is as the elec-
tron that is Life itself; but raised in power and then misdirected may bring
death itself, or—as in the activities of the glands as seen, or ducts—that
used aright may bring serenity, hope, peace, faith, understanding, and the
attributes of its source, as the experience of the entity; or, misdirected, may
bring those doubts, fears, apprehensions, contentions, disorders, disruptions,
in every portion of the body. Hence these may literally be termed, that the

pineal and the Leydig are the *seat* of the soul of an entity.

As to the abilities of physical reproduction, much of the activity of the Leydig makes for that as of embryonic in its activity, or of sterility in its activity. So we have those channels. These are not the psychic forces, please understand! They are the *channels* through which the activities have their impulse! though the manifestations may be in sight, in sound, in speech, in vision, in writing, in dreams, in Urim or Thummim, or in any. For these represent Urim and Thummim in their essence, or in *any* of the *responding* forces in a body; but their impulse arises from or through these sources in much the same manner as the heart and the liver are of the physical body the motivating forces, or impulses, that carry the stream of life itself; or as the brain is that motivating center of impulse or mind. These are merely as illustrations that the student may better understand the activity of that being presented.

444-2

(Q) Please explain more clearly how the body should go about a study of the low electrical vibratory forces.

(A) The low electrical vibratory forces are existent. They *are!* Or, as may be said, the lowest form of electrical vibration *is* the basis of life. The application of such vibrations to the body when it is fagged in mind, in physical endurance, will stimulate the necessary influences for the body to return to the abilities within self to carry on, or to create the life influence for self, or that it may measure out to others. Not necessarily that alone, but that known as the Radio-Active Appliance influence.

(Q) Please explain and give such advice regarding the glandular activity within this body that may be helpful in its development.

(A) Much might be given in this respect. The channels are weak through which this is being given in the present. These may be added, when the channels are cleared sufficient for better expression. But *this* for the body, [444] we are speaking of:

The glands (through experiences which the body is conscious of having passed) are being coordinated in more perfect manners than they have in a great period in the experience. And that the body has chosen through self's own will to make for a study of, and to open self for the acknowledging and experiencing of that which may be raised or lowered in vibration throughout the body, makes for not only a soul advancement but greater abilities in the mental equipment and the mental abilities and scope of activity of this body.

1173-8

(Q) What passages especially should he read in the Bible?

(A) The admonition of Moses, the creation of man in the first three chapters, the admonition of Joshua, the 1st Psalm, the 2nd and 4th Psalm, the 22nd, 23rd and 24th Psalm, the 91st Psalm, the 12th of Romans, the 14th, 15th, 16th, 17th of John, 13th of 2nd Corinthians [1 Cor. 13?], and the Book of Revelation.

And in the Revelation study as this: Know, as there is given each emblem, each condition, it is representing or presenting to self a study of thine own body, with *all* of its emotions, all of its faculties. All of its physical centers represent experiences through which thine own mental and spiritual and physical being pass. For it is indeed the revelation of self.

How much more then should this mean to self? For even as He in the consciousness of the separations bade John to take her, thy mother, His mother, as his own, how much more would be that consciousness in self that the life, the self, the experience is dedicated to His at-onement with the Father in thee; that the glory as He had before the world was is His.

2501-6

(Q) Would a life reading be a help?

(A) Not at present. It's the physical forces that we must combat at the present. That physical conditions exist that are accentuated by influences in the entity's experience is apparent, as does also the [Moon] influence most (This would be very interesting to the physician in charge to watch the changes in the moon and watch the effect it has upon the body). Now, when we have the new moon we will find that for the first two days, as it were, following same, a *wild, hilarious* reaction of the stronger; as the *wane* begins, then we will find the changes will come about, as will of a bettered condition. These are merely *influences, not* those that may not be overcome by the activities as may be changed in a physical organism; for with pressure in the lumbar and sacral region, as has been first indicated, there is that activity to those forces as operate to and through the pineal gland to the upper portion of the body, which corresponds to those forces as are spoken of, even in that of the [Book of] Revelation. Be very good for the doctor here to read [The] Revelation and understand it! especially in reference to this body! These forces as applied to this are the activities as are seen in the sympathetic nerve system, and *advance* in their activities as the force of same impel through the sympathetic and the cerebrospinal plexus from the 9th dorsal to the brain itself—at top, see? Hence in the changes as are being brought about in the system through the activity of the change, there is seen less pressure is on the solar plexus center. Hence there is less *incoordination through* the pineal *from* the effect of the sympathetic system. Hence when there is that of the *usage* of being not *severe* but *positive* has its greatest effect. Be more positive! in the activities *physically* and mentally! That as will be required, that will the body—*in* its development, *in* its being aided—will attempt to supply. Do that. [See 281-28 on 10/26/36 and subsequent rdgs. on The Revelation.]

2501-7

(Q) Explain reference to The Revelation in connection with this body . . .

(A) In The Revelation there is given that illustration of how the mental body is raised from the various degrees of consciousness, and—as is given here—their *activity* are through the correlated centers of an anatomical body, for they are represented by the refuse as comes from the 4th lumbar, emptying into the lower portion of the system. While the consciousness as comes through the system in sympathetic system is raised to the inner court, or in the holy mount, through the pineal gland—that coordinates with sympathetic forces—see?

311-4

In the mental attributes of the body—as has been given, these are exceptional in many directions. Will the body, for its own mental development, make a very close study of that book known as Revelation—in the Holy Book—and apply each indicated force *in* same to the *physical body*, and *understanding* will come within self that will make for the directing of the mental abilities that will be most profitable, most beneficial to self *and* to others. As an illustration—where there is spoken of, as the book becoming bitter within the stomach when eaten, this referring to the application of that as is digested mentally *within* an individual. As again when referring to those of the elders, they refer to those elements within the system, the *body,* the *physical* body, of the *glands* of the body—for, as has been given, the *kingdom* is within *you!* This, then—that the *spirit,* the soul, the *elements* of the *active* forces, use those portions *of* the physical body as their temple *during* an earth's experience.

900-147

(Q) Is this a revelation—a revelation of that I was pondering—what is meant by Life Eternal?

(A) Life Eternal—One with that Oneness, as is seen by the Soul becoming One with the Will, the spirit, of the Father, even as is shown in the ensample of the Man called Jesus—the Christ, the Savior of the World, through compliance to those same laws, as He complied with, see? for with that Force, that Spirit, brought in the World, then becomes the truth, "What thou asketh in My name, believing in thine heart, same shall be unto thee." *Beautiful* is the life and the feet of those who walk in the paths of the righteous One. Lo! The Heavens open and I see Him stand at that Way which leads unto Life Everlasting; *that* then the Way, the Truth, the Light, the Water of Life, the Man made Perfect in that Spirit of Him who gave Himself as the ransom for many.

1473-1

68. (Q) How may I overcome this [inferiority complex], and also my outstanding faults?

(A) Just as indicated.

During such periods of using the Appliance, open thyself to those tenets. Look upon them not as of a man, not as of an entity even, but rather as a universal consciousness to thee in those things given in the 30th chapter of Deuteronomy, in the 150th Psalm, in the 14th, 15th, 16th and 17th of that book called John.

And then the Revelation; knowing *this*—the Revelation—is a description of, a possibility of, thy own consciousness; and not as a historical fact, not as a fancy, but as that thy own soul has sought throughout its experiences, through the phases of thy abilities, the faculties of thy mind and body, the emotions of all of thy complex—as it may appear—system.

And ye will find *peace,* and an awakening—beautiful!

262-14

(Q) [333] & [602]: How may we as members of the group through co-operation grow stronger in faith, and through a knowledge of self attain to those ideals as are set in self for the part in this great work that each would accomplish with the help of all?

(A) Studying to show thyself approved unto God day by day, rightly dividing the words of truth, and keeping self unspotted from the world. There is builded in the meditations, and in the gathering of others here, there, to gain the understanding necessary to bring about a revolution, a revelation, an awakening in *this* place as *has* not been seen in many a day! Making those truths as are known in self *living* truths, through the active force of the *spirit* of *truth* itself. Do that.

262-86

(Q) Should we study to present with this lesson an understanding of the Book of Revelation? If so, how?

(A) Not necessarily; for one is as the spiritual body, that is given in symbolic activity for the learned, while we are beginning with babes!

264-15

(Q) What are the main studies that make known both the physical and metaphysical activities of the organs of the body, as they represent human experiences?

(A) The best of these metaphysical may be studied from [The Book of] Revelation, as applied to Gray's Anatomy.

264-50

(Q) What books or course of study would give me more understanding?

(A) That of a physiology and that of the whole book of first and second John, the 14th, 15th, 16th and 17th chapters of St. John, the 30th chapters of Deuteronomy, the 12th of Romans and the like. And the comparing all with a study of the Book of Revelation, in the thought ever that that indicated, that as is outlined *is* the body, and the body made beautiful.

364-7

(Q) What was meant by the Sons of the Highest in Atlantis and the second coming of souls to the earth, as mentioned in a life reading given thru this channel?

(A) In this period or age, as was seen—There is fault of words here to *project* that as actually *occurs* in the *formations* of that as comes about! There was, with the *will* of that as came into being through the correct channels, of that as created by the Creator, that of the *continuing* of the souls in its projection and projection—see? while in that as was *of* the offspring, of that as pushed itself *into* form to *satisfy, gratify,* that of the desire of that known as carnal forces of the *senses,* of those created, there continued to be the war one with another, and there were then—*from* the other *sources* (worlds) the continuing entering of those that *would* make for the keeping of the balance, as of the first purpose of the Creative Forces, as it magnifies itself in that given sphere of activity, of that that had been *given* the *ability* to *create* with its *own* activity—see? and hence the second, or the *continued* entering of souls into that known as the earth's plane during this period, for that activity as was brought about. Let's *remember* that as was given, in the second, third from Adam, or fourth, or from Amilius, there was "In that day did they *call upon* the *name* of the Lord"—is right! and ever, when the elements that make for littleness, uncleanness, are crucified in the body, the *spirit* of the Lord, of God, is present! When these are overbalanced, so that the body (physical), the mental man, the imagination of its heart, is evil, or his purpose is evil, then is that war continuing—as from the beginning. Just the continued warring of those things within self as from the beginning; for with these changes as brought *sin* into the world, with same came the *fruits* of same, or the seed as of sin, which we see in the material world as those things that corrupt good ground, those that corrupt the elements that are of the compounds of those of the first causes, or elementals, and pests are seen—and the like, see? So does it follow throughout all creative forces, that the fruits of that as is active brings that seed that makes for the corrupting of, or the clearing of, in the activative forces of, that *being* acted upon.

610-1

(Q) What can I do to adjust myself to that situation [problem with son and son's wife]?

(A) This, with each, will aid self in adjusting self. Not that any soul that seeks for the revelation from the Spirit-God into their own lives would become long-faced nor one that mopes or gropes about; for who should be the happiest people in the earth? They that walk and talk with Life day by day! What is Life? God in expression in the earth! For that which has been termed death of the body is but the releasing of the soul, the image of the God in every entity, to find expression and to come closer to that which is Life. So, in preparing self to meet the situations, to counsel with each, draw near to them and they will draw nearer to thee. Draw nearer to the life in thy Maker and He will draw nigh to thee.

What has been the promise? "If ye will be my people, I will be your God." What is the first promise in all? "Honor thy Father, thy mother, that thy days may be long in the land which the Lord thy God giveth thee." Honor, then, thy Father-God. For, if ye would have God to be nigh unto thee, draw *thou* nigh unto Him. Be a savior, a god, to thy fellow man. What may thou do in the earth? What is the standard the Father has set? "Love the Lord, thy God, with all thine heart, thine soul, and thine body, and thy neighbor as thyself." This is the whole law and gospel; there is no other. "Inasmuch as ye do it unto the least of my brethren, of my children, ye do it unto me." This alone, this purpose, this desire, in the heart of any soul, *only* may bring peace when others falter, bring harmony when others become panicky, bring joy when others are afraid. For, "As ye do it unto others, so ye do it unto me." As He has given, first find thine self in this relationship to thy Maker. Then ye may meet with each of these, thy problems; and *their* problems will become not only thy problems in a material way but ye all may lay them at the foot of the Throne of Grace. For His mercies are sufficient unto those that will put their trust in Him. *This* approach, and ye will know Him. Has the Father changed? Has the promise faltered? For He has promised to meet *all* after the pattern in the mount. What is this? That thou knowest well; for it was given that ye "Draw nigh unto me," and that the thoughts in the mind—as the desires in the heart—be spiritualized in thine purpose towards thy *God*, towards thy God in thy fellow man. For no man may hurt thee, wilt thou but know thy soul is of God. For what may be done to the body passeth away, but that which is a mark upon the soul endureth. Then, what art thou doing with *thy* soul as toward thy Maker?

(Q) Just what should be my attitude?

(A) That as thou wouldst have them have toward thee if the conditions and the positions were reversed. Put thyself in the place of each. What would thou have them do to thee? That should be *thy* attitude toward them. But in the light that each soul is the image of thy God; for the *soul* was made in the image, *not* the physical body.

(Q) What can I do to get some happiness in the world?

(A) Would thou be happy? Then make someone else happy! Would thou be that thou would seek? *That* ye find! Knock and it shall be opened. Cry aloud and all stand in awe; but the still small voice from within brings joy and peace—as ye do it unto others.

(Q) Please advise me and give me such guidance necessary to protect my present investments, and warnings to prevent possible errors in the future.

(A) Again would we give the greater basis that that which may be given as warning that this will rise and that will fall. God ever gives the increase. For, when the purposes in life—and the desires of the heart and the mind, soul and body—are made in accord, "all these things shall be added unto you." What was the variation in that Abraham gave from the rest of the world? That the Lord thy God is One? The Lord thy God is *one* in thee! Thy mind, thy soul, thy body being one in purpose, in aim, in desire, He will lead thee in the ways that He will open—even the oneness of heaven, to pour into thine understanding that which will bring the greatest development of thy soul. Put not thy trust in things that are of the earth earthy, but rather in the promises that are sure, that He gives that necessary day by day; and as to whether ye shall sell or invest, whether ye shall trade or whether ye shall gather more and more, this will be shown thee—for thou art sensitive in thine self! Ye have received them rather as hunches, but "Inasmuch as ye do it unto the least, ye do it unto me." And He will show thee the way.

790-1

(Q) What studies would you recommend for my spiritual development?

(A) First the New Testament, especially as related to John and Revelation; then those things that are of the spiritual import that make for the abilities of the entity to receive through its own intuitive influences the greater awakening. For, as seen in the activities of the entity through its research, through its activities, in its study, there are the abilities within each and every entity to not only recall but to experience that through which it has passed, as well as that to which it may attain in the individual experience. For these are the promises that are set in the spiritual import of self.

Do that.

3744-3

(Q) From what source does this body EC derive its information?

(A) The information as given or obtained from this body is gathered from the sources from which the suggestion may derive its information.

In this state the conscious mind becomes subjugated to the subconscious, superconscious or soul mind; and may and does communicate with like minds, and the subconscious or soul force becomes universal. From any subconscious mind information may be obtained, either from this plane or from the impressions as left by the individuals that have gone on before, as we see a mirror reflecting direct that which is before it. It is not the object itself, but that reflected, as in this: The suggestion that reaches through to the subconscious or soul, in this state, gathers information from that as reflected from what has been or is called real or material, whether of the material body or of the physical forces, and just as the mirror may be waved or bended to reflect in an obtuse manner, so that suggestion to the soul forces may bend the reflection of that given; yet within, the image itself is what is reflected and not that of some other.

Through the forces of the soul, through the mind of others as presented, or that have gone on before; through the subjugation of the physical forces in this manner, the body obtains the information.

900-59

(Q) It was first given, Soul and Spirit are "forces." Then in illustrating force as given: "That which is the Spirit of any object, animate or inanimate." Explain "Spirit of an object."

(A) Spirit in an animate object, that giving same life, whether of of that with the attributes of the one, two, three or fourth dimension of same. Spirit in an inanimate object being then that relation as given to same by the mental intelligence of the individual, or person, or thing, giving it a spirit force. As this would be illustrated: To the animal who becomes accustomed to being hitched to a certain post, that post has the spirit for the animal by the mental abilities of the animal's association with same. To man, the stone occupying the place in altar may be of same quarry, of the same strata, of the one occupying the step to the building. The position of one in altar occupying the spirit of reverence. The one on step occupying the position as of one to reach same. Hence the degrees of the relation as is carried in the inanimate conditions. When this relation then is considered, we see how the evolution, or revelation of same comes to the spirit of the herb, of the fly, of the beast, of the companion. Hence how each occupy their position, or as has been better illustrated in the words as were given, "All flesh is not of one flesh. There are the flesh of animal, of bird, of fishes, of men. There are bodies celestial, bodies terrestrial. The glory of one differs in the glory of another, but because one occupies the exalted position would one do away with that of the uncomely parts? for that which is the uncomely becomes the more comely in its action and self when directed in its proper channel and sphere." Hence we find all occupying then the spirit of that acquired by its position, its relation to other conditions, whether of the animate or inanimate condition and position.

(Q) What is meant by: "Mental and Physical with relative forces connecting the soul force and unbalancing of the truth may perform on the soul forces that which brings abnormal results to physical and soul matter"?

(A) Just as has been given in how truth is obtained in the normal or consciousness, may be perverted by the outlook of the individual obtaining same, of as the spirit may view the truth as obtained from a source questionable to the relation of the individual to such conditions. That is, as this: One brought up in the condition of religious liberty does not comprehend a lesson as obtained from one of a faith that would bind the body and the moral and mental forces of an individual, the same as one would understand such lesson brought up in that faith, or as would be seen in this: All religious faiths have their element of truth. Would be hard for the Christian faith to understand the lesson of the Mohammedan faith, and each may gain the lesson to its own destruction, for the relation of each truth bears its relativity of force to the developing of the entity. Then we return to the same premise. What may be viewed by the entity in that plane of the two square, or two fold, or two quantity life, cannot understand the vision of one having reached the threefold or three quantity life.

900-68

(Q) The dream as had on Tuesday night, April 28th, or early morning of Wednesday, April 29th, 1925, at home in bed, was as follows: "I was riding horseback and held the horse by a short rein, which when I pulled to steady the horse caused the beast to rear on his hind legs and nearly dismount me. As I gave the horse his head I seemed to ride easier—more smoothly. Then something happened—I yanked back the reins and was nearly completely thrown off, but finally managed to steady myself and again giving the horse his head rode on in a smoother fashion."

(A) This as we find, with the study of the spiritual elements and environments of the entity [900], will be understandable to the mind of the entity better in the study of those verses in the [Book of] Revelation, pertaining to Horse and Rider, for as has ever been in Urim, the Horse and Rider [represent] the messenger for the waiting world, and the halts and checks those of the indecisions in the entities themselves and is but the warning as the forces may be manifest through the entity, and the entity then should so labor and study to show self approved as the Messenger, the Representative of the Master. In that the Father chooses to use this channel for His representative in the earth at this time, then heed those forces that would prepare the entity for that way in which he may serve his Lord and Redeemer. Just as was chosen in the days of old, when the law-giver [Moses] received those instructions in the highest tribunal in physical learning and thus prepared to give same to the Chosen People through the dictates of the inner communions with the God within, just so *this entity* has been prepared through training in physical planes, and is being drawn out from those conditions wherein the cry may be raised, "Can any good thing come from the Street? Can any force give spiritual understanding that seeks to make monies in such channels?" The Father has chosen the weak things in life to confound the wise. Then *be thou wise* in thine day, and as through the ages thou hast been prepared, be that messenger that will carry on the wings of morn the message to the peoples seeking the understanding, the co-relation [correlation] of the Father with His peoples.

1261-1

In this again, *stand fast* for that as is thy ideal. For choose today. For there is set before thee good and evil, life and death; choose thou. For the spirit of truth maketh alive. Fear, doubt, condemnation, bringeth doubt, illness, fear, and then dissolution (disillusion?); and the hill to be climbed again.

1598-1

(Q) I've been investigating psychic phenomena. Should I write a book about this, in spite of the prejudices in this field? and should I study or try to develop these gifts myself?

(A) This subject is one that is oft misunderstood, and oft misinterpreted. *Psychic* is of the soul, and not *merely* the experience.

It is well to study same, it is well to experience same; but in those manners, in those ways that are in keeping with Him who is thy Ideal! Not, then, by the communion with those *only* of disincarnate entities—or souls! but rather with that direction which comes from within. For how has He given? "Destroy this temple and in three days I will raise it again."

Then thy body is indeed the temple of the living God. *There* He has promised to meet thee, to commune with thee. *There* is the psychic development, the psychic phenomena that ye seek!

For as ye read, as ye study, only that which answers to that being sought within thine *own* self answers to thy prayer, to thy seeking.

Then, it is well to write about these. For the book of Books *is* the greater source of psychic experiences of individuals, and as to *what* they did *about* such! even from Adam to John—or from Genesis to Revelation. These are living examples that are thine. For each day is thy Eden; yea, each evening is the call, "Whosoever *will* let him come and take of the water of life freely."

Study in that manner, and in those that seek for self-effacement—well; but those that seek self-glory, never!

2787-1

Thy body is indeed the temple of the living God. There He hath promised to meet thee. There He does commune with those that seek within the holy of holies.

Then, the physical body is a pattern of the universal consciousness. While it may be as in shadow, if it is interpreted properly, the body is that which interprets The Revelation, that which interprets as to *why* there was the choosing of twelve disciples, twelve tribes.

This, then, is also as the sun, the moon, the planets. All of these have an influence. Rather are all such, however, influenced by the activity of the individual.

For, as has been indicated, man was made in the image of God. Thus he was given the injunction, "Be fruitful, multiply; but subdue the earth."

All things are subject unto thy will. So also the will of the individual entity to know God is subject to the choice that is made in the activity of the impulses that arise.

2879-1

EC: Yes, we have the entity here, [2879].

In giving for this entity a mental and spiritual reading, it is well that the premise be given from which such information is drawn.

We accept the fact that there is the one God and that Jesus the Christ is His manifested messenger in the earth; and that the gift of the Holy Spirit by and through the Christ is ever to be the comforter to those who seek to know the Lord, the Father-God, through Him.

Through the revelations of holy men—as recorded in the Bible—there have been those things oft in man's experience that have caused some confusion, in man's attempt to apply such precepts as indicated there in the daily relationships.

We find that such confusions arise primarily from man's inability to coordinate in his personal experience those precepts that are related to the various phases of man's consciousness in the material plane.

Man finds himself a body, a mind, a soul. The body is self-evident. The mind also is at times understood. The soul or the spiritual portion is hoped for, and one may only discern same from a spiritual consciousness.

The body, the mind and the soul are as the Father, the Son and the Holy Spirit—just as infinity in its expression to the finite mind is expressed in time, space and patience. These are exercised in the consciousness, and yet only the spiritually discerning may interpret. *Spiritually* there becomes no time or space, for they—like the Father—are one. But in man's application they become as one, in the Father, the Son and the Holy Spirit.

Thus in man's interpretation of God's revelation to man through the written word, there becomes confusion at times, and it does not always seem to fit or coordinate from a rational point of reasoning.

Yet man discerns, as within himself, that his body has its attributes, its functionings, its phases of expression. It grows in physical, in the mental, and in its ability of spiritual discernment, through the application of the truths, the tenets, the laws of the spirit, of the mind, and of the body.

There may be, then, definite interpretation. These are not all the laws, to be sure. For, as the body, there are many organs, many functionings. Yet if there is a coordination of these, there is the physical, mental and spiritual discernment of that the body-entity experiences.

In the discerning, then, of the laws—these become one in Him. The first is then as He gave—"Thou shalt love the Lord thy God with all thy body, thy mind, thy soul; thy neighbor as thyself." This, then, is all-inclusive, yet may be better discerned in the study and the application of the tenets set in the thirtieth (30th) of Deuteronomy by the lawgiver in his admonition, in his summing up of the laws, the ordinances that had been indicated for a peculiar people, set aside for a purpose—as a channel through which there might be the discerning of the spirit made manifest in flesh.

Hence it is reminding man that today, now, every day, there is set before him good and evil, life and death. Man does not find other than that answer outside himself as expressed in that spiritual discernment, "My spirit beareth witness with thy spirit."

Thus, as the lawgiver interpreted, "Lo, He is within thee." Man's discerning of that he would worship, then, is within self; how that he, the individual entity, makes manifest in his dealings daily with his fellow men that God is, and that the individual entity is—in body, in mind, in soul—a witness of such; and thus he loveth, he treateth his brother as himself.

Such an admonition has in man's interpretation oft put God, the mighty, the Lord, as far away. And yet he recognizes, if he accepts this admonition of the lawgiver, that He is within self.

This is more clearly demonstrated and interpreted in the words of the Master Himself—"In my Father's house are many mansions—"—many consciousnesses, many stages of enfoldment, of unfoldment, of blessings, of sources. And yet God has not willed that any soul should perish, but has with every temptation, every trial, prepared a way of escape—or a way to meet same; which is indicated here by the Creator, the Maker of heaven and earth and all that in them be.

Thus as He declares, "Behold I stand continuously before the door of thy consciousness, of thine own mansion. For thy body is indeed the temple of the living God." And there He has promised to meet thee. There ye make ready. There ye entertain. There ye meditate upon those influences, those choices ye make day by day.

He, that Christ-Consciousness, is that first spoken of in the beginning when God said, "Let there be light, and there was light." And that is the light manifested in the Christ. First it became physically conscious in Adam. And as in Adam we all die, so in the last Adam—Jesus, becoming the Christ—we are all made alive. Not unto that as of one, then. For we each meet our own selves, even as He; though this did not become possible, practical in a world experience, until He, Jesus, became the Christ and made the way.

Thus He became the first of those that within self arose to righteousness. Thus may we, as individuals—as we apply ourselves—become aware of that abiding presence as He promised—yea, as He maintained—"If I go away I will send the spirit of truth, the spirit of righteousness, and he shall *abide* with you. And I and the Father will come."

Seek ye then to walk with Him. That peace He giveth thee. Not as the world knoweth peace, but as His peace that openeth the door of understanding, of comprehension, of how God maketh peace with man through the law of love. For He *is* law. He is love. He taketh away not the law, but manifesteth love in that He fulfilled the law, in that He gave Himself for that edict, "In the day ye eat thereof, ye shall surely die."

Yet in the day that ye accept Him as thy sacrifice and *live* thyself according to His precepts, *ye* become reconciled—through Him—to the Father, and He—too—walketh and talketh with thee.

Study, then, to show thyself approved unto that as thy ideal.

As to the choices ye make—remember, as He gave, "Who made me a judge of my brother? Who is my brother? He that doeth the will of the Father."

What is the will? "Love one another, even as I have loved you."

3541-1

Just as in the activities in directing those associates about you, if ye become interested in others, others are interested in you! Are ye selfish in all your planning, no matter how you may cover it up with pretty words, if it is for yourself you are using the selfish spirit; then it becomes as the Frankenstein in thyself before it is through. You have experienced some such. You know what is meant. If you attempt to become active in selling to others, unless there is the same sincerity in that approach to selling—as if you were in the other individual's place and you present what you are selling in the spirit of cooperation—again it may turn upon thee and devour thy very self.

4083-1

In giving that as we find may be helpful for the entity, it will be for this entity well that there be given the sources or the reasons and the premises from and for which such information may be drawn.

In analyzing body, mind, soul, all phases of an entity's experience must be taken into consideration. In analyzing the mind and its reactions, oft individuals who would psychoanalyze or who would interpret the reactions that individual entities take, leave out those premises of soul, mind, body.

As we would give, an entity body-mind was first a soul before it entered into material consciousness. Individual entities become aware in a material world of the earth as a three-dimensional consciousness, having its concept or its analysis of good or of Creative Forces or God in a three-dimensional concept, God, the Father, the Son; the Christ the mind, the soul the first cause of an individual entity as it may become aware or conscious in a three-dimensional or material world.

Just so may the soul-entity become aware in the other dimensions, which is indicated when this entity tries to interpret the reactions of a physical and a mental being by its experiences in an unconscious or in a dream state.

Just as these are judgments of an entity outside of itself so is there often left out that which is the motivative influence.

For as you look at or analyze yourself, you find that you have a body-physical with all its attributes. It is in itself combined of flesh, and bone, nerve tissue. Yet the motivative forces through same are the connections in the central nervous system to which the organs of the central body respond. The central nerve and blood supply are in general heart, liver, lungs and kidneys and then there is the general sympathetic nervous system. These control the activities of the organs of the central nerves only in conjunction with or co-ordinating with the activities of the central nervous system or cerebrospinal system. Then there are those activities in the three-dimensional experience of the senses themselves, through which this sympathetic system receives its impressions. Again we have the three-dimensional idea or pattern. All of these in the body are dependent one upon another and the variations that cause the characteristics or the personality or individuality of each entity to vary according to the reaction that is brought into play in the mind. For remember, mind is ever the builder. Mind is represented in the Godhead as the Christ, the Son, the Way. The Father is represented in the earth as the body. The soul is all of those attributes that manifest in the body.

For if you will read the Book of Revelation with the idea of the body as the interpretation, you will understand yourself and learn to really analyze, psychoanalyze, mentally analyze others. But you will have to learn to apply it in self first. For the motivating force in each one of those patterns represented, is that which the individual entity entertains as the ideal. This is the motivating spirit, the motivating purpose. When it is out of attune, or not coordinating with the First Cause, there may not be the greater unfoldment. For, it is in self that it becomes out of attune. It loses its power or ability. It loses creative energy or its hold upon the First Cause that is the Creator or God.

Through what channels do these approach the activity? Through mind! Mind as a stream, not mind as purely physical or as wholly spiritual, but it is that which shapes, which forms, which controls, which directs, which builds, which acts upon. Just as the loss of the sense of sight may attune the touch to such degrees as for the soul to give, to see, to interpret. Just as the loss of hearing. Anyone may attune to the other senses in body.

So, will not the loss in self of the ideal in one direction make for greater attunement in another direction, or for the greater stumblingstone? For individuals who have lost any of the senses as of touch, sight, feeling or what not, and condemn, become, as it were, dependent upon a confusion, a disillusionment, or they become a leech upon others who would find or show the way.

So in the activities of an individual entity, in mind or the mental and spiritual, we find that the mental and spiritual must be in accord with that First Cause in order that it may bring into the material consciousness that which is in accord with the divine purpose. For no soul enters consciousness perchance. For it is indeed true that each entity, each soul, enters into consciousness by and through the grace of the Creator. Compare it with the activity in self: A thought enters the mind. You either entertain it or you discard it. If you discard it, it has little or no effect and yet because you discard it doesn't make or cause the thought to be less productive had it been entertained.

So, as in the self, whether the individual entity or soul entertains its relationship to the Creative Forces or not, the relationship is still existent or possible. For indeed in Him, the Father-God, ye move and have thy being. Act like it! Don't act like ye think ye are a God! Ye may become such, but when ye do ye think not of thyself. For what is the pattern? He thought it not robbery to make Himself equal with God, but He acted like it in the earth. He made Himself of no estate that you, through His grace, through His mercy, through His sacrifice might have an advocate with that First Cause, God; that first principle, spirit.

What are you doing about it? In thine own self ye will find that it is thine self. Selfishness is the basic sin and the soul that sins shall die. What are you going to do about it? His life is offered rather that ye may apply the principles of truth, patience, longsuffering, brotherly love, kindness, gentleness. For if ye would be forgiven, ye must forgive. These are unchangeable laws. Thy body, thyself is the temple of the living God. That is all the God ye may know, that which ye apply in thy relationship to thy fellow man. For the manner in which ye (as an individual entity, a body, a mind, a soul) treat thy fellow man is the manner in which ye treat thy Maker. Remember that what ye sow, thine own soul, thine own entity, thine own mind, thine own body must reap. Ye are already in eternity, thy soul has been since the beginning. What are ye doing about it? Are you using it?

Ready for questions.

(Q) What are the reasons that the entity so often has felt that he has been unable to make full use of his mental and emotional powers?

(A) Lack of finding its own ideal, or the setting of thine own self as that which must be gratified.

(Q) Why has his memory seemed poor—when he really has a very good memory—and he has seemed unable to develop original ideas?

(A) Have ye used thy memory as a creative thing? Only that which is creative grows. Thy memory, remember is as the Way has given: "if ye apply thyself, I will bring to thy remembrance all things since the foundation of the world." What is lacking? It is thine own coordinating of thy mind, thy body, thy soul-purpose to the first cause, the first principle, love. For God so loved the world that He gave His own, His own Son that ye, as an individual, might have access to the Father.

(Q) What has caused the emotional instability?

(A) Just as indicated.

(Q) Psychoanalytically speaking, what is the entity's emotional age?

(A) About two months.

(Q) Is there an Oedipus complex in the entity's psychology?

(A) Read rather that as has been given. Ye are looking for the material. Clean out thy temple. Open it to the powers that are thine. For ye realize, or should, that ye are conscious, that the Father-God hath need of thee.

(Q) Is there some emotional reason for the entity's frequent "clearing" of his throat?

(A) Read that indicated to thee as to how there is need for the perfect unison between Father, Son and Holy Spirit. There must be perfect unison between body, mind and soul, if the physical would be in accord. As ye know, there must be perfect accord between the central nervous system, the sympathetic nervous system and the sensory nervous system if there would be perfect accord. It's a wonder you don't vomit more often than you do!

(Q) What are the reasons that the entity has not found happiness in his marriage?

(A) Ye are seeking the gratification of thyself. Suppose God, suppose Christ had done that same for Himself, where would you be?

(Q) Psychoanalytically speaking, does the entity have a split personality?

(A) It has a split desire rather than personality. The individuality lacks stability. With the individuality being stabilized in an ideal that takes hold upon the infinite, the possibilities of the entity are unlimited, but self gets in the way and becomes the stumblingblock.

(Q) To what extent have childhood home influences incapacitated the entity for a normal, happy marriage?

(A) Just as much as the individual entity lets it have. For when ye were

a child, ye thought as a child, but when ye became a man ye should have
put away childish things and not blamed others for same. For each soul is
an entity, body, mind, soul. If it will use its will, in applying the fruits of
the spirit to those conditions about it, the entity may attune itself to the
infinite. If it attempts to abuse such, the entity pays the price. Just as ye may
see about thee. As a tree grows you may bear it and use it and grind it in
the shape desired. So may an individual entity, as it is trained, grow. It has
those complexes but it also has its own individuality, and apple trees don't
produce peaches, neither does a son of Satan produce saints. But ye are the
son of the Almighty, the Creative Forces, even as Satan. Whose side are you
on? Ye alone can determine! Will ye?

(Q) Have any adolescent experiences incapacitated the entity for a normal, happy marriage?

(A) Read what has been given. All of thy problems are here within self.
Know, as has been indicated, all of the world (as ever has been, as ever will
be) is represented in thee, thine own self. Look within. There ye will find
the answer to every problem. Ye cannot ask a question that ye cannot answer
within thine own self, if or when ye attune thyself to the infinite. Thy soul is
eternal, thy soul-mind is eternal. Will ye as a child of the Most High listen
to the voice within? For He has promised to meet thee within thyself if and
when you attune to that. How? By the manner in which ye treat thy wife,
the manner in which ye treat thy friend, the manner in which ye treat thy
enemy. For the Lord, thy God is not mocked and thy troubles arise within
thyself. Attune thyself to the God within. Begin with that which is best
expressed in Deuteronomy 30 and in Exodus 19:5. There you may begin
and you will find the answer if you will make of thyself not a slave, no, but
one in accord with His will. For the knowledge of God, the Father is that
which indeed sets thee free.

5322-1

Then the whole disturbance or the whole suggested activity, not as a
disturbance, save that it disturbs the entity, is that there must be the choice
of ideals, spiritually, mentally, materially. These should not be merely as
tenets that you will think about or that you would copy from a prayer book
or even from the Book itself, the Bible. But rather as the result of the entity
"thinking same through" but referring to at least ten promises of the Lord

and Master. Find these, yes. What is the first that would come to you of a promise? "Come unto me, all that are weak and heavy laden, and I will give you rest." Does this to you mean the promise, or something that a good man said and "I hope I'll understand it some day"? Isn't it a direct challenge to yourself in some of the moods in which you find yourself? Isn't it a scientific fact that He is the savior of the world? Or have ye thought of it in that manner? It is true. For from the very first of the Old Testament to the very last even of Revelation, He is not merely the subject of the book, He is the author in the greater part, having given to man the mind and the purpose for its having been put in print. For it is in Him ye live and move and have thy being and as He gave, "Search ye the scriptures, for they be they that testify of me, and in them ye *think* ye have eternal life."

If ye know Him, ye know that in Him ye have eternal life. For He is the beginning and the end of all things.

So, as the entity analyzes its own purposes in the earth, as it determines what its ideals are, know they must ever be as beginning and ending in Him. But, as to how to make application of same, do not merely say "I'll take this from this prayer book, this from another book or this quotation from the Bible," but draw the line around each of these: Physical, Mental and Spiritual, and write under each heading the ideals. Write the sort of mother ye should be to your boy, or what sort of a wife would be the ideal one. These are material, not mental even. For these are physical things. What is thy son's concept of thee? What is thy concept of thy Lord thy God? These do, and ye will make life more worthwhile.

5749-14

(Q) Should the Christ-Consciousness be described as the awareness within each soul, imprinted in pattern on the mind and waiting to be awakened by the will, of the soul's oneness with God?

(A) Correct. That's the idea exactly!

1210-1

For to the entity also we would give, *know* that *will* supersedes those influences that may express themselves even as material desires; and certainly

supersedes those influences that may be had from sojourns in the earth. For
it is true that that influence, that force which is of the Creative Force, hath
not willed that a soul should become so overburdened, so discouraged, so
disheartened as not to be given hope for its regeneration, but hath prepared
the means, the ways of escape. Not from self but in the *aid* in self, manifested
in *will*. For he that wills to do sets in motion those influences that have in
the experience of the entity in the present sojourn brought about activity
from the various realms of development. Not a wise choice always taken by
the entity in the present, but *know* that thou hast in thine inner self in thine
temple, in thine tabernacle within, the advocate with that Creative Force
that may give those influences. For he that maketh the will one *with* those
Creative Forces or constructive influences may build and *build* and *build!*

877-27

Not that the light, then, is other than to bring encouragement. And ye
may *indeed* say, then, even as they, "Let us make here a tabernacle." What
indeed is thy tabernacle? It is thy body, thy mind, thy soul! Present them,
therefore, as things holy, acceptable unto Him who *is* the Giver of all good
and perfect gifts!

He *is* giving Himself in power to those who, as many as use that they
have in hand to the *glory* of Him who thought it not robbery to be equal
with God yet made Himself of *no* estate that He might enter into the holy
of holies with thee in thy *own* tabernacle!

Study then to show thyself approved unto God, a workman not ashamed;
keeping self from condemnation by not condemning thy neighbor yet showing a more excellent way by the very glory of the Lord in thy dealings with
thy fellow man day by day!

338-4

(Q) Please explain the meaning of "even as it was given as to when the
tabernacle was to be builded—or when it was shown even as in the Master's
directing when the day when each should stand as a messenger," given in a
previous reading.

(A) As has been indicated, each—or this soul makes the application personal. In the expressions as shown in the tabernacle, in the orders as given for its construction—the size, the shape, the measurements, the figures above the holy of holies, the directions of the colors as indicated for the hangings, the manner in which each board was to be set, the manner in which each skin was to be used or dyed—these were not only for the physical protection but for the expressions that would come in the experience of individuals that took the service or the worship there as being a thing within themselves. Hence became material, emblematical, and the experience of the application of same in the worship there became as a living thing in the experience of the individuals.

Now the expression as given by Him, the Maker, the Creator of the earth and all therein, was "the day arrives when not in this mountain nor in this temple, but in the hearts of men and women everywhere, is that service, that manner, that means of expression." [John 4:21]

So as it has been given for the entity in its depicting of those expressions of things in life, those expressions of man's obligations and duties, those expressions that may hold before the beholder that ideal, that idea of the fruits of the spirit—as the entity then labors in its giving of itself in expression, it becomes even as those things given by the pattern in the mount as well as the pattern given by the Master that they become as *living* experiences, not only in the activities of the individuals but create that atmosphere, that vibration, that environment for the beholder of those things that *are* expressions of the fruits of the spirit as manifested things in their lives and experiences, see?

987-4

He has promised to meet thee within the temple of thine own body. For as has been given, thy body is the temple of the living God; a tabernacle, yea, for thy soul. And in the holy of holies within thine own consciousness He may walk and talk with thee.

How? How?

Is it the bringing of sacrifice? Is it the burning of incense? Is it the making of thyself of no estate?

Rather is it that ye *purpose!* For the try, the purpose of thine inner self, to *him* is the righteousness. For He hath known all the vicissitudes of the earthly experience. He hath walked through the valley of the shadow of death. He hath seen the temptations of man from every phase that may come into thine own experience; and, yea, He hath given thee, "If ye will love me, believing I am able, I will deliver thee from that which so easily besets thee at *any* experience."

And it is thus that He stands; not as a Lord but as thy Brother, as thy Savior; that ye may know indeed the truth that gentleness, kindness, patience, brotherly love, beget—in thy heart of hearts, with Him—that peace, that harmony. Not as the world knoweth peace but as He gave: "That peace I give you; that ye may know that thy spirit, yea thy soul, beareth witness with me that ye are mine—I am thine," even as the Father, the Son, the Holy Spirit.

Even so may thy soul, thy mind, thy body, become aware of that which renews the hope, the faith, the patience within thee.

And until ye show forth in His love that patience, ye cannot become aware of thy relationship with Him. Even as He has given, in patience ye become aware of being that soul—that seeketh the Father's house that is within even thine own consciousness.

How? How, then, may ye approach the throne?

Turn thou within. As ye meditate, give forth in thine *own* words these thoughts:

"Father, God, Maker of heaven and earth! I am Thine—Thou art mine! As I claim that kinship with that holy love, keep Thou me in that consciousness of Thy presence abiding with me: that I may be that channel of blessings to others, that I may know Thy grace, Thy mercy, Thy love—even as I show such to my fellow man!"

And ye may be very sure the answer comes within.

Thus, as ye apply—the answer comes. Not—by applying—do we mean a separation from the world. For even as He, ye are *in* the world but not *of* the world. But putting away the worldly things ye take hold upon the spiritual things, knowing that the worldly are but the shadows of the real.

And thus, as ye come into the light of His countenance, it maketh thy heart glad in the consciousness of *"I am Thine—Thou art mine."*

3744-5

(Q) Where does the soul come from, and how does it enter the physical body?

(A) It is already there. "And He breathed into him the breath of life, and he became a living soul," as the breath, the ether from the forces as come into the body of the human when born breathes the breath of life, as it becomes a living soul, provided it has reached that developing in the creation where the soul may enter and find the lodging place.

All souls were created in the beginning, and are finding their way back to whence they came.

281-3

(Q) Being named and called to be a healer, in what way and manner will I be able to heal?

(A) In the manner that, as those are *called,* the self will be able to guard and guide as it is accomplished. Even as self chose to be the one as looked after detail, so in this be thou the one as looks after the *little* things, that will make it possible for the group to *be* healers *to* those that seek. As *is* brought *to* self that necessary for the *accomplishing of* this, so does *healing* arise. Here, let's analyze healing for the moment, to those that must consciously—as this body—see and reason, see a material demonstration, *occasionally* at least! Each atomic force of a physical body is made up of its units of positive and negative forces, that brings it into a *material* plane. These are of the ether, or atomic forces, being electrical in nature as they enter into a material basis, or become *matter* in its ability to take on or throw off. So, as a *group* may raise the atomic vibrations that make for those positive forces as bring divine forces in action into a material plane, those that are destructive are broken down by the raising of that vibration! That's *material,* see? This is *done* through *creative* Forces, which are God in manifestation! Hence, as self brings those *little* things necessary, as each is found to be necessary, for position, posture, time, period, place, name, understanding, *study* each, and assist each in their respective sphere. So does the *entity become* the healer.

281-27

(Q) During a recent group meditation when we asked for a blessing from the Lord I felt a pulsation on the top of my head; it was like a pulsation of the heart. Please explain.

(A) Read just that as has been given, respecting the emotions going through the system (as for [585]), and we will find these are *one*. For there is, as given, the contact between the spiritual emotions and the bodily activity. And these are as the experiences then, the sources arising to, throughout the body, the ability for the giving through the single eye of service, the single eye's expression in the glandular forces in the brain itself, to *send out!* Rather know, as the knowledge of the material conveniences is that messages of others from far or near may be wafted upon the ether so as to become a materialization in thine own home, so in the wafting of those influences or emotions that arise in such experience—send them *out! He*, God, bringeth the contact *where needed!*

195-70

EC: Yes, we have the body, the enquiring mind, [195], and the article as written by this body as regards Positive and Negative Force. In making suggestions for the better presentation of such data in such an article, this should be kept in mind—that these may be made either in answer *to* that written or in keeping *with* that written; or, to put in *different* words, may be answered in a positive or a negative manner, even as the article; or it may be given as in keeping with, and presenting in, a different angle. Ready for questions.

(Q) Page 2—lines 9 to 12. ["The positive may be considered as the active forces in their activity and the negative as those tending to keep the balance."] Please expand on this and give better explanation of Positive and Negative Force.

(A) This [is] as *good* an explanation as may be given, other than illustrating same; for it *is* a positive or a *plain statement* as to the conditions as regarding relativity of force; for *positive* is the active and negative is passive, as illustrated by the article in its various phases. The statement we would *not* expand upon in *this* instance, for it (the statement) must react with the individual *development* of each individual who takes the time to become positive *or* negative to the statement, and as one responds to same may the activity of the statement be seen.

(Q) Page 3—lines 1 to 8—["Consider Gravity—This applies right here, there and everywhere. This, too, may be considered a negative force, for it tends to balance the positive forces. Gravitational forces are vibratory forces and might be defined as the centralization of vibratory 195-70 Page 2 forces ready to change into power by non-activity."] Is gravity a negative force? How could this be better explained here?

(A) Gravity in this *sense*—as explained in that, in the activity that becomes passive in its force—gravity becomes the negative force, see? even as is illustrated. Better illustration may be had in that of the Radio-Active Appliance, as [to] how one becomes positive, the other negative, dependent upon which way the cycle begins by the change in the active force by which one is applied to a body in the first place, see?

(Q) Page 3—lines 16 to 24—["With the assumption that their radial forces are thrown off this planet at or near Cancer and Capricorn, then it were possible when the vibrations of sun's rays at a certain deflection on passing through these emanating radial vibrations to set up a partial vacuum, thereby causing winds."] Is this correct?

(A) This correct.

(Q) Page 4—lines 6 to 13—["The one substance vibrates in different dynamic degrees, and sound, heat, light, electricity, are the effections of the one substance by specific degrees of the One Energy, and there is no difference between anything such as electricity and, say iron, save in rate of effection."] Is this correctly stated?

(A) Correctly stated.

(Q) Page 5—lines 5 to 20—["The heart in the human body may be compared to the sun of a solar system. Then by analogy the sun is the center of forces of the solar system. Similarly to the blood flowing from the heart through the arterial system, Force emerges from the sun drawn to the opposite polarity of the planets and in this outgoing flow it would be possible to develop magnetism, electricity, light, color, heat, sound, and lastly matter, in the order of lessening dynamic degrees of vibration. Matter then would be the offspring of energy and not the parent, as is often thought."] Is this correctly stated?

(A) Correctly stated, and just what happens in the human organism.

(Q) Page 5—lines 21 to 25—["It is more than probable that at the sun's surface there are many higher degrees of vibrations than are known or understood on this planet."] Is this correct?

(A) Correct.

(Q) Page 5—lines 27 to 31—["When this force, decreasing in vibrations to light and light waves, enter spectroscope, they will emerge as colors. Evidence of flames and metals 195-70 Page 3 on fire on sun and stars is in all probability due to etheric vibrations being broken into color by formation of natural spectroscope at the sun or satellite under observation."] Is this correct?

(A) This correct.

(Q) Page 6—lines 3 and 4—["As given above these radial emanations are negative forces."] Are radial forces negative forces?

(A) Not always are radial forces negative forces. Only when they become passive, or of being acted upon as gravitation, do they become negative forces—while they are emanating from the positive; else they would not be drawn to the earth's force, in *its* emanation with the positive rays—and they are positive rays. From the sun's emanation does it produce the heat, see? This is seen in a *better* application, in that the deflection from—and the direct rays *of*—the sun's emanation *to* the earth, *through* the various stages of its activity, brings summer, or the heat wave, or the moving *of* the various forms; for these acting *upon*—become negative, and then are *positive* in their action, though at times these, to be sure, become negative in their action; for each has its radial activity and is throwing *off,* as well as drawing *to.* Hence the various positions or conditions as is seen in sun, through the activity of the various forms of gas or metal, or those various conditions that seem to cause the various eruptions as apparent within the sun itself. It receives as well as throws off, is positive as well as negative, see? and only until it becomes in such a force that it is altogether negative, as the gravitation that holds in place—for when each are lost in their relative position, these then are thrown off, as was the moon from the earth, or as is the various satellites of the various planets, as *well* as the various effects out in space.

(Q) Page 6—lines 15 to 18—["Therefore, there could be in the solar system a dynamic reservoir or solar storage battery that would correspond to the lungs of a human system."] Is there a solar power reservoir corresponding to lungs of a human system?

(A) Solar power corresponding.

(Q) Page 7—lines 16 to 20—["Ether may be defined as the combination of a higher plane, leading us to metaphysics, to where every consideration of the atom finally leads one."] Is this statement concerning ether correct? Will you please give a better definition?

(A) There's no *better* definition! This is correct for, same as the statement of positive and negative forces as relating to gravitation, they act upon the individual's *development,* or individual's application of thought as applied *to* metaphysical condition or position as is occupied from 195-70 Page 4 within itself. Hence, as is seen, there are (This may be an illustration for this same condition) certain *characters* of disease that accentuate mental forces, or the metaphysical activity of a human body. There are others that so *dull* the senses as that they become onesided, or only passive, not positive; yet a *normal,* perfectly well and normal mind may be so active as to be considered by others in its activity as of being unbalanced, but only are they considered *peculiar.*

(Q) Page 8—lines 1 to 15—["A mechanical device might be constructed where a vacuum even excluding ether could be drawn and maintained, developing thereby a levitating force; this similar to that force which exerts pressure upward when air is pumped into a steel barrel while submerged below surface of a medium such as water. This levitating force will be utilized in many ways, particularly in so-called heavier than air ships, with the result that air navigation will be possible without the use of wings or gas."] Is this correct?

(A) This correct when the elements must be made so condensed in their form as to prevent the ether in its finer sense from being, or escaping through the various elements that are ordinarily used for creating of such vacuums. [195] will understand that! You don't get it, but [195] will! That is, the container—you can get it here—a container in which a vacuum may be made must be of such a *condensed* element as to prevent ether from going through the atomic forces of the element itself, as is seen in that of an electric bulb—this is *not* a vacuum, only a portion! To the finite mind this is *considered* as such, but were the same character—or these same conditions produced in a *different* way—*then* these may be made to *become* an element that would act in that way and manner, see? As is seen at present, helium becomes the greater usage in containers that may be made; yet these *themselves* (This is working from the opposite side, see?)—but were those gases, or those metals used that the supply of helium itself becomes the container *for* the vacuum itself, see? this condensed, see? into a metal form, *then* the vacuum may be made that would lift without being lifted, see?

(Q) Page 9—lines 12 to 16—["Pressure of metals on earth could possibly be accounted for by the breaking up of solar rays through formation of national spectroscopes during formation era of the planet earth."] Is this correct?

(A) This [is a] very good expression of that. Very good, and very well stated—that it may be possible, for it *is* very well stated.

(Q) Give suggestion as to how to improve on the article and how to better explain positive and negative aspects of force?

(A) This as is given is *very well* presented, and with the various comments as will come *from* such presentation, these 195-70 Page 5 will develop for the body-mind that necessary. Begin with that as is expressed here.

(Q) With motor as now laid out, embodying new leverages and gears with same pitch, will this work as designed?

(A) When balanced properly, it will work.

(Q) What argument would be most conclusive to prove that sun is not hot at surface?

(A) The breaking up of the rays, just as has been described, in that it takes *back* as well as gives off, being both positive and negative.

(Q) What could be given as cause for appearance of corona of sun?

(A) Just as has been explained, in that the forces as are thrown off by the various activities of the forces in all—that is, the planets, the stars, and those about it that are thrown off from same in their active principle, as draws to and throws off at the same time—these may be seen as the forces which produce or cause the various effects as seen.

(Q) What could be given as cause for appearance of solar flames and metal coloring in these so-called solar flames?

(A) *This* is as has been given.

262-49

(Q) [303]: What is the significance of my dream about two weeks ago, in which Mr. Cayce was watching clouds come together, expecting something unusual—and when they met, crystals came down like fireworks?

(A) This is a vision that will come to the body again, and with same will come an awakening as to the import of the vision.

294-17

Then the incoming of those in the flying machines and of other passage, we find these, as it were, must come from out of the clouds in different manners to earth for the establishing of such work and such phenomena.

440-10

(Q) Is the Radio-Active battery doing its work? (A) We have just given that it is creating a balance! It is an active force that prevents other reactions through the creating of a balance in the circulation. Doing its work. Keep these up, as we have outlined. We will find the results, if the body will keep its feet on the ground—but keep your head in the clouds also!

585-10

On the left of this figure [on life seal] indicate the sign of Mercury, in green and gold; while the manner of activity would be depicted in Leo—four in number—small and black—these above and below and upon each side.

1877-2

(Q) Is there any way in which the entity at this time could serve her Father-God, as she has an intense desire to do so?

(A) As indicated—it is not by might, nor by some great deed (as the entity saw illustrated in that experience), nor by something that may be spoken of by others, but as He has given so oft, it is here a little, there a little, line upon line, precept upon precept; *sowing* the fruits of the spirit, *leaving* the fruition of same to God!

So oft do individuals stumble over their own abilities, because of not seeing, not experiencing, great revolutions because of their attempts. Remember, as it was told to those of old, as it was told to *thee* by those who answered when ye beheld Him enter the glory of the clouds, the sky—"Think not He has left thee, for His promise has been, Lo, I am with thee always, even unto the end of the world."

So—all who open their hearts—all who keep their purpose in Him, are as under the protecting wing of that promise.

Faint not—but keep the faith.

10

THE TEXT OF THE REVELATION
WORLD ENGLISH BIBLE
(WEB) TRANSLATION

Author's Note: The World English Bible (WEB) translation is the latest in many attempts to keep the Scriptures alive for modern readers. In its attempt to convey the Bible in modern English, the WEB has held as closely as possible to words and literal meanings of the original texts. The creators of this translation placed their translation on the Internet and opened it to the world for commentary, criticism, suggestions, and changes. I have found it to be excellent. You will notice that it is in modern sentence and paragraph format, but the superscript verse numbers are maintained for easy cross-referencing. You will also notice that the classic Revelation word *church* has been replaced by *assembly,* which is a good English word for the original Greek *ekkleio,* which literally means *a calling out* so as to meet together, and, therefore, a body of the meeters, the assembly, or congregation. Overall, it is a good translation and has the added benefit of being freely in the public domain—the translators retained no copyrights and wanted no royalties for its use:

^{1:1}This is the Revelation of Jesus Christ, which God gave him to show to his servants the things which must happen soon, which he sent and made known by his angel to his servant, John, ^{1:2}who testified to God's word, and of the testimony of Jesus Christ, about everything that he saw.

^{1:3}Blessed is he who reads and those who hear the words of the prophecy, and keep the things that are written in it, for the time is at hand.

^{1:4}John, to the seven assemblies [churches] that are in Asia: Grace to you and peace, from God, who is and who was and who is to come; and from the seven Spirits who are before his throne; ^{1:5}and from Jesus Christ, the faithful witness, the firstborn of the dead, and the ruler of the kings of the earth. To him who loves us, and washed us from our sins by his blood; ^{1:6}and he made us to be a kingdom, priests to his God and Father; to him be the glory and the dominion forever and ever. Amen.

^{1:7}Behold, he is coming with the clouds, and every eye will see him, including those who pierced him. All the tribes of the earth will mourn over him. Even so, Amen. ^{1:8}"I am the Alpha and the Omega," says the Lord God, "who is and who was and who is to come, the Almighty."

^{1:9}I John, your brother and partner with you in oppression, kingdom, and perseverance in Christ Jesus, was on the isle that is called Patmos because of God's Word and the testimony of Jesus Christ. ^{1:10}I was in the Spirit on the Lord's day, and I heard behind me a loud voice, like a trumpet ^{1:11}saying, "What you see, write in a book and send to the seven assemblies: to Ephesus, Smyrna, Pergamum, Thyatira, Sardis, Philadelphia, and to Laodicea."

^{1:12}I turned to see the voice that spoke with me. Having turned, I saw seven golden lampstands.

^{1:13}And among the lampstands was one like a son of man, clothed with a robe reaching down to his feet, and with a golden sash around his chest. ^{1:14}His head and his hair were white as white wool, like snow. His eyes were like a flame of fire. ^{1:15}His feet were like burnished brass, as if it had been refined in a furnace. His voice was like the voice of many waters. ^{1:16}He had seven stars in his right hand. Out of his mouth proceeded a sharp two-edged sword. His face was like the sun shining at its brightest. ^{1:17}When I saw him, I fell at his feet like a dead man.

He laid his right hand on me, saying, "Don't be afraid. I am the first and the last, ^{1:18}and the Living one. I was dead, and behold, I am alive forevermore. Amen. I have the keys of Death and of Hades.

^{1:19}Write therefore the things which you have seen, and the things which are, and the things which will happen hereafter; ^{1:20}the mystery of the seven

stars which you saw in my right hand, and the seven golden lampstands. The seven stars are the angels of the seven assemblies. The seven lampstands are seven assemblies.

²:¹To the angel of the assembly in Ephesus write:

"He who holds the seven stars in his right hand, he who walks among the seven golden lampstands says these things:

²:²"I know your works, and your toil and perseverance, and that you can't tolerate evil men, and have tested those who call themselves apostles, and they are not, and found them false. ²:³You have perseverance and have endured for my name's sake, and have not grown weary. ²:⁴But I have this against you, that you left your first love. ²:⁵Remember therefore from where you have fallen, and repent and do the first works; or else I am coming to you swiftly, and will move your lampstand out of its place, unless you repent. ²:⁶But this you have, that you hate the works of the Nicolaitans, which I also hate. ²:⁷He who has an ear, let him hear what the Spirit says to the assemblies. To him who overcomes I will give to eat of the tree of life, which is in the Paradise of my God.

²:⁸"To the angel of the assembly in Smyrna write:

"The first and the last, who was dead, and has come to life says these things:

²:⁹"I know your works, oppression, and your poverty (but you are rich), and the blasphemy of those who say they are Jews, and they are not, but are a synagogue of Satan. ²:¹⁰Don't be afraid of the things which you are about to suffer. Behold, the devil is about to throw some of you into prison, that you may be tested; and you will have oppression for ten days. Be faithful to death, and I will give you the crown of life. ²:¹¹He who has an ear, let him hear what the Spirit says to the assemblies. He who overcomes won't be harmed by the second death.

²:¹²"To the angel of the assembly in Pergamum write:

"He who has the sharp two-edged sword says these things:

²:¹³"I know your works and where you dwell, where Satan's throne is. You hold firmly to my name, and didn't deny my faith in the days of Antipas my witness, my faithful one, who was killed among you, where Satan dwells. ²:¹⁴But I have a few things against you, because you have there some who hold the teaching of Balaam, who taught Balak to throw a stumbling block before the children of Israel, to eat things sacrificed to idols, and to commit sexual immorality. ²:¹⁵So you also have some who hold to the teaching of the Nicolaitans likewise. ²:¹⁶Repent therefore, or else I am coming to you

quickly, and I will make war against them with the sword of my mouth. [2:17]He who has an ear, let him hear what the Spirit says to the assemblies. To him who overcomes, to him will I give of the hidden manna, and I will give him a white stone, and on the stone a new name written, which no one knows but he who receives it.

[2:18]"To the angel of the assembly in Thyatira write:

"The Son of God, who has his eyes like a flame of fire, and his feet are like burnished brass, says these things:

[2:19]I know your works, your love, faith, service, patient endurance, and that your last works are more than the first. [2:20]But I have this against you, that you tolerate your woman, Jezebel, who calls herself a prophetess. She teaches and seduces my servants to commit sexual immorality, and to eat things sacrificed to idols. [2:21]I gave her time to repent, but she refuses to repent of her sexual immorality. [2:22]Behold, I will throw her into a bed, and those who commit adultery with her into great oppression, unless they repent of her works. [2:23]I will kill her children with Death, and all the assemblies will know that I am he who searches the minds and hearts. I will give to each one of you according to your deeds. [2:24]But to you I say, to the rest who are in Thyatira, as many as don't have this teaching, who don't know what some call 'the deep things of Satan,' to you I say, I am not putting any other burden on you. [2:25]Nevertheless, hold firmly that which you have, until I come. [2:26]He who overcomes, and he who keeps my works to the end, to him I will give authority over the nations. [2:27]He will rule them with a rod of iron, shattering them like clay pots; as I also have received of my Father: [2:28]and I will give him the morning star. [2:29]He who has an ear, let him hear what the Spirit says to the assemblies.

[3:1]"And to the angel of the assembly in Sardis write:

He who has the seven Spirits of God, and the seven stars says these things:

"I know your works, that you have a reputation of being alive, but you are dead. [3:2]Wake up, and keep the things that remain, which you were about to throw away, for I have found no works of yours perfected before my God. [3:3]Remember therefore how you have received and heard. Keep it, and repent. If therefore you won't watch, I will come as a thief, and you won't know what hour I will come upon you. [3:4]Nevertheless you have a few names in Sardis that did not defile their garments. They will walk with me in white, for they are worthy. [3:5]He who overcomes will be arrayed in white garments, and I will in no way blot his name out of the book of life, and I will confess his name before my Father, and before his angels. 3:6He who has an ear, let him hear what the Spirit says to the assemblies.

3:7"To the angel of the assembly in Philadelphia write:

"He who is holy, he who is true, he who has the key of David, he who opens and no one can shut, and who shuts and no one opens, says these things:

3:8"I know your works (behold, I have set before you an open door, which no one can shut), that you have a little power, and kept my word, and didn't deny my name. 3:9Behold, I give of the synagogue of Satan, of those who say they are Jews, and they are not, but lie. Behold, I will make them to come and worship before your feet, and to know that I have loved you. 3:10Because you kept my command to endure, I also will keep you from the hour of testing, which is to come on the whole world, to test those who dwell on the earth. 3:11I am coming quickly! Hold firmly that which you have, so that no one takes your crown. 3:12He who overcomes, I will make him a pillar in the temple of my God, and he will go out from there no more. I will write on him the name of my God, and the name of the city of my God, the new Jerusalem, which comes down out of heaven from my God, and my own new name. 3:13He who has an ear, let him hear what the Spirit says to the assemblies.

3:14"To the angel of the assembly in Laodicea write:

"The Amen, the Faithful and True Witness, the Head of God's creation, says these things: 3:15"I know your works, that you are neither cold nor hot. I wish you were cold or hot. 3:16So, because you are lukewarm, and neither hot nor cold, I will vomit you out of my mouth. 3:17Because you say, 'I am rich, and have gotten riches, and have need of nothing'; and don't know that you are the wretched one, miserable, poor, blind, and naked; 3:18I counsel you to buy from me gold refined by fire, that you may become rich; and white garments, that you may clothe yourself, and that the shame of your nakedness may not be revealed; and eye salve to anoint your eyes, that you may see. 3:19As many as I love, I reprove and chasten. Be zealous therefore, and repent. 3:20Behold, I stand at the door and knock. If anyone hears my voice and opens the door, I will come in to him, and will dine with him, and he with me. 3:21He who overcomes, I will give to him to sit down with me on my throne, as I also overcame, and sat down with my Father on his throne. 3:22He who has an ear, let him hear what the Spirit says to the assemblies."

4:1After these things I looked and saw a door opened in heaven, and the first voice that I heard, like a trumpet speaking with me, was one saying,

"Come up here, and I will show you the things which must happen after this."

⁴·²Immediately I was in the Spirit. Behold, there was a throne set in heaven, and one sitting on the throne ⁴·³that looked like a jasper stone and a sardius. There was a rainbow around the throne, like an emerald to look at. ⁴·⁴Around the throne were twenty-four thrones. On the thrones were twenty-four elders sitting, dressed in white garments, with crowns of gold on their heads. ⁴·⁵Out of the throne proceed lightnings, sounds, and thunders. There were seven lamps of fire burning before his throne, which are the seven Spirits of God. ⁴·⁶Before the throne was something like a sea of glass, similar to crystal. In the midst of the throne, and around the throne were four living creatures full of eyes before and behind. ⁴·⁷The first creature was like a lion, and the second creature like a calf, and the third creature had a face like a man, and the fourth was like a flying eagle. ⁴·⁸The four living creatures, each one of them having six wings, are full of eyes around about and within. They have no rest day and night, saying, Holy, holy, holy, holy, holy, holy, holy, holy, holy is the Lord God, the Almighty, who was and who is and who is to come!"

⁴·⁹When the living creatures give glory, honor, and thanks to him who sits on the throne, to him who lives forever and ever, ⁴·¹⁰the twenty-four elders fall down before him who sits on the throne, and worship him who lives forever and ever, and will throw their crowns before the throne, saying, ⁴·¹¹"Worthy are you, our Lord and God, the Holy One, to receive the glory, the honor, and the power, for you created all things, and because of your desire they existed, and were created!"

⁵·¹I saw, in the right hand of him who sat on the throne, a book written within and outside, sealed shut with seven seals. ⁵·²I saw a mighty angel proclaiming with a loud voice, "Who is worthy to open the book, and to break its seals?" ⁵·³No one in heaven above, or on the earth, or under the earth, was able to open the book, or to look in it. ⁵·⁴And I wept much, because no one was found worthy to open the book, or to look in it. ⁵·⁵One of the elders said to me, "Don't weep. Behold, the Lion who is of the tribe of Judah, the Root of David, has overcome; he who opens the book and its seven seals." ⁵·⁶I saw in the midst of the throne and of the four living creatures, and in the midst of the elders, a Lamb standing, as though it had been slain, having seven horns, and seven eyes, which are the seven Spirits of God, sent forth into all the earth. ⁵·⁷Then he came, and he took it out of the right hand of him who sat on the throne. ⁵·⁸Now when he had taken the book, the four

living creatures and the twenty-four elders fell down before the Lamb, each one having a harp, and golden bowls full of incense, which are the prayers of the saints. ^{5:9}They sang a new song, saying,

> "You are worthy to take the book,
> And to open its seals:
> For you were killed,
> And bought us for God with your blood,
> Out of every tribe, language, people, and nation,
> ^{5:10}And made them kings and priests to our God,
> And they reign on earth."

^{5:11}I saw, and I heard something like a voice of many angels around the throne, the living creatures, and the elders; and the number of them was ten thousands of ten thousands, and thousands of thousands; ^{5:12}saying with a loud voice, "Worthy is the Lamb who has been killed to receive the power, wealth, wisdom, strength, honor, glory, and blessing!"

^{5:13}I heard every created thing which is in heaven, on the earth, under the earth, on the sea, and everything in them, saying, "To him who sits on the throne, and to the Lamb be the blessing, the honor, the glory, and the dominion, forever and ever! Amen!"

^{5:14}The four living creatures said, "Amen!" The elders fell down and worshiped.

^{6:1}I saw that the Lamb opened one of the seven seals, and I heard one of the four living creatures saying, as with a voice of thunder, "Come and see!" ^{6:2}And behold, a white horse, and he who sat on it had a bow. A crown was given to him, and he came forth conquering, and to conquer.

^{6:3}When he opened the second seal, I heard the second living creature saying, "Come!" ^{6:4}Another came forth, a red horse. To him who sat on it was given power to take peace from the earth, and that they should kill one another. There was given to him a great sword.

^{6:5}When he opened the third seal, I heard the third living creature saying, "Come and see!" And behold, a black horse, and he who sat on it had a balance in his hand. ^{6:6}I heard a voice in the midst of the four living creatures saying, "A choenix[1] of wheat for a denarius, and three choenix of barley for a denarius! Don't damage the oil and the wine!"

^{6:7}When he opened the fourth seal, I heard the fourth living creature saying, "Come and see!" ^{6:8}And behold, a pale horse, and he who sat on it, his

name was Death. Hades followed with him. Authority over one fourth of the earth, to kill with the sword, with famine, with death, and by the wild animals of the earth was given to them.

⁶:⁹When he opened the fifth seal, I saw underneath the altar the souls of those who had been killed for the Word of God, and for the testimony of the Lamb which they had. ⁶:¹⁰They cried with a loud voice, saying, "How long, Master, the holy and true, until you judge and avenge our blood on those who dwell on the earth?" ⁶:¹¹A long white robe was given to each of them. They were told that they should rest yet for a while, until their fellow servants and their brothers, who would also be killed even as they were, should complete their course.

⁶:¹²I saw when he opened the sixth seal, and there was a great earthquake. The sun became black as sackcloth made of hair, and the whole moon became as blood. ⁶:¹³The stars of the sky fell to the earth, like a fig tree dropping its unripe figs when it is shaken by a great wind. ⁶:¹⁴The sky was removed like a scroll when it is rolled up. Every mountain and island were moved out of their places. ⁶:¹⁵The kings of the earth, the princes, the commanding officers, the rich, the strong, and every slave and freeperson, hid themselves in the caves and in the rocks of the mountains. ⁶:¹⁶They told the mountains and the rocks, "Fall on us, and hide us from the face of him who sits on the throne, and from the wrath of the Lamb, ⁶:¹⁷for the great day of his wrath has come; and who is able to stand?"

⁷:¹After this, I saw four angels standing at the four corners of the earth, holding the four winds of the earth, so that no wind would blow on the earth, or on the sea, or on any tree. ⁷:²I saw another angel ascend from the sunrise, having the seal of the living God. He cried with a loud voice to the four angels to whom it was given to harm the earth and the sea, ⁷:³saying, "Don't harm the earth, neither the sea, nor the trees, until we have sealed the bondservants of our God on their foreheads!" ⁷:⁴I heard the number of those who were sealed, one hundred forty-four thousand, sealed out of every tribe of the children of Israel:

⁷:⁵Of the tribe of Judah were sealed twelve thousand,

Of the tribe of Reuben twelve thousand,
Of the tribe of Gad twelve thousand,
⁷:⁶Of the tribe of Asher twelve thousand,
Of the tribe of Naphtali twelve thousand,
Of the tribe of Manasseh twelve thousand,

> ^{7:7}Of the tribe of Simeon twelve thousand,
> Of the tribe of Levi twelve thousand,
> Of the tribe of Issachar twelve thousand,
> ^{7:8}Of the tribe of Zebulun twelve thousand,
> Of the tribe of Joseph twelve thousand,
> Of the tribe of Benjamin were sealed twelve thousand.

^{7:9}After these things I looked, and behold, a great multitude, which no man could number, out of every nation and of all tribes, peoples, and languages, standing before the throne and before the Lamb, dressed in white robes, with palm branches in their hands. ^{7:10}They cried with a loud voice, saying, "Salvation be to our God, who sits on the throne, and to the Lamb!"

^{7:11}All the angels were standing around the throne, the elders, and the four living creatures; and they fell on their faces before his throne, and worshiped God, ^{7:12}saying, "Amen! Blessing, glory, wisdom, thanksgiving, honor, power, and might, be to our God forever and ever! Amen."

^{7:13}One of the elders answered, saying to me, "These who are arrayed in white robes, who are they, and from where did they come?"

^{7:14}I told him, "My lord, you know."

He said to me, "These are those who came out of the great tribulation. They washed their robes, and made them white in the Lamb's blood. ^{7:15}Therefore they are before the throne of God, they serve him day and night in his temple. He who sits on the throne will spread his tent over them. ^{7:16}They will never be hungry, neither thirsty any more; neither will the sun beat on them, nor any heat; ^{7:17}for the Lamb who is in the midst of the throne shepherds them, and leads them to springs of waters of life. And God will wipe away every tear from their eyes."

^{8:1}When he opened the seventh seal, there was silence in heaven for about half an hour. ^{8:2}I saw the seven angels who stand before God, and seven trumpets were given to them. ^{8:3}Another angel came and stood over the altar, having a golden censer. Much incense was given to him, that he should add it to the prayers of all the saints on the golden altar which was before the throne. ^{8:4}The smoke of the incense, with the prayers of the saints, went up before God out of the angel's hand. ^{8:5}The angel took the censer, and he filled it with the fire of the altar, and threw it on the earth. There followed thunders, sounds, lightnings, and an earthquake.

^{8:6}The seven angels who had the seven trumpets prepared themselves to sound. ^{8:7}The first sounded, and there followed hail and fire, mixed with

blood, and they were thrown on the earth. One third of the earth was burnt up, and one third of the trees were burnt up, and all green grass was burnt up.

8:8The second angel sounded, and something like a great burning mountain was thrown into the sea. One third of the sea became blood, 8:9and one third of the living creatures which were in the sea died. One third of the ships were destroyed.

8:10The third angel sounded, and a great star fell from the sky, burning like a torch, and it fell on one third of the rivers, and on the springs of the waters. 8:11The name of the star is called "Wormwood." One third of the waters became wormwood. Many men died from the waters, because they were made bitter.

8:12The fourth angel sounded, and one third of the sun was struck, and one third of the moon, and one third of the stars; so that one third of them would be darkened, and the day wouldn't shine for one third of it, and the night in the same way. 8:13I saw, and I heard an eagle, flying in mid heaven, saying with a loud voice, "Woe! Woe! Woe for those who dwell on the earth, because of the other voices of the trumpets of the three angels, who are yet to sound!"

9:1The fifth angel sounded, and I saw a star from the sky which had fallen to the earth. The key to the pit of the abyss was given to him. 9:2He opened the pit of the abyss, and smoke went up out of the pit, like the smoke from a burning furnace. The sun and the air were darkened because of the smoke from the pit. 9:3Then out of the smoke came forth locusts on the earth, and power was given to them, as the scorpions of the earth have power. 9:4They were told that they should not hurt the grass of the earth, neither any green thing, neither any tree, but only those people who don't have God's seal on their foreheads. 9:5They were given power not to kill them, but to torment them for five months. Their torment was like the torment of a scorpion, when it strikes a person. 9:6In those days people will seek death, and will in no way find it. They will desire to die, and death will flee from them. 9:7The shapes of the locusts were like horses prepared for war. On their heads were something like gold crowns, and their faces were like people's faces. 9:8They had hair like women's hair, and their teeth were like those of lions. 9:9They had breastplates, like breastplates of iron. The sound of their wings was like the sound of chariots, or of many horses rushing to war. 9:10They have tails like those of scorpions, and stings. In their tails they have power to harm men for five months. 9:11They have over them as king the angel of the abyss. His name in Hebrew is "Abaddon," but in Greek, he has the name "Apollyon."[2] 9:12The first woe is past. Behold, there are still two woes coming after this.

9:13The sixth angel sounded. I heard a voice from the horns of the golden altar which is before God, 9:14saying to the sixth angel who had one trumpet, "Free the four angels who are bound at the great river Euphrates."

9:15The four angels were freed who had been prepared for that hour and day and month and year, so that they might kill one third of mankind. 9:16The number of the armies of the horsemen was two hundred million. I heard the number of them. 9:17Thus I saw the horses in the vision, and those who sat on them, having breastplates of fiery red, hyacinth blue, and sulfur yellow; and the heads of lions. Out of their mouths proceed fire, smoke, and sulfur. 9:18By these three plagues were one third of mankind killed: by the fire, the smoke, and the sulfur, which proceeded out of their mouths. 9:19For the power of the horses is in their mouths, and in their tails. For their tails are like serpents, and have heads, and with them they harm. 9:20The rest of mankind, who were not killed with these plagues, didn't repent of the works of their hands, that they wouldn't worship demons, and the idols of gold, and of silver, and of brass, and of stone, and of wood; which can neither see, nor hear, nor walk. 9:21They didn't repent of their murders, nor of their sorceries,[3] nor of their sexual immorality, nor of their thefts.

10:1I saw a mighty angel coming down out of the sky, clothed with a cloud. A rainbow was on his head. His face was like the sun, and his feet like pillars of fire. 10:2He had in his hand a little open book. He set his right foot on the sea, and his left on the land. 10:3He cried with a loud voice, as a lion roars. When he cried, the seven thunders uttered their voices. 10:4When the seven thunders sounded, I was about to write; but I heard a voice from the sky saying, "Seal up the things which the seven thunders said, and don't write them."

10:5The angel who I saw standing on the sea and on the land lifted up his right hand to the sky, 10:6and swore by him who lives forever and ever, who created heaven and the things that are in it, the earth and the things that are in it, and the sea and the things that are in it, that there will no longer be delay, 10:7but in the days of the voice of the seventh angel, when he is about to sound, then the mystery of God is finished, as he declared to his servants, the prophets. 10:8The voice which I heard from heaven, again speaking with me, said, "Go, take the book which is open in the hand of the angel who stands on the sea and on the land."

10:9I went to the angel, telling him to give me the little book.

He said to me, "Take it, and eat it up. It will make your stomach bitter, but in your mouth it will be as sweet as honey."

10:10I took the little book out of the angel's hand, and ate it up. It was as sweet as honey in my mouth. When I had eaten it, my stomach was made bitter. 10:11They told me, "You must prophesy again over many peoples, nations, languages, and kings."

11:1A reed like a rod was given to me. Someone said, "Rise, and measure God's temple, and the altar, and those who worship in it. 11:2Leave out the court which is outside of the temple, and don't measure it, for it has been given to the gentiles. They will tread the holy city under foot for forty-two months. 11:3I will give power to my two witnesses, and they will prophesy one thousand two hundred sixty days, clothed in sackcloth. 11:4These are the two olive trees and the two lampstands, standing before the Lord of the earth. 11:5If anyone desires to harm them, fire proceeds out of their mouth and devours their enemies. If anyone desires to harm them, he must be killed in this way. 11:6These have the power to shut up the sky, that it may not rain during the days of their prophecy. They have power over the waters, to turn them into blood, and to strike the earth with every plague, as often as they desire. 11:7When they have finished their testimony, the beast that comes up out of the abyss will make war with them, and overcome them, and kill them. 11:8Their dead bodies will be in the street of the great city, which spiritually is called Sodom and Egypt, where also their Lord was crucified. 11:9From among the peoples, tribes, languages, and nations people will look at their dead bodies for three and a half days, and will not allow their dead bodies to be laid in a tomb. 11:10Those who dwell on the earth rejoice over them, and they will be glad. They will give gifts to one another, because these two prophets tormented those who dwell on the earth. 11:11After the three and a half days, the breath of life from God entered into them, and they stood on their feet. Great fear fell on those who saw them. 11:12I heard a loud voice from heaven saying to them, "Come up here!" They went up into heaven in the cloud, and their enemies saw them. 11:13In that day there was a great earthquake, and a tenth of the city fell. Seven thousand people were killed in the earthquake, and the rest were terrified, and gave glory to the God of heaven. 11:14The second woe is past. Behold, the third woe comes quickly.

11:15The seventh angel sounded, and great voices in heaven followed, saying, "The kingdom of the world has become the Kingdom of our Lord, and of his Christ. He will reign forever and ever!"

¹¹:¹⁶The twenty-four elders, who sit on their thrones before God's throne, fell on their faces and worshiped God, ¹¹:¹⁷saying: "We give you thanks, Lord God, the Almighty, the one who is and who was; because you have taken your great power, and reigned. ¹¹:¹⁸The nations were angry, and your wrath came, as did the time for the dead to be judged, and to give your bondservants the prophets, their reward, as well as to the saints, and those who fear your name, to the small and the great; and to destroy those who destroy the earth."

¹¹:¹⁹God's temple that is in heaven was opened, and the ark of the Lord's covenant was seen in his temple. Lightnings, sounds, thunders, an earthquake, and great hail followed.

¹²:¹A great sign was seen in heaven: a woman clothed with the sun, and the moon under her feet, and on her head a crown of twelve stars. ¹²:²She was with child. She cried out in pain, laboring to give birth. ¹²:³Another sign was seen in heaven. Behold, a great red dragon, having seven heads and ten horns, and on his heads seven crowns. ¹²:⁴His tail drew one third of the stars of the sky, and threw them to the earth. The dragon stood before the woman who was about to give birth, so that when she gave birth he might devour her child. ¹²:⁵She gave birth to a son, a male child, who is to rule all the nations with a rod of iron. Her child was caught up to God, and to his throne. ¹²:⁶The woman fled into the wilderness, where she has a place prepared by God, that there they may nourish her one thousand two hundred sixty days.

¹²:⁷There was war in the sky. Michael and his angels made war on the dragon. The dragon and his angels made war. ¹²:⁸They didn't prevail, neither was a place found for him any more in heaven. ¹²:⁹The great dragon was thrown down, the old serpent, he who is called the devil and Satan, the deceiver of the whole world. He was thrown down to the earth, and his angels were thrown down with him. ¹²:¹⁰I heard a loud voice in heaven, saying, "Now is come the salvation, the power, and the Kingdom of our God, and the authority of his Christ; for the accuser of our brothers has been thrown down, who accuses them before our God day and night. ¹²:¹¹They overcame him because of the Lamb's blood, and because of the word of their testimony. They didn't love their life, even to death. ¹²:¹²Therefore rejoice, heavens, and you who dwell in them. Woe to the earth and to the sea, because the devil has gone down to you, having great wrath, knowing that he has but a short time."

¹²:¹³When the dragon saw that he was thrown down to the earth, he persecuted the woman who gave birth to the male child. ¹²:¹⁴Two wings of

the great eagle were given to the woman, that she might fly into the wilderness to her place, so that she might be nourished for a time, and times, and half a time, from the face of the serpent. ¹²:¹⁵The serpent spewed water out of his mouth after the woman like a river, that he might cause her to be carried away by the stream. ¹²:¹⁶The earth helped the woman, and the earth opened its mouth and swallowed up the river which the dragon spewed out of his mouth. ¹²:¹⁷The dragon grew angry with the woman, and went away to make war with the rest of her seed, who keep God's commandments and hold Jesus' testimony.

¹³:¹Then I stood on the sand of the sea. I saw a beast coming up out of the sea, having ten horns and seven heads. On his horns were ten crowns, and on his heads, blasphemous names. ¹³:²The beast which I saw was like a leopard, and his feet were like those of a bear, and his mouth like the mouth of a lion. The dragon gave him his power, his throne, and great authority. ¹³:³One of his heads looked like it had been wounded fatally. His fatal wound was healed, and the whole earth marveled at the beast. ¹³:⁴They worshiped the dragon, because he gave his authority to the beast, and they worshiped the beast, saying, "Who is like the beast? Who is able to make war with him?" ¹³:⁵A mouth speaking great things and blasphemy was given to him. Authority to make war for forty-two months was given to him. ¹³:⁶He opened his mouth for blasphemy against God, to blaspheme his name, and his dwelling, those who dwell in heaven. ¹³:⁷It was given to him to make war with the saints, and to overcome them. Authority over every tribe, people, language, and nation was given to him. ¹³:⁸All who dwell on the earth will worship him, everyone whose name has not been written from the foundation of the world in the book of life of the Lamb who has been killed. ¹³:⁹If anyone has an ear, let him hear. ¹³:¹⁰If anyone has captivity, he will go. If anyone is with the sword, he must be killed. Here is the endurance and the faith of the saints.

¹³:¹¹I saw another beast coming up out of the earth. He had two horns like a lamb, and he spoke like a dragon. ¹³:¹²He exercises all the authority of the first beast in his presence. He makes the earth and those who dwell in it to worship the first beast, whose fatal wound was healed. ¹³:¹³He performs great signs, even making fire come down out of the sky to the earth in the sight of people. ¹³:¹⁴He deceives my own people who dwell on the earth because of the signs he was granted to do in front of the beast; saying to those who dwell on the earth, that they should make an image to the beast who had the sword wound and lived. ¹³:¹⁵It was given to him to give breath to

it, to the image of the beast, that the image of the beast should both speak, and cause as many as wouldn't worship the image of the beast to be killed. [13:16]He causes all, the small and the great, the rich and the poor, and the free and the slave, to be given marks on their right hands, or on their foreheads; [13:17]and that no one would be able to buy or to sell, unless he has that mark, the name of the beast or the number of his name. [13:18]Here is wisdom. He who has understanding, let him calculate the number of the beast, for it is the number of a man. His number is six hundred sixty-six.

[14:1]I saw, and behold, the Lamb standing on Mount Zion, and with him a number, one hundred forty-four thousand, having his name, and the name of his Father, written on their foreheads. [14:2]I heard a sound from heaven, like the sound of many waters, and like the sound of a great thunder. The sound which I heard was like that of harpists playing on their harps. [14:3]They sing a new song before the throne, and before the four living creatures and the elders. No one could learn the song except the one hundred forty-four thousand, those who had been redeemed out of the earth. [14:4]These are those who were not defiled with women, for they are virgins. These are those who follow the Lamb wherever he goes. These were redeemed by Jesus from among men, the first fruits to God and to the Lamb. [14:5]In their mouth was found no lie, for they are blameless.

[14:6]I saw an angel flying in mid heaven, having an eternal gospel to proclaim to those who dwell on the earth, and to every nation, tribe, language, and people. [14:7]He said with a loud voice, "Fear the Lord, and give him glory; for the hour of his judgment has come. Worship him who made the heaven, the earth, the sea, and the springs of waters!"

[14:8]Another, a second angel, followed, saying, "Babylon the great has fallen, which has made all the nations to drink of the wine of the wrath of her sexual immorality."

[14:9]Another angel, a third, followed them, saying with a great voice, "If anyone worships the beast and his image, and receives a mark on his forehead, or on his hand, [14:10]he also will drink of the wine of the wrath of God, which is prepared unmixed in the cup of his anger. He will be tormented with fire and sulfur in the presence of the holy angels, and in the presence of the Lamb. [14:11]The smoke of their torment goes up forever and ever. They have no rest day and night, those who worship the beast and his image, and whoever receives the mark of his name. [14:12]Here is the patience of the saints, those who keep the commandments of God, and the faith of Jesus."

[14:13]I heard the voice from heaven saying, "Write, 'Blessed are the dead who die in the Lord from now on.'"

"Yes," says the Spirit, "that they may rest from their labors; for their works follow with them."

¹⁴:¹⁴I looked, and behold, a white cloud; and on the cloud one sitting like a son of man, having on his head a golden crown, and in his hand a sharp sickle. ¹⁴:¹⁵Another angel came out from the temple, crying with a loud voice to him who sat on the cloud, "Send forth your sickle, and reap; for the hour to reap has come; for the harvest of the earth is ripe!" ¹⁴:¹⁶He who sat on the cloud thrust his sickle on the earth, and the earth was reaped.

¹⁴:¹⁷Another angel came out from the temple which is in heaven. He also had a sharp sickle. ¹⁴:¹⁸Another angel came out from the altar, he who has power over fire, and he called with a great voice to him who had the sharp sickle, saying, "Send forth your sharp sickle, and gather the clusters of the vine of the earth, for the earth's grapes are fully ripe!" ¹⁴:¹⁹The angel thrust his sickle into the earth, and gathered the vintage of the earth, and threw it into the great winepress of the wrath of God. ¹⁴:²⁰The winepress was trodden outside of the city, and blood came out from the winepress, even to the bridles of the horses, as far as one thousand six hundred stadia.⁴

¹⁵:¹I saw another great and marvelous sign in the sky: seven angels having the seven last plagues, for in them God's wrath is finished. ¹⁵:²I saw something like a sea of glass mixed with fire, and those who overcame the beast, his image, and the number of his name, standing on the sea of glass, having harps of God. ¹⁵:³They sang the song of Moses, the servant of God, and the song of the Lamb, saying,

"Great and marvelous are your works, Lord God, the Almighty;
Righteous and true are your ways, you King of the nations.
¹⁵:⁴Who wouldn't fear you, Lord,
And glorify your name?
For you only are holy.
For all the nations will come and worship before you. For your righteous acts have been revealed.

¹⁵:⁵After these things I looked, and the temple of the tabernacle of the testimony in heaven was opened. ¹⁵:⁶The seven angels who had the seven plagues came out, clothed with pure, bright linen, and wearing golden sashes around their breasts.

¹⁵:⁷One of the four living creatures gave to the seven angels seven golden bowls full of the wrath of God, who lives forever and ever. ¹⁵:⁸The temple was filled with smoke from the glory of God, and from his power. No one

was able to enter into the temple, until the seven plagues of the seven angels would be finished.

[16:1]I heard a loud voice out of the temple, saying to the seven angels, "Go and pour out the seven bowls of the wrath of God on the earth!"

[16:2]The first went, and poured out his bowl into the earth, and it became a harmful and evil sore on the people who had the mark of the beast, and who worshiped his image.

[16:3]The second angel poured out his bowl into the sea, and it became blood as of a dead man. Every living thing in the sea died.

[16:4]The third poured out his bowl into the rivers and springs of water, and they became blood. [16:5]I heard the angel of the waters saying, "You are righteous, who are and who were, you Holy One, because you judged these things. [16:6]For they poured out the blood of the saints and the prophets, and you have given them blood to drink. They deserve this." [16:7]I heard the altar saying, "Yes, Lord God, the Almighty, true and righteous are your judgments."

[16:8]The fourth poured out his bowl on the sun, and it was given to him to scorch men with fire. [16:9]People were scorched with great heat, and people blasphemed the name of God who has the power over these plagues. They didn't repent and give him glory.

[16:10]The fifth poured out his bowl on the throne of the beast, and his kingdom was darkened. They gnawed their tongues because of the pain, [16:11]and they blasphemed the God of heaven because of their pains and their sores. They didn't repent of their works.

[16:12]The sixth poured out his bowl on the great river, the Euphrates. Its water was dried up, that the way might be made ready for the kings that come from the sunrise. [16:13]I saw coming out of the mouth of the dragon, and out of the mouth of the beast, and out of the mouth of the false prophet, three unclean spirits, something like frogs; [16:14]for they are spirits of demons, performing signs; which go forth to the kings of the whole inhabited earth, to gather them together for that war of that great day of God, the Almighty.

[16:15]"Behold, I come like a thief. Blessed is he who watches, and keeps his clothes, so that he doesn't walk naked, and they see his shame." [16:16]He gathered them together into the place which is called in Hebrew, Megiddo.

[16:17]The seventh poured out his bowl into the air. A loud voice came forth out of the temple, from the throne, saying, "It is done!" [16:18]There were lightnings, sounds, and thunders; and there was a great earthquake, such as was not since there were men on the earth, so great an earthquake, so mighty. ¹⁶:¹⁹The great city was divided into three parts, and the cities of the nations fell. Babylon the great was remembered in the sight of God, to give to her the cup of the wine of the fierceness of his wrath. ¹⁶:²⁰Every island fled away, and the mountains were not found. ¹⁶:²¹Great hailstones, about the weight of a talent, came down out of the sky on people. People blasphemed God because of the plague of the hail, for this plague is exceedingly severe.

¹⁷:¹One of the seven angels who had the seven bowls came and spoke with me, saying, "Come here. I will show you the judgment of the great prostitute who sits on many waters, ¹⁷:²with whom the kings of the earth committed sexual immorality, and those who dwell in the earth were made drunken with the wine of her sexual immorality." ¹⁷:³He carried me away in the Spirit into a wilderness. I saw a woman sitting on a scarlet-colored animal, full of blasphemous names, having seven heads and ten horns. ¹⁷:⁴The woman was dressed in purple and scarlet, and decked with gold and precious stones and pearls, having in her hand a golden cup full of abominations and the impurities of the sexual immorality of the earth. ¹⁷:⁵And on her forehead a name was written, "MYSTERY, BABYLON THE GREAT, THE MOTHER OF THE PROSTITUTES AND OF THE ABOMINATIONS OF THE EARTH." ¹⁷:⁶I saw the woman drunken with the blood of the saints, and with the blood of the martyrs of Jesus. When I saw her, I wondered with great amazement. ¹⁷:⁷The angel said to me, "Why do you wonder? I will tell you the mystery of the woman, and of the beast that carries her, which has the seven heads and the ten horns. ¹⁷:⁸The beast that you saw was, and is not; and is about to come up out of the abyss and to go into destruction. Those who dwell on the earth and whose names have not been written in the book of life from the foundation of the world will marvel when they see that the beast was, and is not, and shall be present. ¹⁷:⁹Here is the mind that has wisdom. The seven heads are seven mountains, on which the woman sits. ¹⁷:¹⁰They are seven kings. Five have fallen, the one is, the other has not yet come. When he comes, he must continue a little while. ¹⁷:¹¹The beast that was, and is not, is himself also an eighth, and is of the seven; and he goes to destruction. ¹⁷:¹²The ten horns that you saw are ten kings who have received no kingdom as yet, but they receive authority as kings, with the beast, for one hour. ¹⁷:¹³These have one mind, and they give their power and authority to the beast. ¹⁷:¹⁴These will war against the Lamb, and the Lamb will overcome them, for he is Lord of lords, and King of kings. They also will overcome who are with him, called and chosen and faithful." ¹⁷:¹⁵He said

to me, "The waters which you saw, where the prostitute sits, are peoples, multitudes, nations, and languages. [17:16]The ten horns which you saw, and the beast, these will hate the prostitute, and will make her desolate, and will make her naked, and will eat her flesh, and will burn her utterly with fire. [17:17]For God has put in their hearts to do what he has in mind, and to be of one mind, and to give their kingdom to the beast, until the words of God should be accomplished. [17:18]The woman whom you saw is the great city, which reigns over the kings of the earth."

[18:1]After these things, I saw another angel coming down out of the sky, having great authority. The earth was illuminated with his glory. [18:2]He cried with a mighty voice, saying, "Fallen, fallen is Babylon the great, and has become a habitation of demons, a prison of every unclean spirit, and a prison of every unclean and hateful bird! [18:3]For all the nations have drunk of the wine of the wrath of her sexual immorality, the kings of the earth committed sexual immorality with her, and the merchants of the earth grew rich from the abundance of her luxury."

[18:4]I heard another voice from heaven, saying, "Come out of her, my people, that you have no participation in her sins, and that you don't receive of her plagues, [18:5]for her sins have reached to the sky, and God has remembered her iniquities. [18:6]Return to her just as she returned, and repay her double as she did, and according to her works. In the cup which she mixed, mix to her double. [18:7]However much she glorified herself, and grew wanton, so much give her of torment and mourning. For she says in her heart, 'I sit a queen, and am no widow, and will in no way see mourning.' [18:8]Therefore in one day her plagues will come: death, mourning, and famine; and she will be utterly burned with fire; for the Lord God who has judged her is strong. [18:9]The kings of the earth, who committed sexual immorality and lived wantonly with her, will weep and wail over her, when they look at the smoke of her burning, [18:10]standing far away for the fear of her torment, saying, 'Woe, woe, the great city, Babylon, the strong city! For your judgment has come in one hour.' [18:11]The merchants of the earth weep and mourn over her, for no one buys their merchandise any more; [18:12]merchandise of gold, silver, precious stones, pearls, fine linen, purple, silk, scarlet, all expensive wood, every vessel of ivory, every vessel made of most precious wood, and of brass, and iron, and marble; [18:13]and cinnamon, spices, incense, perfume, frankincense, wine, olive oil, fine flour, wheat, sheep, horses, chariots, bodies, and people's souls. [18:14]The fruits which your soul lusted after have been lost to you, and all things that were dainty and sumptuous have perished from you, and you will find them no more at all. ^{18:15}The merchants of these things, who were made rich by her, will stand far away for the fear of her torment, weeping and mourning; ^{18:16}saying, 'Woe, woe, the great city, she who was dressed in fine linen, purple, and scarlet, and decked with gold and precious stones and pearls! ^{18:17}For in an hour such great riches are made desolate.' Every shipmaster, and everyone who sails anywhere, and mariners, and as many as gain their living by sea, stood far away, ^{18:18}and cried out as they looked at the smoke of her burning, saying, 'What is like the great city?' ^{18:19}They cast dust on their heads, and cried, weeping and mourning, saying, 'Woe, woe, the great city, in which all who had their ships in the sea were made rich by reason of her great wealth!' For in one hour is she made desolate. ^{18:20}Rejoice over her, O heaven, you saints, apostles, and prophets; for God has judged your judgment on her." ^{18:21}A mighty angel took up a stone like a great millstone and cast it into the sea, saying, "Thus with violence will Babylon, the great city, be thrown down, and will be found no more at all. ^{18:22}The voice of harpists, minstrels, flute players, and trumpeters will be heard no more at all in you. No craftsman, of whatever craft, will be found any more at all in you. The sound of a mill will be heard no more at all in you. ^{18:23}The light of a lamp will shine no more at all in you. The voice of the bridegroom and of the bride will be heard no more at all in you; for your merchants were the princes of the earth; for with your sorcery all the nations were deceived. ^{18:24}In her was found the blood of prophets and of saints, and of all who have been slain on the earth."

^{19:1}After these things I heard something like a loud voice of a great multitude in heaven, saying, "Hallelujah! Salvation, power, and glory belong to our God: ^{19:2}for true and righteous are his judgments. For he has judged the great prostitute, who corrupted the earth with her sexual immorality, and he has avenged the blood of his servants at her hand."

^{19:3}A second said, "Hallelujah! Her smoke goes up forever and ever." ^{19:4}The twenty-four elders and the four living creatures fell down and worshiped God who sits on the throne, saying, "Amen! Hallelujah!"

^{19:5}A voice came forth from the throne, saying, "Give praise to our God, all you his servants, you who fear him, the small and the great!"

^{19:6}I heard something like the voice of a great multitude, and like the voice of many waters, and like the voice of mighty thunders, saying, "Hallelujah! For the Lord our God, the Almighty, reigns! ^{19:7}Let us rejoice and be exceedingly glad, and let us give the glory to him. For the marriage of the Lamb has come, and his wife has made herself ready." ^{19:8}It was given to

her that she would array herself in bright, pure, fine linen: for the fine linen is the righteous acts of the saints.

19:9He said to me, "Write, 'Blessed are those who are invited to the marriage supper of the Lamb.'" He said to me, "These are true words of God."

19:10I fell down before his feet to worship him. He said to me, "Look! Don't do it! I am a fellow bondservant with you and with your brothers who hold the testimony of Jesus. Worship God, for the testimony of Jesus is the Spirit of Prophecy."

19:11I saw the heaven opened, and behold, a white horse, and he who sat on it is called Faithful and True. In righteousness he judges and makes war. 19:12His eyes are a flame of fire, and on his head are many crowns. He has names written and a name written which no one knows but he himself. 19:13He is clothed in a garment sprinkled with blood. His name is called "The Word of God." 19:14The armies which are in heaven followed him on white horses, clothed in white, pure, fine linen. 19:15Out of his mouth proceeds a sharp, double-edged sword, that with it he should strike the nations. He will rule them with a rod of iron. He treads the winepress of the fierceness of the wrath of God, the Almighty. 19:16He has on his garment and on his thigh a name written, "KING OF KINGS, AND LORD OF LORDS."

19:17I saw an angel standing in the sun. He cried with a loud voice, saying to all the birds that fly in the sky, "Come! Be gathered together to the great supper of God, 19:18that you may eat the flesh of kings, the flesh of captains, the flesh of mighty men, and the flesh of horses and of those who sit on them, and the flesh of all men, both free and slave, and small and great." 19:19I saw the beast, and the kings of the earth, and their armies, gathered together to make war against him who sat on the horse, and against his army. 19:20The beast was taken, and with him the false prophet who worked the signs in his sight, with which he deceived those who had received the mark of the beast and those who worshiped his image. They two were thrown alive into the lake of fire that burns with sulfur. 19:21The rest were killed with the sword of him who sat on the horse, the sword which came forth out of his mouth. All the birds were filled with their flesh.

20:1I saw an angel coming down out of heaven, having the key of the abyss and a great chain in his hand. 20:2He seized the dragon, the old serpent, which is the devil and Satan, who deceives the whole inhabited earth, and bound him for a thousand years, 20:3and cast him into the abyss, and shut it, and sealed it over him, that he should deceive the nations no more, until the thousand years were finished. After this, he must be freed for a short time. ²⁰:⁴I saw thrones, and they sat on them, and judgment was given to them. I saw the souls of those who had been beheaded for the testimony of Jesus, and for the word of God, and such as didn't worship the beast nor his image, and didn't receive the mark on their forehead and on their hand. They lived, and reigned with Christ for the thousand years. ²⁰:⁵The rest of the dead didn't live until the thousand years were finished. This is the first resurrection. ²⁰:⁶Blessed and holy is he who has part in the first resurrection. Over these, the second death has no power, but they will be priests of God and of Christ, and will reign with him one thousand years.

²⁰:⁷And after the thousand years, Satan will be released from his prison, ²⁰:⁸and he will come out to deceive the nations which are in the four corners of the earth, Gog and Magog, to gather them together to the war; the number of whom is as the sand of the sea. ²⁰:⁹They went up over the breadth of the earth, and surrounded the camp of the saints, and the beloved city. Fire came down out of heaven from God, and devoured them. ²⁰:¹⁰The devil who deceived them was thrown into the lake of fire and sulfur, where the beast and the false prophet are also. They will be tormented day and night forever and ever.

²⁰:¹¹I saw a great white throne, and him who sat on it, from whose face the earth and the heaven fled away. There was found no place for them. ²⁰:¹²I saw the dead, the great and the small, standing before the throne, and they opened books. Another book was opened, which is the book of life. The dead were judged out of the things which were written in the books, according to their works. ²⁰:¹³The sea gave up the dead who were in it. Death and Hades gave up the dead who were in them. They were judged, each one according to his works. ²⁰:¹⁴Death and Hades were thrown into the lake of fire. This is the second death, the lake of fire. ²⁰:¹⁵If anyone was not found written in the book of life, he was cast into the lake of fire.

²¹:¹I saw a new heaven and a new earth: for the first heaven and the first earth have passed away, and the sea is no more. ²¹:²I saw the holy city, New Jerusalem, coming down out of heaven from God, made ready like a bride adorned for her husband. ²¹:³I heard a loud voice out of heaven saying, "Behold, God's dwelling is with people, and he will dwell with them, and they will be his people, and God himself will be with them as their God. ²¹:⁴He will wipe away from them every tear from their eyes. Death will be no more; neither will there be mourning, nor crying, nor pain, any more. The first things have passed away."

21:5He who sits on the throne said, "Behold, I am making all things new."
He said, "Write, for these words of God are faithful and true." 21:6He said to
me, "It is done! I am the Alpha and the Omega, the Beginning and the End.
I will give freely to him who is thirsty from the spring of the water of life.
21:7He who overcomes, I will give him these things. I will be his God, and
he will be my son. 21:8But for the cowardly, unbelieving, sinners, abominable,
murderers, sexually immoral, sorcerers, idolaters, and all liars, their part is in
the lake that burns with fire and sulfur, which is the second death."

21:9One of the seven angels who had the seven bowls, who were laden with
the seven last plagues came, and he spoke with me, saying, "Come here. I
will show you the wife, the Lamb's bride." 21:10He carried me away in the
Spirit to a great and high mountain, and showed me the holy city, Jerusalem,
coming down out of heaven from God, 21:11having the glory of God. Her
light was like a most precious stone, as if it was a jasper stone, clear as crystal;
21:12having a great and high wall; having twelve gates, and at the gates twelve
angels; and names written on them, which are the names of the twelve
tribes of the children of Israel. 21:13On the east were three gates; and on the
north three gates; and on the south three gates; and on the west three gates.
21:14The wall of the city had twelve foundations, and on them twelve names
of the twelve Apostles of the Lamb. 21:15He who spoke with me had for a
measure, a golden reed, to measure the city, its gates, and its walls. 21:16The
city lies foursquare, and its length is as great as its breadth. He measured the
city with the reed, Twelve thousand stadia.5 Its length, breadth, and height
are equal. 21:17Its wall is one hundred forty-four cubits,6 by the measure of
a man, that is, of an angel. 21:18The construction of its wall was jasper. The
city was pure gold, like pure glass. 21:19The foundations of the city's wall were
adorned with all kinds of precious stones. The first foundation was jasper;
the second, sapphire; the third, chalcedony; the fourth, emerald; 21:20the fifth,
sardonyx; the sixth, sardius; the seventh, chrysolite; the eighth, beryl; the
ninth, topaz; the tenth, chrysoprasus; the eleventh, jacinth; and the twelfth,
amethyst. 21:21The twelve gates were twelve pearls. Each one of the gates was
made of one pearl. The street of the city was pure gold, like transparent glass.
21:22I saw no temple in it, for the Lord God, the Almighty, and the Lamb,
are its temple. 21:23The city has no need for the sun, neither of the moon, to
shine, for the very glory of God illuminated it, and its lamp is the Lamb.
21:24The nations will walk in its light. The kings of the earth bring the glory
and honor of the nations into it. 21:25Its gates will in no way be shut by day
(for there will be no night there), 21:26and they shall bring the glory and the

honor of the nations into it so that they may enter. [21:27]There will in no way enter into it anything profane, or one who causes an abomination or a lie, but only those who are written in the Lamb's book of life.

[22:1]He showed me a river of water of life, clear as crystal, proceeding out of the throne of God and of the Lamb, [22:2]in the middle of its street. On this side of the river and on that was the tree of life, bearing twelve kinds of fruits, yielding its fruit every month. The leaves of the tree were for the healing of the nations. [22:3]There will be no curse any more. The throne of God and of the Lamb will be in it, and his servants serve him. [22:4]They will see his face, and his name will be on their foreheads. [22:5]There will be no more night, and they need no lamp light; for the Lord God will illuminate them. They will reign forever and ever.

[22:6]He said to me, "These words are faithful and true. The Lord God of the spirits of the prophets sent his angel to show to his bondservants the things which must happen soon."

[22:7]"Behold, I come quickly. Blessed is he who keeps the words of the prophecy of this book."

[22:8]Now I, John, am the one who heard and saw these things. When I heard and saw, I fell down to worship before the feet of the angel who had shown me these things. [22:9]He said to me, "See you don't do it! I am a fellow bondservant with you and with your brothers, the prophets, and with those who keep the words of this book. Worship God." [22:10]He said to me, "Don't seal up the words of the prophecy of this book, for the time is at hand. [22:11]He who acts unjustly, let him act unjustly still. He who is filthy, let him be filthy still. He who is righteous, let him do righteousness still. He who is holy, let him be holy still."

[22:12]"Behold, I come quickly. My reward is with me, to repay to each man according to his work. [22:13]I am the Alpha and the Omega, the First and the Last, the Beginning and the End. [22:14]Blessed are those who do his commandments, that they may have the right to the tree of life, and may enter in by the gates into the city. [22:15]Outside are the dogs, the sorcerers, the sexually immoral, the murderers, the idolaters, and everyone who loves and practices falsehood. [22:16]I, Jesus, have sent my angel to testify these things to you for the assemblies. I am the root and the offspring of David; the Bright and Morning Star."

[22:17]The Spirit and the bride say, "Come!" He who hears, let him say, "Come!" He who is thirsty, let him come. He who desires, let him take the water of life freely. [22:18]I testify to everyone who hears the words of the prophecy of this book, if anyone adds to them, may God add to him the plagues which are written in this book. [22:19]If anyone takes away from the words of the book of this prophecy, may God take away his part from the tree of life, and out of the holy city, which are written in this book. [22:20]He who testifies these things says, "Yes, I come quickly."

Amen! Yes, come, Lord Jesus.

[22:21]The grace of the Lord Jesus be with all the saints. Amen.

*   *   *

Endnotes

[1]A choenix is a dry volume measure that is a little more than a liter.

[2]"Abaddon" is a Hebrew word that means *ruin, destruction,* or *the place of destruction,* and "Apollyon" is a Greek word that means *destroyer.*

[3]The word for "sorceries" (pharmakeia) can also imply the use of poisons and drugs.

[4]1,600 stadia = 296 kilometers or 184 miles.

[5]12,000 stadia = 2,219 kilometers or 1,379 miles.

[6]144 cubits is about 65.8 meters or 216 feet.

About the Author

John Van Auken is the founder of Inner Vision and a former executive director of the Association for Research and Enlightenment, Inc. (A.R.E.), the organization founded by Edgar Cayce in 1931.

His personal experience with living the tenets and practicing the techniques he teaches, combined with his storytelling ability, make him a popular author and speaker on topics of spirituality, reincarnation, prophecy, rejuvenation of the body, and Egyptian mysticism. He is a skilled teacher of meditation—from kundalini meditation to his unique "passage in consciousness" process. He lectures and conducts workshops around the world and has appeared on several television programs.

He is the author of seven books and many audio- and videotapes as well as the editor and publisher of a monthly letter, *Living in the Light*. The author can be contacted at:

John Van Auken
P.O. Box 4942
Virginia Beach, VA 23454-0942
E-mail: johnvanauken@att.net

Discover How the Edgar Cayce Material Can Help You

The Association for Research and Enlightenment, Inc. (A.R.E.), was founded in 1931 by Edgar Cayce. Its international head-quarters are in Virginia Beach, Virginia, where thousands of visitors come year round. Many more are helped and inspired by A.R.E.'s local activities in their own hometowns or by contact via mail (and now the Internet!) with A.R.E. headquarters.

People from all walks of life, all around the world, have discovered meaningful and life-transforming insights in the A.R.E. programs and materials, which focus on such areas as personal spirituality, holistic health, dreams, family life, finding your best vocation, reincarnation, ESP, meditation, and soul growth in small-group settings. Call us today on our toll-free number:

1-800-333-4499

or

Explore our electronic visitors center on the
Internet: http://www.edgarcayce.org.

We'll be happy to tell you more about how the work of the A.R.E. can help you!

A.R.E.
215 67th Street
Virginia Beach, VA 23451-2061